Defend Life!

David Prentice

11-10-07
LLDF

HUMAN DIGNITY IN THE BIOTECH CENTURY

A CHRISTIAN VISION FOR PUBLIC POLICY

Charles W. Colson and
Nigel M. de S. Cameron, editors

InterVarsity Press
Downers Grove, Illinois

InterVarsity Press
P.O. Box 1400, Downers Grove, IL 60515-1426
World Wide Web: www.ivpress.com
E-mail: mail@ivpress.com

InterVarsity Press® is the book-publishing division of InterVarsity Christian Fellowship/USA®, a student movement active on campus at hundreds of universities, colleges and schools of nursing in the United States of America, and a member movement of the International Fellowship of Evangelical Students. For information about local and regional activities, write Public Relations Dept., InterVarsity Christian Fellowship/USA, 6400 Schroeder Rd., P.O. Box 7895, Madison, WI 53707-7895, or visit the IVCF website at <www.ivcf.org>.

All Scripture quotations, unless otherwise indicated, are taken from the Holy Bible, New International Version®. NIV®. Copyright ©1973, 1978, 1984 by International Bible Society. Used by permission of Zondervan Publishing House. All rights reserved.

Cover design: Cindy Kiple

Cover images: Gandee Vasan/Getty Images (babies in eggs); Andrew Lambert Photography/Photo Researchers (test tube)

ISBN 0-8308-2783-8

Printed in the United States of America ∞

Library of Congress Cataloging-in-Publication Data

Human dignity in the biotech century: a Christian vision for public policy/Charles W. Colson and Nigel M. de S. Cameron, editors.
   p. cm.
Includes bibliographical references and index.
ISBN 0-8308-2783-8 (pbk.: alk. paper)
1. Genetic engineering—Religious aspects—Christianity. I. Colson, Charles W. II. Cameron, Nigel M. de S.
TP248.6.H85 2004
241'.64957—dc22

                                                                                      2004006654

P	19	18	17	16	15	14	13	12	11	10	9	8	7	6	5	4	3	2	1
Y	19	18	17	16	15	14	13	12	11	10	09	08	07	06	05	04			

CONTENTS

PREFACE

In August of 2001 something truly remarkable took place. President George W. Bush made his first televised broadcast to the American people. Its subject? Embryo research—specifically, whether the federal government should fund embryonic stem cell research that involved the destruction of the embryo. While the events of 9/11 were soon to overshadow this, as they did every other element in the nation's politics, we need to remember that the dominant issue of the first year of the Bush presidency was bioethics. What had been obscure, academic debates had spilled over into the center of our national life. The pundits who had declared this to be "the biotech century" had very rapidly been proved right.

In fact, since the announcement in February of 1997 that Dolly the sheep had been cloned, biotechnology has generated political and media controversy as never before. Our new abilities to manipulate the building blocks of human life have sparked alarm and hope in equal proportions. On the one hand, biotech industry advocates have hyped their hopes of what can be accomplished in the cure of dreadful diseases—if they are given a free hand with human embryos, cloned in vast numbers. On the other hand, the specter of scientists and their corporate backers pursuing ghoulish projects that manipulate and destroy human life has led millions of Americans to be deeply skeptical of those claims. They have sought constraints on biotechnology to ensure that experiments are ethical and scientists accountable.

Christians have been playing key roles in these debates, since we are acutely aware of the dignity of human life—made in the image of God—and the limitless capacity of fallen men and women to do evil. We also believe that God has given us "dominion" over creation, to rule it as his stewards; so while we are aware of its dangers, we are not anti-technology. The pro-life movement soon recognized that cloning was as much an assault on human dignity as was abortion itself. And, in ways that some have found surprising, pro-choice advocates have worked side by side with the pro-life movement, equally alarmed by the prospect of science that is out of control, seeking to turn human life into a commodity.

The biotechnology agenda is already long, and it is getting longer. Beyond cloning and embryo research lies the sinister question of "germline" genetic engineering—making inheritable changes in human genes. The patenting of genes and other human tissue has already begun to turn human nature into property. The misuse of genetic information will enable insurers and employers to exercise the ultimate form of discrimination. Meanwhile, advances in nanotechnology and cybernetics threaten to "enhance" and one day perhaps rival or replace human nature itself—in what some thinkers are already calling "transhumanism."

How are Christians to prepare themselves and engage, under God, in what promises to be a vast struggle in the coming decades? At one level, we are already uniquely prepared, because in a culture that has lost its bearings on what it means to be human, we have not lost ours. To be human is to be made in God's image; and if we find that amazing truth hard to grasp, we are reminded of it by God himself—since in his son he took human form as Jesus of Nazareth, a fellow member of our species, *Homo sapiens*. So as believers our worldview gives us the key to the uniqueness and dignity of human nature. Yet at another level, we are woefully unprepared. Decades of "pietistic" withdrawal have left the church little engaged in public questions, disinterested in science and technology, and wide open to the secular values that constantly creep into the thinking of Christian men and women. We face an enormous educational task: to build on Christian commitment to the pro-life cause a broad understanding of the biotech challenge and the kind of cultural and political response that will make a difference for Jesus Christ. If ever there was need and opportunity for Christians to shape culture, it is now.

Here at the Wilberforce Forum we have taken several initiatives to help the church play its vital role. We developed the Council for Biotechnology Policy to bring together key leaders and thinkers. The essays in this volume are all by fellows or friends of the council. We are developing resources, including our "Playing God?" curriculum for adult Sunday school classes, an online bioethics certificate program, a biotechpolicy.org website and our monthly Biotech Update e-mail newsletter. We have been active, in concert with others, in developing briefings for members of Congress and their staff on Capitol Hill. Many of these essays were conceived at a conference we convened in Washington, D.C., in February 2002 with participants from across the nation and also from the White House, the Senate and the House of Representatives.

The chapters that follow survey the emerging biotech agenda and draw on the expertise of individuals in the fields of theology, ethics, medicine, bioscience, law and public policy. Some chapters are more technical and intellectually demanding than others, although the writers assume little of their readers beyond a commitment to address the agenda. We explore both distinctively Christian arguments and strategies, and public arguments. As an appendix we include the text and key signatories of "The Sanctity of Life in a Brave New World: A Manifesto on Biotechnology and Human Dignity," in which we set out a public argument that covers cloning and other major questions we confront.

We hope these chapters will inform you and encourage you to make the case for biotech that enhances, and does not subvert, the dignity of human beings, made in the image of God himself.

Charles W. Colson
Nigel M. de S. Cameron

The Wilberforce Forum
Council for Biotechnology Policy
Washington, D.C.

INTRODUCTION

Can We Prevent the "Abolition of Man"?

C. S. Lewis's Challenge to the Twenty-first Century

CHARLES W. COLSON

There has long been a simmering debate about the respective merits of the two most influential books about the future that were written during the twentieth century. They are both alike in one respect: they are dystopias, visions of a world that has gone profoundly wrong, warnings from the future to the present.

George Orwell's 1984 *sets out a vision of political oppression and control that foresees the triumph of technology in the service of totalitarianism: Big Brother is watching you. By contrast, Aldous Huxley's* Brave New World *offers a more subtle nightmare, in which technology and choice have combined to bring about a world where, as one commentator has written, pain and suffering have been almost entirely alleviated at the cost of everything that makes life worth living.*

In the closing years of the twentieth century it became obvious whose vision was right. As totalitarianisms crumbled around the world, the biotech revolution set out on its exponentially growing path. We have reason to be grateful that Orwell seems to have been wrong. We have reason to be fearful that Huxley may have been right.

This is not business as usual for the human race. The global community confronts a defining opportunity to declare the primacy of human dignity in the development of biotechnology. Its extraordinary benefits are mingled with threats of equal proportion.

The closing years of the twentieth century demonstrated that Orwell's totalitarian vision did not represent the human future. It lies in our hands at the start of the twenty-first to ensure that Huxley is also proved wrong.

NIGEL M. DE S. CAMERON

Let us visit a laboratory in a gray building in London. A conveyer belt is moving from one side of the room to the other. On that conveyer belt are little glass jars, and in those glass jars are fertilized ova, and they are clattering back and forth on the conveyer as they go across the room. Those fertilized ova will break into ninety-six separate buds, each of those buds will mature into an embryo, and each one of those embryos will mature into a human being.

Interestingly enough, the people who are conducting this experiment have figured out how to genetically preprogram what each person created in that test tube will be. Some will be laborers, some will be members of Congress, some will be business leaders. Each is predestined—not by God, as those of us who are of the Reformed tradition believe, but by scientists and bureaucrats who make a genetic determination in the test tube based on the society's needs. Human beings have become nothing more than a replaceable commodity.

The scene, of course, comes from Aldous Huxley's novel *Brave New World*, published in 1931. And it may be the most prophetic writing of the twentieth century—even more prophetic than George Orwell's *1984*—for we have seen in the new millennium the real potential for precisely the kind of society about which Huxley wrote.

The story of *Brave New World* is fascinating because of the parallels it offers to what is happening today in the biotechnology revolution. *Brave New World* is about implementing a utopian vision of the perfect society, brought about by biotechnology.

In the book all people are genetically preprogrammed to fit in and do particular jobs. They all take "soma," a narcotic that brings about a mild state of euphoria. When someone feels any momentary depression or distress, he or she just pops another soma.

Brave New World prompted the late Neil Postman, a television critic and professor at New York University, to write his marvelous book *Amusing Ourselves to Death*. In his introduction, Postman points out that Huxley foresaw something that Orwell missed: Orwell wrote about the tyranny that resulted from totalitarian powers holding citizens in their grip.[1] Huxley foresaw a tyranny in which the people were lulled into passivity. The state in Huxley's novel kept people amused and entertained and provided all the sex and all the drugs they wanted. Control was exercised through pleasure, not pain.

The book illustrates the biotech dream of fit bodies and happy minds.

---

[1] Neil Postman, *Amusing Ourselves to Death: Public Discourse in the Age of Show Business* (New York: Penguin, 1985), pp. vii-viii.

While the laboratories turn out better babies, the pharmacies turn out the solution to all emotional or spiritual problems. Clearly, it illustrates dangers we face today.

Morality

Biotechnology has, in a myriad of ways, been a huge blessing. I am grateful every day for the advances in medicine and medical technology that improve the quality and the length of our lives. My own friends and family have recovered from diseases or conditions that fifty years ago would have killed them. Human creativity and industry are wonderful gifts from God which have enabled us to make extraordinary discoveries that enhance and extend life for us all. I stand in awe of developments such as artificial joints, fetal surgery, artificial hearts and the medical successes from adult stem cell therapies. The growth of biotechnology has been, for the most part, a very positive development.

Christians should never be anti-science or anti-progress. Part of the creation mandate is to make life on Earth better, and biomedical advances do just that. In addition, the more science discovers about DNA, the more it reveals that we are the products of an "intelligent designer." The structures and workings of genetics did not come about as the result of a chance collision of atoms in a primordial soup. Science shows that there is a lot more to it than that; and the more we learn, the better our apologetic defense of Christian truth becomes. So I am all for progress. But that does not mean we can disregard circumspection or neglect ethical discretion in such matters.

For not all the developments biotechnology has brought about are positive. Among those that are less than positive are embryonic stem cell research, fetal tissue research, cloning, genetic engineering, genetic discrimination and eugenics. Issues such as these are on the leading edge of biotechnology and on the leading edge of controversy.

It is important in the controversy to distinguish between biotechnology and bioethics. Biotechnology refers to scientific processes that enable us to develop new prescription drugs, to develop artificial heart valves, to break down cell structure, to be able to see the structure of DNA, and a host of other scientific and genetic feats that were unimaginable even a decade ago. It also includes technologies surrounding cloning, genetic engineering and embryonic stem cell research.

Bioethics deals with right conduct in biotechnology and this is really where Christians have a particular responsibility. What Huxley saw (and what C. S. Lewis also saw, from a very different perspective) is that we can never separate science from morality. While Christians should welcome biotechnology because it will bring about great advances in human progress, we need to insist that bioethics have equal stature with biotechnology. We need to be able to look at what is right and wrong in the conduct of science.

Western culture has been dominated over the past two hundred years or so by what I call the "technological imperative." This says that if something *can* be done, it *ought* to be done. If scientists can invent something, they should invent it. So, for example, if we can clone human beings, we should. Those who hold to this call it progress.

Over the past few years, Dr. Panos Zavos, Dr. Severino Antinori and the Raelians have claimed that they have cloned human embryos and implanted them in women's wombs despite protests from many quarters. Dr. Zavos told a congressional committee that live-birth cloning will take place, and he is probably right.[2] If it can be done, someone is sure to do it.

The great need, however, is a consideration of whether we *should* do it. Ethics, you see, deals with the "ought" factor: that is, it asserts what we ought to do and ought not to do. Science, by contrast, deals with the "is" factor: it describes what is. Thus science tells us what can be done, not what ought to be done. This is the province of moral and ethical judgment—of bioethics—and Christians must be prepared to bring this particular dimension to the debate. We should listen to science when it tells us what can be done, but technology must always be tempered by the ethics of what ought to be done.

That raises a difficult, contemporary problem. How can we have meaningful ethics in a relativistic era? Relativism is the prevailing spirit of our age. People today tend to believe that there is no absolute truth. It is taken as obvious that truth is whatever you say it is and that absolute truth is unknowable. Therefore, one person's formulation of truth is as good as anyone else's. When we try to establish what we ought to do, we soon discover that relativistic ethics are an oxymoron. The best approach secular thinking can aspire to today is a utilitarian one. Outcomes alone dictate what we ought and ought not do.

The leading bioethicist in America today—or at least the most famous bioethicist in America—is Princeton professor Peter Singer. Singer, a utilitarian, is eminently logical in his thinking. He rigorously follows his basic presuppositions about life and concludes, for example, that infanticide is perfectly permissible within a person's first two years of life.[3] Since he believes that life is the result of natural processes and his reasoning is logical, his conclusion makes sense. It makes all the difference, in his view, whether a baby is normal or whether a baby is deformed or suffers from Down syndrome, autism or some other abnormality, however slight.[4] (I have a grandson who is autistic, so

---

[2]Panos Zavos, testifying on March 15, 2002 before the House Subcommittee on Oversight and Investigation, during a hearing on issues raised by human cloning research.
[3]Peter Singer, *Practical Ethics*, 2nd ed. (Cambridge: Cambridge University Press, 1993), p. 182.
[4]Ibid., p. 181.

I'm especially alert to this.) If we believe a child is not going to live a worth-while life, then, he reasons, why not just get rid of it? We can dispose of any children if we believe they are imperfect or are going to be a burden on society or even merely a burden on their caretakers.

Singer is a utilitarian who wants to minimize suffering in the world by pro-viding the greatest good for the greatest number. And so he also argues that each of us should live on only $30,000 a year. That way there would be enough money for everybody.[5] He believes that there is no point in keeping disabled old people alive because the elderly are no longer productive or use-ful to society.[6] "The greatest good for the greatest number" encourages us to get rid of old people and other "useless eaters," as John Stuart Mill famously called them.

In an example of tragic-comic irony, actor Christopher Reeve made the same utilitarian argument before a congressional committee.[7] As a result of a riding accident, Reeve is a quadriplegic and is unable even to breathe without mechanical assistance. He believes that biotech holds the key to his walking again, and he has been a vocal proponent of human cloning and destructive embryonic stem cell research. At the hearing, Reeve repeated that adage that the purpose of government is to provide the greatest good for the greatest number. And everyone nodded agreement.

The irony, of course, is that Reeve should rejoice that the purpose of govern-ment is *not* the greatest good for the greatest number, for if it were, Reeve would not be testifying before Congress. His own utilitarian calculus would have turned its deadly cost benefit analysis on him, and no one would have spent the time, money and effort required to keep him alive. He would have been left to die after his accident. We care for Reeve and those like him—and oppose cloning and embryonic stem cell research—because the government's responsibility is not the "greatest good for the greatest number" but rather the protection of the weak from the strong who would exploit them.

Christians believe in what God tells us by divine revelation, and we believe that God's truth can be empirically validated. But you can't empirically vali-date Singer's worldview. In fact, he himself can't live with it. Not long ago he announced that bestiality is morally permissible even though he doesn't en-gage in it.[8] (At least, I hope he doesn't.) In spite of his arguments about the eld-

---

[5]Peter Singer, "Peter Singer's Solution to World Poverty," *The New York Times*, September 5, 1999.
[6]Singer, *Practical Ethics*, p. 184.
[7]Christopher Reeve, testifying on March 5, 2002 before the Senate Health, Education, Labor and Pensions Committee.
[8]Peter Singer, "Heavy Petting," *Nerve*, March 1, 2001 <http://www.nerve.com/Opinions/Singer/heavyPetting/main.asp>. (The URLs cited in this chapter were accessed on January 16, 2004.)

erly, he spends his own money to keep his mother, who has Alzheimer's disease, in extended care.[9] The implications of his worldview are so monstrous that he can't live with their logical conclusions, and neither can Reeve. Their views don't hold up because they are not true. And yet Singer's books and speeches are still taken very seriously in academic circles, where he's viewed as a top bioethicist, and Reeve keeps getting invited back to Congress to hype destructive embryonic research based on reasoning that would deny him his own life.

The moral issue at stake in the biotech debate is no less than what it means to be human. Does being human mean that we are made in the image of God, have dominion over creation and are valuable simply because we exist? Or is being human something that other humans decide for us based on some utilitarian standard? Is our status as human beings given to us at some point in our development, and can it be taken away at another based on some criteria of ability or potential ability?

From a biblical point of view, human value and dignity do not depend on what we can do or have the potential to do. A human embryo does not have value and dignity simply because he or she will someday be able to perform to a certain standard and, thus, reflect the image of God. Likewise, the aged or infirmed don't lose their value and dignity even if they have permanently lost the ability to perform to a standard. Being human gives us value and dignity and entitles us to protection and life because to be human is to be created in the image of God. This applies throughout our journey through life.

Research cloning creates an embryonic human being—someone who bears the image of God— in order for it to be "disaggregated" for medical purposes. That is a polite way of saying that it is pulled to pieces for its stem cells. The embryo is killed for the benefit of a sick person who is different from the embryo only because he or she is older. It is barbaric and has been correctly characterized as "high-tech cannibalism."

What has been called "reproductive" cloning (in truth, all cloning is reproductive) presents a slightly different twist on the same theme of human value and dignity. Cloning in order to bring about live births turns a child into a product. God intended that all children should be begotten in the loving embrace of a husband and a wife and be received—as he or she is—as a gift. In stark contrast, a cloned child is manufactured in a sterile laboratory. The clone is made for a fee and is, like all the things we manufacture, subject to quality control. It turns children into mere commodities, stripping them of value and dignity. As President George W. Bush said in a speech on April 10, 2002,

---

[9]George F. Will, "Life and Death at Princeton," *Newsweek*, September 7, 1999.

Our children are gifts to be loved and protected, not products to be designed and manufactured. Allowing cloning would be taking a significant step toward a society in which human beings are grown for spare body parts, and children are engineered to custom specifications; and that is not acceptable.[10]

Biotech research must be governed by more than a utilitarian standard of morality. It is not acceptable to our culture as a whole, and it is certainly not acceptable to serious Christians, to make decisions based on the technological imperative. Bioethical reasoning based on the meaning and value of human beings must precede and guide biotechnology.

The debates over today's biotech revolution and the public policy that must be put into place bring us back to foundational truth. This is no easy matter since there is big money invested in this revolution and potential fortunes to be made. In light of the enormous amount of money behind biotech, we have to insist that we are not against scientific progress. We simply want that progress tied to moral truth. Without that connection, we will end up creating the ultimate *Brave New World*, where we can decide ahead of time what a person is going to be and where human dignity, human freedom and human rights are things of the past.

Policy

Aldous Huxley, it should be pointed out, was the grandson of T. H. Huxley, who was known as "Darwin's bulldog." Like Charles Darwin, THuxley was an evolutionist. He was also involved in the eugenics fads of that day, attempting to speed evolution along according to a human design. Margaret Sanger came under the same influences and began Planned Parenthood to reduce the population of what she considered inferior classes.[11] Planned Parenthood was based on eugenic philosophy and practice. The misguided thinking, laws and policies of the eugenics movement of the early twentieth century are the precursors to much of biotechnology today, which is, at its core, a modern eugenics movement—an attempt to build the better human, the ultimate utopian project.

C. S. Lewis, a professor of medieval literature, was a true prophet in the sense that he saw then what others could not. In his great book *The Abolition of Man*, Lewis critiqued what he saw as the triumph of science over humanity, warning that this would bring about "the abolition of man," turning him into a project and product:

---

[10]George W. Bush, "Remarks by the President on Human Cloning Legislation," speech given on April 10, 2002 at the White House, Washington, D.C. <http://www.whitehouse.gov/news/releases/2002/04/20020410-4.html>.

[11]Margaret Sanger, *The Pivot of Civilization* (New York: Bretano, 1922), chap. 4.

If any one age really attains by eugenics and scientific education the power to make its descendents what it pleases, all men who live after it are the patients of that power. Man's conquest of nature, if the dreams of some scientific planners are realized, means the rule of a few hundreds of men (in the present that is) over billions upon billions of men born later. Human nature would be the last part of nature to surrender to man, but then the battle would be won.[12]

Lewis spoke about what he called the *Tao*. By that he meant the idea of a transcendent body of truth, an understanding of right and wrong shared by all people in all cultures throughout history. He saw the abandonment of the *Tao* as the opening through which the "Conditioners," as he called them, would come and decide how we should live. The biotech revolution demands that we ask this pivotal question: Will our future be decided by the Conditioners or by each of us as individuals? The answer to this is the one on which the future of humanity succeeds or fails. Will we experience the abolition of humanity through the potions and technology of biotech's Conditioners?

Lewis went on to say that the Conditioners "have sacrificed their own share in traditional humanity in order to devote themselves to the task of deciding what 'Humanity' shall henceforth become."[13] "Good" and "bad" applied to them are mere words without content, for it is from them that the content of these words is from now on to be derived. The Conditioners have placed themselves above humanity as the oligarchic rulers of humanity.

Lewis concluded that "man's final conquest has proved to be the abolition of Man."[14] Lewis prophesied that if you got rid of the *Tao*—the transcendent truth, which I would call Judeo-Christian law and what others call "natural revelation"—there would be no restraints. Eventually the Conditioners, through the progress of science, would decide what humanity should be. And that is precisely the issue before us today. It is precisely why biotechnology policy must be met by sound *bioethics*, which is made possible only through Christian reflection.

Christians must bring that influence to bear in public policy in order to keep moral truth attached to scientific progress. The whole idea of producing humans for body parts or for stem cells may sound appealing to some, but it will lead inevitably to the abolition of humankind and the ultimate end of Western civilization as we know it.

The stakes really are that large. Over the next ten years I believe we will see all this played out in public debates, and Christians, who represent the

---

[12]C. S. Lewis, *The Abolition of Man* (San Francisco: HarperSanFrancisco, 2001), p. 58.
[13]Ibid., p. 63.
[14]Ibid., p. 64.

moral conscience of this nation, need to be a bulwark against what would otherwise be an incredibly appealing sentimental argument. Many will cry, "Save my uncle from his Parkinson's disease. All we need is a little more embryonic stem cell research to do it." We must weep for such a man and his family and show deep compassion for the sick and suffering, but if we allow sentiment to overthrow truth or natural law—the *Tao*—then the decisions about biotechnology will soon be overwhelmed by public passions. And those public passions are, for the most part, ill-informed and deaf to the weightier philosophical and ethical issues biotechnology is forcing us to consider.

In our public policy, we have got to say yes to science, yes to every ethical means to curing someone's Parkinson's. Nonetheless, we must insist on policy which insures that the advances of science will always be tied to moral truth.

Involvement

The road ahead is littered with additional traps for the human race. Cloning and embryonic stem cell research offer us a bridge into a series of life-or-death issues that pro-life Christians have hardly started to consider.

Gene patenting. It is already possible to patent human genes, to "own" a part of our human nature.

Genetic discrimination. People are people, and one should not face discrimination because of one's genes anymore than one's skin color. Yet if businesses can get genetic information about customers or prospective employees, discrimination will surely follow. Health and life insurance rates and availability, for example, could be tied to genetic predisposition to a disease or condition. Opportunities to abuse such information are vast unless we ensure that it remains private and that employment and insurance decisions are not made on genetic grounds. This is ultimately a form of eugenics.

Germline intervention. Just as the eugenics of the early twentieth century was an attempt to "improve" the human race by selective breeding, germline intervention refers to genetic engineering that does the same thing. An individual's genes are altered so as to produce inheritable changes. This might include anything from resistance to inherited diseases, to hair color, to being taller, smarter and faster. Germline intervention may be the most critical issue that will ever confront the human race, because once we can make changes that will be passed on to subsequent generations, we will have changed the human species itself. Some thinkers are now talking about "post-human" nature as we "take control" of our identity by taking control of our genetics.

Nanotechnology and cybernetics. Already a tremendous amount of money is being spent researching new technologies that will mix human beings and machines.

Conclusion

Just as most Christians were asleep thirty years ago when *Roe* v. *Wade* was decided and abortion on demand became legal, we are again in danger of sleeping through another moral catastrophe. With the latest advances in biotechnology, not only are we taking upon ourselves the god-like prerogative of ending human life as we choose (as we have done with abortion and euthanasia), but we are attempting to appropriate the god-like prerogative of making human life as we choose. The most profound question we are being asked today is which is the more grievous sin against God—to take life created in his image or to make life created in man's image?

We need to get a grip on biotechnology and the bioethical considerations that go along with it. It is time for people to get educated, to think about these profound moral questions that affect the future of the human race. Your reading this book is a good beginning. These essays are designed to give a good, basic education on how to approach the ethical questions being raised by the biotech advances.

If we make right choices here, if we refuse to throw off moral restraints, if we deny the postmodern dictum that there is no truth and if we insist that science keep its ventures and enterprises tied to moral truth, then we may avoid Lewis's distressing vision. We may yet prevent the "abolition of man."

1

CHRISTIAN VISION
FOR THE BIOTECH CENTURY

Toward a Strategy

NIGEL M. de S. CAMERON, Ph.D.

The point of departure for Christian reflection on medicine and biotechnology is the fact that God made us in his image, imparting to humankind a unique dignity that radically distinguishes humans from other creatures and also from the inanimate creation, and declaring the "sanctity" of life—a safeguarding of human life by the holy God. For many centuries this fundamental assumption governed the thinking of our civilization and had powerful effects on the development of medicine and science, as well as on the shape of public policy. That forms the context for the challenge posed by abortion, with its notion that unborn human life is at the disposal of maternal choice, and the challenge posed by euthanasia, with its notion that whether one lives or dies (outside the womb) depends on someone's choice. Christians and even some non-Christians have identified abortion and euthanasia as evils to be challenged through distinctive Christian living, through education and caring, and through public policy.

Yet as we move into the twenty-first century, it is clear that potentially greater evils lie ahead, ones in which we move from taking life made in God's image, to making it in our own through our manipulation of human biology, and, finally, to faking it from inanimate materials.

The human race faces a challenge of a new kind, for which our churches are ill-prepared and which poses enormous problems to governments. Yet those who seek to defend the integrity of human life—to work for a "human future" free from the technological reductionism of the Brave New World *scenario—will confront some unusual advantages, since they have allies among the very liberal Christians and secularists who have given leadership to the "pro-choice" cause on abortion. This has been evident in an ad hoc fashion in debates about human cloning, but it promises to be of vast significance as the century progresses and the biotech agenda unfolds. The prospect of long-term collaboration between conservative Christians, liberal Christians and secularists seems strange to many and will raise many difficulties. Yet it offers the best hope under God of a human*

society that will strive to ensure that biotechnology sustains, and does not supplant, the
dignity of the individual.

NIGEL M. DE S. CAMERON

The announcement in February of 1997 that Dolly the sheep had been cloned took the media by storm and offered cover copy to news magazines, many of which showed an uncomprehending sheep staring out at a scarcely more comprehending public around the globe. Yet for all the news hype its significance was, and continues to be, underestimated.[1]

The first mammalian cloning bifurcates the history of the world. It announces to humankind as has nothing before that we are in line to become the creatures, the products, of our own inventive selves: *Homo sapiens* in the hands of *Homo faber*.[2] As the talk shows jumped straight from reporting on the Scottish sheep to discussing the meaning of this story for the human future, Dolly became instantly famous as the centerpiece of a growing debate about biotechnology and human nature. On trial, alongside human nature itself, is the capacity of our public institutions to respond to what many now see as their greatest challenge.

By curious coincidence, the year 1997 also witnessed the formalization of the first two international responses intended to set policy parameters for the development of biotechnology: the Council of Europe's European Convention on Human Rights and Biomedicine and UNESCO's Universal Declaration on the Human Genome and Human Rights.[3] Between them they represent the attempts of the more prescient members of the international community to anticipate the policy challenges of the biotech revolution. Yet the slow rate of their progress (both these projects began in the mid-1980s) shows the limits to their prescience, the vastness of the challenge and the problems of multilateral decision making.

---

[1]Earlier versions of this paper were presented at the Council for Biotechnology Policy conference in Washington, D.C., on February 22, 2002, and at a meeting of congressional staff on April 23, 2002.

[2]*Homo faber* means "man the maker," a term used by anthropologists to focus on our capacity to use tools to make things.

[3]Of the two, the European Convention is both more comprehensive in scope and more substantive in its positions. For example, in the area that it addresses in common with the UNESCO statement, it seeks to prohibit germline (inheritable) genetic interventions. By contrast, the UNESCO declaration states that this central question needs to be studied further, since it "could" affect human dignity.

It has become customary for historians to see the so-called nineteenth century as beginning in 1789 and ending in 1914. There is little doubt that in due time they will deem the twenty-first, and indeed the third millennium anno domini, to have begun in 1997.

Four Contexts for Cloning

The simplest way to illustrate the significance of these developments is to set cloning itself in a fourfold context.

First, it represents the latest intervention in the process of mammalian reproduction. Religious authorities and some secularists were deeply troubled in the middle of the twentieth century by the application to human beings of artificial insemination (AI), long a technique of animal husbandry. Some focused on the technique itself (in which sperm is implanted "artificially" in the womb); others focused on the use of "donor sperm," that is, sperm from a third party. While that debate is now hardly in evidence, the AI controversy raised some of the key issues that remain at stake in the current debate. The idea of medical intervention to enable conception also gained wide social acceptance, even when it involves a gamete from another party. AI led directly to its more sophisticated sibling, in vitro fertilization (IVF), in which either gamete could now come from a third party and the fertilization process is attained under controlled conditions in the lab.[4] This raised fresh ethical issues and greatly increased the options and dilemmas involved. But while it generated publicity, there was surprisingly little controversy found outside the Roman Catholic Church, even among evangelical Christians.

Against the backdrop of AI and IVF, cloning is plainly revolutionary. Indeed, one of the many ironies of current debate is the degree to which assisted reproduction technologies (ARTs) involving AI, IVF and their variants radiate by contrast an aura of normalcy, since they seek to replicate the natural process of conception—even though in "unnatural" and controlled circumstances. In cloning we have a completely different technique, a mechanism for asexual reproduction. Yet it is one for which the public mind (and the unreflective Christian mind that tracks with it) has been prepared, its moral sensibilities dulled. AI and IVF, aside from their respective merits and demerits, have built a bridge between procreation as natural process (the consequence of sexual union) and reproduction as an act of human will and technique in which science and medicine combine to enable a range of choice in childbearing. When combined with such techniques as the selection of gametes, preimplantation genetic diagnosis (PGD) to ensure genetically attractive offspring, surrogacy and other manipulative com-

---

[4]Louise Brown, the world's first test-tube baby, was born in England more than twenty-five years ago, in 1978.

ponents, "reproduction" in the late twentieth century had already taken on key lineaments of the custom building of a product with features selected by the customer.[5] *Homo faber* is already getting to work on the design of himself.

The second context for cloning lies in abortion. Indeed, it is almost entirely for this reason that Christians have become engaged both morally and politically to seek its prohibition. Abortion has not only loomed over the landscape of political and cultural life in the United States for the past generation, it has served as *the* major focus for political interest and activity on the part of conservative Christians. It has served as the framework for their engagement with questions in medicine and science. We may wish to note that the relative lack of interest in euthanasia, potentially a greater question than abortion, is disturbing, for we face in biotechnology a growing agenda of issues that are more obscure and often less directly threatening to human life than the killing of the sick and elderly.

There is a double connection between abortion and cloning. Cloning advocates fall into two groups: those who favor the birth of live-born cloned children, and those who may or may not favor cloned children but who seek cloned human embryos for purposes of experimentation. Advocates of this latter use of the somatic cell nuclear transfer (SCNT) technology (by which Dolly was cloned) have devised two confusing terms by which they seek to distinguish themselves from the much smaller number of baby-cloning advocates: *therapeutic cloning,* that is, cloning for research in which the embryo is destroyed (to produce embryonic stem cells or for some other reason); and *reproductive cloning,* in which the cloned embryo is implanted and leads to a live birth. We should note that all cloning is in fact "reproductive," and none is "therapeutic" to the clone (note the parallel with therapeutic abortion, so-called).

The point to note here is that while cloning for research invariably would destroy the cloned embryo, cloning that is intended to lead to live-born children would cause many deaths along the way. (Dolly was the one relatively healthy survivor out of 277.) So the pro-life movement has lined up behind a ban on all human cloning.

But the abortion context goes wider, since liberal abortion has undoubtedly paved the way for a laissez-faire approach to experimentation on the early embryo, itself one of the keys to IVF and other reproductive technologies.[6]

The third context is more fundamental. Abortion, like cloning, is no mere accident; neither (to shift the metaphor) is it a disease to be treated in itself.

---

[5]A market for gametes is evidenced in the solicitation of sperm on the Internet and ads for egg donation in college newspapers.

[6]In the UK it is approved and regulated; in the United States the controversy has focused on funding, but there are no restrictions in federal law on privately funded research.

Rather, it is a symptom of a far-wider-ranging disease process in our culture. Failure to grasp this foundational fact threatens the strategic effectiveness of the pro-life movement, and as new questions of biotechnology are raised, a strategic misstep could have tragic consequences for the human future. For abortion, like so many of the new approaches of bioethics and public policy in this last generation, is a subset of the steady reconstruction of the Western vision of human nature.

At one level this is simple to illustrate. Much of the earlier debate about abortion focused on what seemed to many on both sides to be the central question: when does life begin? That debate has moved on. It is at heart now no longer about when life begins, but about what life is and whose right it is to make decisions about life and death. We might say that the debate has moved back, from one about embryology to one about anthropology—what it means to be human. In ways that are complex but discernible, our culture is engaged in an often blind effort to remake the meaning of human nature. That is nowhere as evident as it is in the questions raised by bioethics, since here we deal directly with whether and under what circumstances human life may be taken; whether it may be copied; whether, finally, it may be radically reshaped—as a matter of our choice and design.

Here we note the fourth context, since cloning, in tandem with the culture's engagement in rethinking human nature, offers the firstfruits of a technology that is destined to raise for humankind the most profound of all questions. For cloning is just the beginning. The scope of biotech's possibilities has yet to be imagined. What we do know is that its capacities will press the human conscience, and its capacity to develop and implement public policy responses, to the limit.

The Shape of the Biotech Debate

It is common for the many questions raised by medicine and biotechnology to be listed as if they were disconnected from one another. Yet, as we have noted, debates about abortion and euthanasia prepared the way for our discussion of issues in biotechnology both directly, by undermining our assumptions about the sanctity of life, and also indirectly, by giving shape to gathering cultural unease and confusion about what it means to be human—and, therefore, about how humans should be treated.

The first major policy document in the field, like the first "test-tube baby," was produced in the United Kingdom, under the guidance of moral philosopher Mary Warnock. In an infamous passage that has set the lamentable pattern for policy development in much of the world, the Warnock Report states that "instead of trying to answer" the questions of "when life or personhood begins," the report's contributors have "gone straight to the question of *how it is right to treat the human embryo."*[7] It is an elementary question, but unless we know what something is, how we can know how to treat it? This admission of ignorance in relation to the nature of the human embryo is symbolic of our more general willing ignorance of the nature of human being itself that has pervaded public discussion of issues in medicine and biotechnology. If we do not know what it means to be human, how shall we know how to treat humans, even as we begin to develop powers over our own selves—not simply taking life but shaping it according to our wishes?

In summary, we should note here a threefold development. In Bioethics 1 (my term for the discussions of the past generation), the focus has been on whether and when we should *take* life. Abortion and euthanasia form the bookends of this debate, though it has many more subtle components, such as definitions of brain death, transplant protocols, "do not resuscitate" (DNR) orders, questions about the so-called persistent vegetative state, the debate of whether withdrawing food and drink is permissible as the withdrawal of "treatment," and more besides. The great questions of Bioethics 1 have focused on the taking of life. Its disagreements and lack of resolution stem directly from the unresolved questions of who is alive and who is human, and of whether and when human life may be deliberately taken.

In Bioethics 2 we turn from the *taking* of life to the *making* of life—decisions intended to enable us to design a child to order. That may be with current technologies such as certain options made available by IVF: positive options include the selection of desirable gametes; negative options include the use of preimplantation genetic diagnosis (PGD) to "weed out" the less desirable embryos. But it will find its fulfillment in the far more sophisticated options that will be enabled by the application of our growing knowledge of human genetics to the design of human life.

In Bioethics 3 we move from *taking* life through *making* life to what I have somewhat crudely termed the *faking* of life: the capacity of developments in the fields of nanotechnology and cybernetics to manipulate, enhance and finally perhaps supplant biological human nature.[8]

The theological questions emerge here with great clarity, for this entire debate is addressed with extraordinary relevancy in Genesis 1. In summary, the narrative of the creation sets out the unique significance of human being,

---

[7]*Report of the Committee of Inquiry into Human Fertilisation and Embryology,* Cmnd. 9314 1984, p. 60.
[8]I gladly acknowledge the contribution of my friend and colleague C. Christopher Hook, M.D., who persuaded me that these developments qualified as a third division within the bioethics agenda and proposed the term Bioethics 3 to cover them. They share, of course, the same goals as Bioethics 2. His essay in this book (see chap. four) surveys these questions and their implications.

made in the "image of God"—the imago Dei—to rule over the rest of God's creation. The image of God is, as has been said, species-specific: *only* human-kind and *all* of humankind—every member of *Homo sapiens*—is made in God's image. The so-called dominion mandate lays out the role of God's human crea-tures as his stewards not simply of the agricultural world of fish and animals enumerated, but of every thing and every creature God has made. So side by side with the unique character of human nature, we have also the mandate for science and technology. The dilemma of the twenty-first century lies precisely here in the fateful confluence of these two principles, that is, as created human beings confront the new powers of technology over our own selves—the meet-ing point of the dominion mandate and the imago Dei. What is more, at the heart of Christian theology lies the incarnation. This "human nature" that God has made in his image has been assumed by God himself. In Jesus of Nazareth we see "the Word made flesh"; and although Jesus was crucified, dead, and buried, and then rose and ascended to the right hand of God, he has not laid down his human nature. A neglected though core Christian belief is that the second person of the Trinity, the Son of God, having once taken human nature, has not laid it down. The doctrine of the continuing humanity of Christ comes into fresh focus as we reflect on our new powers to change human nature it-self. If the fact that every human being bears the image of God is fundamental to Christian perspectives on every traditional issue in bioethics—affirming as it does the radical equality and dignity of every member of the species, from zygote onward—then the point of departure in Christian bioethics as we con-front the new manipulative technologies of germline interventions and "trans-humanism," which hold out the promise of reshaping human nature, is the hu-manity of Christ.

Democracy on Trial

Behind the many particular issues of this debate lurks the underlying question for public policy: can our democratic institutions frame a proportionate re-sponse to the exponential demands that biotechnology will make on the fabric of human society? As government pursues its traditional priorities of national defense and adroit economic management, a stealth agenda of greater import has begun to break the surface—the question of the future of human nature. Since democratic government has evolved in a period of settled conviction about such fundamental questions, it is little surprise that our institutions find this fateful challenge to be traumatic.

How are ordinary folk to grasp what is at stake? What are they to make of the "experts" who rule the airwaves and the op-ed pages? And once they have grasped what is going on, how are they to influence events? The more insis-tently we ask these questions, the bigger loom the challenges to democracy.

For biotech questions are not what we have been used to. At one level, the basic expertise required for democratic participation in this debate is not high, given that our culture requires biology in both college and high school. But the "expert" factor is of grave political consequence, as I note below.

We must confront huge questions that the democratic process was not designed to handle—fast-paced changes in our understanding of science that challenge all of us who want to stay on top of developments, challenges that focus on controlling and changing the nature of human being itself. We need to note four interrelated factors in the emerging policy debate.

1. Technology and ignorance. There is no shortcut to expecting responsible citizens to develop a basic familiarity with developments in biology. Our local newspaper carried a recent report on a high school senior who had just graduated despite the challenges of life in a wheelchair. "Stem-cell research" might cure her problem, she told the reporter, but "the government won't allow it." Well, those who follow the debate will note at least three basic mistakes in that statement: work on adult stem cells is hugely promising and is being funded energetically by the federal government; basic work on embryonic stem cell lines is also being funded; and there is in any case no federal prohibition on privately funded work that involves destroying embryos to obtain embryonic stem cells. Moreover, the pending federal legislation that would prohibit cloning would affect not destructive embryo research itself, but merely cloning to mass-produce the embryos.

Unless citizens (and journalists) can learn to appreciate such distinctions as the biotech agenda becomes even more sophisticated, democracy will find itself increasingly dislocated, the victim of slogans and hype, and biotech—with its huge corporate influence—will run out of control.

2. The "expert" problem. Feeding on public ignorance and fear, the biotech industry has taken on a defensive posture: its "experts"—whether scientists or "bioethicists" or plain public-relations people (BIO, the industry group, recently renamed its chief lobbyist "vice president of bioethics")—have fallen back on the use of mantras such as the meaningless slogan "Cures now." They claim to favor cures for disease; they imply that their opponents do not. So hearings are peppered with wheelchairs, and the endorsement of disease-advocacy organizations is cultivated as a trump card. The public in general is both ignorant of the science and scared of disease. The biotech industry and its scientist-entrepreneurs tell us not to worry but to trust them to seek cures for our woes. Meanwhile, their political sponsors deny that there should be any limitation on their freedom. We should leave it all to the experts, we are told; they know best and we can trust them. This claim, we should note, is thoroughly disingenuous since all scientific and medical research is regulated by ethics rules, and no responsible scientist would suggest that they are unnecessary.

3. A new kind of politics. As the cloning debate has already shown, the questions raised by biotechnology are not the same as those that have traditionally divided our politics. The very fact that opposition to cloning has come from both sides of the pro-life and pro-choice divide illustrates this forcefully. Conservatives and progressives share a respect for human nature and a distrust of manipulative interventions that will enable certain men and women to reshape others. This pits the more radical progressives against the mainstream liberals they thought were their friends; for those who want the freedom to do what they choose, ironically, want to let big biotech business do what it chooses. And on the conservative side, it pits those who treasure the sanctity of life against both libertarians and others who tend to uncritically favor corporate interests.

It is hard to predict how this newfound alliance between those divided by their general political philosophy, and their view on issues like abortion, will develop. What is clear is that the bio questions (what the Germans call *Biopolitic*) do not fit neatly into our traditional politics, and they therefore present us with special political challenge. This combination of pro-life and pro-choice forces could prove a novel and potent political force, and I discuss it further below.

4. Biotech and international policy debate. The biotech issues are being considered in many multilateral forums, from the Council of Europe to UNESCO and other agencies of the United Nations. It has been recognized that these are fundamental questions affecting all of humankind, and that it is hard to see how individual nations can control the direction of biotechnology.[9] Yet these international bodies are to exercise democratic accountability. Indeed, it can be hard to discover what it is they are doing. This has become a pressing issue with the United States' decision to rejoin UNESCO (the United Nations Educational, Social and Cultural Organization). UNESCO's work includes the International Bioethics Committee, which is working on the long-term goal of a "universal instrument" in bioethics—that is, a convention that covers the biotech waterfront. The Universal Declaration on the Human Genome, to which I referred above, is intended to be the first step toward such an international convention.

It may make sense for us to work for global agreement on these issues, but ensuring that such bodies are responsive to public opinion presents a huge challenge.

The Need for Action

More than ten years ago I wrote an essay that reviewed the meager Christian

---

[9]The United States, which dominates global biotechnology markets (having three-quarters of biotechnology revenues in 2003), has a unique opportunity to exercise policy leadership.

contributions to bioethics debate, citing Sir Edward Creasey's famous book
The Fifteen Decisive Battles of the World.[10] History does not turn entirely on military strategy and the tactics that can make all the difference to an individual
engagement. There are vast forces at work in what Samuel Huntington has
memorably called the "clash of civilizations,"[11] and we know well that so
much of the modern world is explicable only in terms of the internal clash
within Western culture of its Judeo-Christian roots and their Enlightenment
critique. But to note that there are great historical forces at work is never to
suggest inaction or fatalism on our part. As I have argued elsewhere, the history of warfare makes plain that there is nothing "inevitable" about the outcomes of the clashes of great powers and their military forces.[12]

This has been neatly illustrated by the recent surge of interest in so-called
counterfactuals, scholarly explorations of what might have been had the great
decisions and engagements gone another way.[13] We could elaborate on some
of our own counterfactuals. Had Christians been fatalists in the eighteenth
century, the church would have taken Enlightenment advice and essentially
resigned itself to some kind of Unitarian accommodation with nascent secu-
larism. And the nineteenth century as we know it—the greatest century of mis-
sionary expansion in which, not least, America was comprehensively evangel-
ized and bequeathed the deep-rooted religious conviction to which we have
fallen heir—would simply not have happened.

Fatalism is no part of the Christian worldview. One thing we do learn from
history is that action can pay; strategically focused, timely activism, modeled
in such heroes as William Wilberforce, can change the future. By steadily and
skillfully engaging the slave trade and slavery itself in the British Empire, Wilberforce fought one of our civilization's most decisive battles, laying the foundations for abolition here in the United States and its belated echo in the civil
rights movement a century later.

During the past several years I have been invited to debate human cloning
on college and university campuses, often along with Gregory Pence, whose
book *Who's Afraid of Human Cloning?* is an eloquent defense of baby cloning as
a reproductive right.[14] I well recall that during one such debate he made his

---

[10]Nigel M. de S. Cameron, "Bioethics: The Twilight of Western Hippocratism," in *God and Cul-
ture: Essays in Honor of Carl F. H. Henry*, ed. D. A. Carson and John D. Woodbridge (Grand
Rapids. Mich.: Eerdmans, 1993), pp. 321-40; citing Sir Edward Creasey, *The Fifteen Decisive
Battles of the World*, first edition 1851.

[11]Samuel Huntington, *The Clash of Civilizations and the Remaking of World Order* (New York: Si-
mon & Schuster, 1996).

[12]Cameron, "Bioethics."

[13]The best recent example is Niall Ferguson, ed., *Virtual History: Alternatives and Counterfactuals* (London: Macmillan, 1997).

[14]Gregory Pence, *Who's Afraid of Human Cloning?* (Lanham, Md.: Rowman & Littlefield, 1998).

usual rights claims and coupled them with a common and cancerous argument that we hear on all sides: biotechnology is here to stay; we can't prevent it; the industry and the market will shape it; so whatever our views may be, there is not very much we can do.[15] In my rebuttal, I asked the question, who, in fact, is in favor of choice? Pence was saying that as a community we *have* no choices. My case was that, by contrast, we can, we must, shape our future, under God. We must decide what it is we choose for the human community. It is in our hands to frame policy that will give us a biotechnology which serves us. The alternative, a biotechnology that we serve, is the greatest threat that hangs over the twenty-first century.

So we may wish to welcome the cloning of Dolly as an object lesson, one that we could hardly have expected so early in the new biotech. Here is our opportunity to educate ourselves and our community, to discern what Leon Kass has called the wisdom of repugnance and to develop the outlines of policy.[16] In the prospect of human cloning we gaze into an image of biotechnology setting its own pace for the human species; we see the twin dimensions of biotech as hubris and horror (the conjoining of Faust and Frankenstein, as it were) and a sampling of the new powers that we are taking to ourselves.

Cloning is the first in a succession of waves of technological development that, one after another and in combinations we cannot predict, are set to break on the moral structures of our culture. Cloning is intertwined with the patenting of genetic material that has suddenly made this field hugely attractive to investors and crippled the public-good motivation of researchers. Behind it lies the prospect of germline gene interventions—modifications of the germ cells that are inheritable by succeeding generations—as we become able not just to pick but to "design" our babies. And in back of that lie developments in cybernetics and nanotechnology that take us beyond biology to its control and replication in the manufacture of devices of intelligence and enhancement, and to the integration of the human and the mechanical. While there are serious debates about whether artificial intelligence will in fact be able to empower us to replicate and supersede the life of the mind, there is no question that each of these waves of technological advance and corporate opportunity will pose afresh the question at the heart of our culture: what does it mean to be human?

For in each case we are confronted with a cornucopia of possibility—whether for healing or enhancement or control. We may expect that the appeal will be intense, and the attraction of particular applications marketed to us with full force. The policy parameters to which we agree today will set the tone for tomorrow

---

[15]This debate was at the University of North Dakota in early 2002.
[16]Leon Kass, "The Wisdom of Repugnance," *The New Republic*, June 2, 1997, pp. 17-26.

and what it will bring. And that of course is the reason some leaders of the bio-industrial complex are so deeply committed to resisting policy development of any kind. For them, as for us, this is round one of a great struggle; and every succeeding round will be easier for the side that wins at the outset.

And these considerations distinguish the significance of this debate from every preceding discussion. There are basic connections with the moral and policy discussions over the experimental use of in vitro embryos, and one of the side effects of cloning has been shedding light on the degree to which the entire clutch of in vitro questions qualify as unfinished business.[17]

Cloning, by contrast, represents the first decisive step across the line that separates the kind of beings we are from the kind of things we make; thus *Homo sapiens,* who has always been *Homo faber,* man the maker, turns his making on himself—and in the sublimest of ironies, in a single fateful act both elevates himself to the role of creator and degrades that same self to the status of a manufacture.

This act is stupefying in its scope. Humankind simultaneously claims the role of God and reduces itself to playing the part of a mere thing, the dust of the earth out of which we were made and to which we foolish creatures choose to return ourselves; to become, in President Bush's recent phrase, commodity rather than creation.

From a theological perspective the significance of both sides of the coin is plain. In our attempt to serve as our own creator, we are revealed as usurpers, capable only of manufacture. That Faustian bargain is the only one offered. For the task of creator is personal to God, and his election of the interpersonal mystery of human sexuality as the context for procreation preserves his creator-hood absolutely. The most that his human creatures can do is, as we say, to "ape" his role, parody it, and reduce it to the mechanistic and industrial processes at which we are so good and for which indeed—among other things—we were made. The ambiguity of the clonal human, as both creature and product, as *Homo sapiens* hijacked by *Homo faber,* moves us decisively toward what the posthumanists call the "singularity"—that state they envisage in which the distinction between human being and manufactured being is over, and a seamless dress weaves together our humankind and what we have made. It anticipates the union of *mecha* and *orga.*[18]

It is worth noting that outside narrow academic circles this discussion is being carried on almost entirely in science fiction literature and movies,

---

[17]This is well illustrated by the fact that the President's Council on Bioethics held hearings on the question in 2003 (see <http://bioethics.gov>). (The URLs cited in this chapter were accessed on January 16, 2004.)

[18]These useful terms are from director Steven Spielberg's 2001 movie *AI: Artificial Intelligence,* generally memorable only for its special effects.

from *Frankenstein* and *Brave New World* onward, including *The Matrix*, which anticipates a world in which the machines have taken over. Perhaps the most powerful recent commentary was the movie *Gattaca*, which portrayed a society in which the use and abuse of genetic information destroys human dignity.[19]

In his famous jeremiad, "Why the Future Doesn't Need Us," Bill Joy, cofounder of Sun Microsystems, claims that genetics, robotics and nanotechnology are the three great threats to the human race in the twenty-first century.[20] Through some mixture of accident and intent, they are likely to destroy the human species, or supplant it, through some biological or mechanical meltdown or through the triumph of machine intelligence. One does not need to buy the whole thesis to acclaim his comprehensive framing of the issues. And at the heart of this secular analysis lies what Christians recognize as a single theological issue: the threat to human nature posed by fallen human creativity, that is, the dominion mandate from Genesis 1 to "subdue the earth" divorced from its biblical context, which is human dignity made in the image of God.

With human cloning we therefore cross the Rubicon. We venture for the first time into the manufacture of our own kind. Until now the depth of our imaginative depravity had to be content with new forms of killing, the legacy of Cain and Abel. We confront now a new kind of sin, a fresh fulfillment of our conflicted fallen nature, the sequel of the Tower of Babel. This is our best opportunity to begin to frame public policy for biotechnology around an issue of high profile that has resonated with the public conscience.

The challenge comes to us at that time in the history of our civilization when we are least able to resist. While our churches remain full (at least here in the United States), the Judeo-Christian defaults that have long nourished the values of our culture and fed its moral vision are steadily being reset by our cultural elite in a process aided by the generally pietistic and withdrawn character of our Christianity. It remains to be seen whether Christian commitment to the pro-life cause, the single most striking exception, can evolve into a broad engagement with biotechnology.

---

[19]*Gattaca* (1997, written and directed by Andrew Niccol) is a fine movie for many reasons, not least as a celebration of an unusual friendship between men that is entirely devoid of eroticism. Part of its message is that genetic reductionism (*genoism* is one of the many terms coined in the script) undermines the freedom and dignity of those with "good genes" (the "valid") and weaker genes (the "in-valid") alike. Indeed, two of the characters emerge as tragic figures whose lives are blighted since they have failed to fulfill genetic expectations, in contrast to those with weaker genes who transcend their predicated destiny.

[20]Bill Joy, "Why the Future Doesn't Need Us," *Wired*, April 2000 <http://www.wired.com/wired/archive/8.04/joy.html>.

The Need for a Christian Strategy

Asked what was his strategy on coming into office, Winston Churchill famously temporized, "It is to wage war, by land and sea." At that same level, ours is always to resist evil and to promote good. But how shall we do it?

We have noted that the debate over human cloning has offered a powerful opportunity for the education of the conscience of the world, as we move toward the prospect of C. S. Lewis's chilling vision in *The Abolition of Man*. The pro-life movement has been drawn, not without some hesitation, into energetic support for a comprehensive ban on human cloning. At the same time, as pro-choice law professor Lori Andrews and I declared in a joint op-ed in the *Chicago Tribune*, a watershed has been crossed in collaboration between political progressives and conservatives, between pro-choice and pro-life.[21] The occasion of the editorial was a House Commerce hearing on cloning at which, we noted, one of the great moments of political theater of our generation was being acted out, as representative pro-choice and progressive environmental figures lined up behind legislation that originated with the pro-life community.

Two strategic issues here emerge. First, the pro-life community needs to upgrade both its understanding of and commitment to questions that go beyond abortion and yet are of equal gravity to our conscience and our civilization in their threat to the sanctity of human life.[22]

Second, cooperation between those who have been and those who remain foes of abortion will be central to the long-term task of engaging the emerging biotech agenda on issues as diverse as germline interventions (inherited genetic modifications), gene patenting issues, genetic discrimination and, later, nanotechnology and artificial intelligence. We have moved to consolidate this emerging coalition. The *Tribune* op-ed was followed by the first of a series of private meetings that have now led to the formation of the Institute on Biotechnology and the Human Future (which I codirect with Andrews).

We turn now to review these issues of strategy.

---

[21]Lori Andrews and Nigel M. de S. Cameron, "Cloning and the Debate on Abortion," *Chicago Tribune*, August 8, 2001, p. 17.

[22]Several initiatives have led to increasing reflection and action on this emerging agenda within the conservative Christian community, including the Council for Biotechnology Policy <http://www.biotechpolicy.org>, an affiliate of the Wilberforce Forum, and the Center for Bioethics and Culture <http://thecbc.org>. I addressed these questions in "Biotechnology and the Struggle for Human Dignity: Whatever Happened to the Human Race?" my keynote speech to the National Right to Life Committee's convention in 2002, published in *Representative American Speeches, 2002-2003*, ed. Calvin M. Logue and Lynn Messina (New York: H. W. Wilson, 2003).

Strategy 1: We Must Develop a New Pro-life Paradigm

The strategic situation of the Christian church on the cusp of the biotech century is not strong. Widespread disengagement from public debate and political-cultural action has been characteristic of the American church. Abortion has proved, to some degree, an exception. It has galvanized Christians to engage in policy issues and has become a keynote of cultural critique. Not only has this had profound effects on the church, but it has also made abortion one of the dominant factors in contemporary American politics.

While those who lead the pro-life movement include sophisticated intellectuals and strategists well aware of broader issues in medicine, science and policy, most of their followers would summarize the pro-life message as the need to "save babies." This simple message as the basis for mission focus has proved a major factor in the success of the movement. Yet, as is evident from the meager engagement of pro-life individuals and organizations in the potentially greater challenge posed by euthanasia, the obverse of this commendable mission focus is strategic weakness for the wider cause of human dignity in the contexts in medicine and biotechnology.

What is seen by some as "mission-creep" is rather a dawning awareness that the dignity of human life, focused in the threat posed by abortion, will require in the twenty-first century a more comprehensive defense. As I said above, we are moving from Cain and Abel to the Tower of Babel. In this new situation, the killing of the unborn is rivaled by the transcendent crimes of genetic manipulation—the redesign of human nature—and, through mechanisms such as cloning, the manufacture of whole classes of compromised human beings.

The problem is well illustrated by the fact that for pro-lifers experimental (so-called therapeutic) cloning is considered to be plainly wrong since it kills the unborn. Live-birth (so-called reproductive) cloning may be ruled out on safety grounds. But as to cloning *in itself*, on the assumption, let us say, that it were to prove as "safe" as natural conception, some find it harder to take a view. Thus what would a pro-life position be if, *per impossibile*, it could be shown that it was actually "safer" to clone babies than to conceive and carry them the natural way? Would it then be pro-life to favor cloning?

We do not, of course, have a moral calculus readily to hand—one of the many problems of utilitarianism. Goods and evils may be incommensurable. How do we compare, let us say, an abortion with lifelong enslavement? How do we compare a crime of violence with a lifetime of discrimination based on the misuse of genetic information? When we assess the new crimes made possible by developments in biotechnology, we find ourselves confronting fresh features in the moral landscape.

It is important that we see elective abortion as symptom and not disease. The symptoms of a diseased, inhumane medical and scientific culture are mounting—a culture in which manipulative technologies place in our hands capacities for the abuse of human beings that go even beyond abortion in their sinister sophistication. It has been said that it is at least an open question whether in God's eyes to take a human life made in his image is as serious a challenge to the moral order as making a human life in our own. The compounding technological and moral threat to human nature becomes ever more serious.

This multiplication of challenges to the sanctity of life requires a proportionate response, both in the development of our vision for human dignity and in our political-cultural engagement. This is necessary not simply in order to enable Christians to influence legislation and broader cultural forces, but in order to enable them to lead distinctive lives. One of the little-noted yet pervasive and malign effects of the disengagement of much conservative Christianity from culture has been the steady secularization of the Christian mind. This effect is tragic, since much of the well-intentioned if ignorant pressure on Christians to disengage from public culture has been motivated by the desire to preserve the distinctive features of their beliefs and their way of life. Yet while that has had some success in areas such as the *adiaphora* of smoking and drinking alcohol, its net effect has been to encourage the secularization of Christians' thinking on all matters not explicitly addressed as part of their religion. On these questions (all the way from, in many cases, issues of wealth and poverty to attitudes toward in vitro fertilization) the influences are not from the church and its teaching. The influences therefore come from the ambient secular culture. Unless "secular" questions are energetically addressed within the context of a Christian worldview, the steady secularization of Christian thinking results. Unless the church awakens to the profound significance of the biotech agenda, its distinctive lifestyle will be eroded as Christians join non-Christians in the uncritical acceptance of the commodification of humankind.

Yet Christians are called to be both distinctive and engaged—to be not of the world, but in it; to be light, yet also to be salt. The pro-family and more sharply focused pro-life organizations that have developed to represent the Christian worldview in the public square face a radical challenge in the emerging biotech agenda. If, as is argued consistently in these essays, biotech represents the gravest threat to human dignity and therefore to the Christian vision for our culture, these organizations need to overhaul their mission and their activities in proportion to that threat.

"The Sanctity of Life in a Brave New World: A Manifesto on Biotechnology and Human Dignity," drafted by the editors of this volume and endorsed by an impressive range of conservative Christian leaders, sets forth the major questions.[23] It offers a public overview of the Christian agenda for biotechnology and has begun the process of defining the pro-family/pro-life movement's position on the greatest questions of the twenty-first century.

Strategy 2: We Must Develop Durable Collaboration with "Progressive" Critics of Biotech

The critique of biotechnology has come chiefly from the predominantly secular, progressive end of the political spectrum. Much of the interest, especially in Europe, has been in agricultural biotech, focusing on the development of "genetically modified" foods, known widely in Europe as Frankenfoods. But it extends also to human biotech and is most in evidence in Germany, where public policy has set severe restraints on the development of ethically problematic medicine and biotechnology. The "German conscience," the result of the experience of medicine and science under the Nazi regime, has led to the most cautious and principle-based approach to human biotech in the world. Thus human cloning was outlawed as far back as 1990, on pain of five years' imprisonment. Preimplantation genetic diagnosis is illegal. The import of certain embryonic cell lines has recently been permitted, but it was done in a highly restrictive decision modeled on that of President Bush in 2001. The strength of the environmental movement in Europe has given a conservative cast to biotech policy development in many countries and also in the Council of Europe (as I have already noted).

In the United States several environmental groups and other progressives have been energetically engaged in this debate. The Council for Responsible Genetics, which is staunchly pro-choice, opposes all research on human embryos. The Boston Women's Health Book Collective, publishers of *Our Bodies, Ourselves*—the best-known feminist women's health book—was associated with a letter by feminist and other progressive leaders seeking a moratorium on the cloning of embryos for research. On the liberal religious front, the United Methodist Church, an explicitly pro-choice denomination, has taken a lead in pressing for a comprehensive cloning ban. At a political level, the bill that would ban all human cloning is cosponsored by pro-life and pro-choice members of the House and Senate.

This growing rapprochement with the generally pro-choice progressive community must form the keystone to a comprehensive biotech strategy for the twenty-first century. Politics has always produced ad hoc coalitions on is-

---

[23]This manifesto is printed in the appendix. It was launched in February 2003 in a press conference on Capitol Hill. Signatories included the editors of this volume as well as James Dobson, Joni Eareckson Tada and other Christian leaders. See <http://www.biomanifesto.org>.

sues such as religious freedom and human rights. Some of these projects are narrower than others, but they tend to focus on one bill or one debate. In this case, we must move into an enduring coalition that will last for a generation and spread its networks around the globe.

Cloning has served as a catalyst to bring various parties together, although ironically there is less common ground here than on some other biotech issues; thus some progressives favor a moratorium rather than a ban on experimental cloning.

But reflection on the ramifications of cloning and the broad issues raised by biotechnology has led to growing awareness of common ground and our capacity for long-term political collaboration. It has been noted that the conscientious forces within our culture are grouped on the right and the left, wearing political labels that are assuming less significance as politics become more eclectic and all our political traditions face the pressures of secularization. A creeping libertarianism across the entire spectrum contrasts with the "social conservatism" of both left and right that upholds the central place of values and conviction in the framing of public policy.

The tactical political cooperation that has been sparked by the cloning debate needs to give place to strategic alignment on the biotech agenda between the pro-family/pro-life movement and progressives in the environmental and feminist communities. This will not be easily achieved, but it will prove to be central to effective policy development and advocacy both in the United States and in other nations and within the multilaterals. "Strategic" alignment will entail the development of institutions, long-term networks and durable working relationships in which areas of disagreement are noted while long-term common goals are explored, articulated and advanced. It will therefore be focused not simply on ad hoc political collaboration, but on the building of a common understanding of the moral and policy issues that are in prospect. While some of this will be at the level of white papers and legislative proposals, these will need to be nourished by fundamental intellectual work as centers, conferences and publishing projects are developed to sustain such activities. The need to respond to immediate policy debate (as in the current focus on human cloning) must not detract from the building of an infrastructure adequate to support a generation of incremental engagement.

The need for this realignment is especially evident when the global context of policy development is in view. It could be argued that the two most vigorous forces in Western culture are the pro-family/pro-life movement (which has its greatest strength in the United States) and the progressive/environmental/green movement (strongest in Europe). This strategic realignment can be seen as the linking of these two centers of cultural influence in a common focus on human biotech. It will be focused not simply in individual nations but also in multilaterals such as the United Nations, in which biotech policy development will increasingly be focused. It will entail the emergence of a powerful third force between the right and the broadly secular left, drawing on the intellectual resources and political energies of both and steadily reshaping the political-cultural landscape. As biotech developments unfold, through dramatic announcements like the cloning of Dolly as well as through incremental change on a vast scale, we may expect these questions to take a dominant place in the public mind. The marriages of convenience that presently hold together the conservative and liberal political coalitions will find themselves fractured with increasing frequency as the social conservatives on both wings break ranks with the libertarians. The central question confronting policymakers in the post-Dolly world will be put into the limelight: can the human community focus the wonders of biotech to serve the human good, or shall the new powers emerging from Pandora's box finally eclipse human dignity and usher in the Brave New World?

Conclusion

Christians have been placed as stewards in God's world to hold it in trust—exercising dominion with accountability. At the heart of our stewardship is that of our own selves, made in his image. And Jesus Christ has taken that nature as his own: in the Palestine of the first century and today in glory, the Son of God bears the nature of a member of our own species, *Homo sapiens*. In the words of Charles Wesley, writing of the one who sits on the throne of the universe and who will one day come to be our judge, "Of our flesh and of our bone, Jesus is our brother now."

So in our twin challenge to be both light and salt—to live distinctive lives and to engage the culture, transforming it for Christ—the church of the twenty-first century confronts a daunting challenge: to resist the commodification of humankind and ensure that biotechnology serves human dignity. For there can be no higher dignity than that of those who bear the image of their Maker, found in the human nature that he, in turn, has now taken to himself in Jesus Christ.

2

THE BIOTECH REVOLUTION

Major Issues in the Biosciences

DAVID A. PRENTICE, Ph.D.

Part of the problem confronted by us all as we seek to address the challenge of biotechnology is the fact that most of us are not very familiar with the science involved. Moreover, even if we were attentive when we studied science in school, the field is changing fast. The very possibility of somatic cell nuclear transfer (the Dolly cloning technique) and the extraordinary properties we have discovered in adult and embryonic stem cells do not simply represent new developments; they contradict the textbooks from which we learned. Yet while some of these techniques are highly specialized, the principles involved can be grasped and discussed without the need for nonspecialists to be retrained in bioscience. Indeed, this education is vital for democratic control of the biotech industry and our capacity to engage the moral and cultural significance of these technologies. The alternative is rule by experts, and recent debates about stem cell therapies and cloning have often been conducted as if Nobel prizewinners should determine the future of the human race. Expertise is to be respected, but the basic questions at stake here concern not what science can do, but whether it should do all it is able to do.

Dr. David Prentice therefore summarizes for a nonspecialist readership the basic science questions that underlie these debates. He is well-qualified to do so. Not only has he spent his career teaching bioscience, but he is engaged in research on adult stem cells. Moreover, he has extensive experience on Capitol Hill, having served as science adviser to U.S. Senator Sam Brownback (R-KS) in the drafting and advocacy of legislation to ban human cloning and in testifying before Congress and the President's Council on Bioethics.

NIGEL M. DE S. CAMERON

Biotechnology is an age-old science in many respects. At its simplest, biotechnology involves the use, manipulation and even creation of living organisms for humanity's purposes. The use of yeast in making bread and wine are applications of biotechnology, as is the cultivation of molds for antibiotics such as penicillin. In more recent times, recombinant DNA technology has allowed scientists to manipulate the genetic material of organisms, starting first with bacteria and now with other, more complex organisms, including humans. The creation of human life in the laboratory, starting with the birth of the first in vitro fertilization (IVF) baby in 1978, has ushered in an era where biotechnology can be brought to bear directly on humans.

The current revolution in the biosciences has focused our attention on new technologies related to human life itself, with the idea of creating, manipulating, even controlling life. Ostensibly the goal of the new technologies is to "make life better," but this phrase can have different meanings. One meaning is obvious: to make life easier by improving overall health and vitality, by treating or preventing disease, by extending the lifespan or even by enhancing physical or mental abilities. A second meaning can be taken from the phrase, however, a meaning that has more ominous undertones: the implication that there can be an aspect of designing life, of manufacturing humans such that this new version is an improved model. An implicit assumption is that the designers know that what is manufactured is truly better than the original and that the modifications will be a positive step for not only the individual, but also for the species. However, this assumption is questionable.

The major question that underlies concerns regarding biotechnology (and both meanings behind the phrase *make life better*) involves our basic definition of human life. What does it mean to be human? To whom do we choose to assign value? Who decides, and who benefits? This chapter will address the major issues regarding the science and the biotechnologies that are forcing us to ask the basic question of just what it means to be human.

Stem Cells and Regenerative Medicine: Destroying Life for Our Own Purposes

Why are people interested in stem cells, and why are stem cells such a controversial topic? To begin, stem cells offer the possibility of treating numerous degenerative diseases that affect millions of people in the United States alone. These include diseases such as heart disease, stroke, Alzheimer's disease, Parkinson's disease, diabetes and other chronic conditions. Degenerative diseases involve the slow, gradual breakdown of tissues and organs; or they are the result of death of some cells in an organ, which weakens the organ and leads to further breakdown and eventually organ failure. These are the major killers in the United States and other industrialized nations. For example, when someone has a heart attack, the entire heart doesn't die; instead, *part* of the heart muscle dies due to lack of oxygen (from a blocked or obstructed blood vessel).

The weakened heart muscle can lead to further problems and death. Stem cells might be used to repair or replace the damaged heart muscle, essentially "regenerating" the heart and restoring it to full function, hence the term *regenerative medicine*.

Stem cells have two basic characteristics that make them such attractive candidates for regenerating damaged organs and tissues: first, they continue to grow and proliferate, maintaining a pool of cells for possible use; and, second, given the correct signals, they can differentiate into a particular specialized cell type. Thus, a stem cell could be directed to become an insulin-secreting cell to treat diabetes, a dopaminergic neuron to treat Parkinson's or a cardiac muscle cell to treat heart disease. The implications for treating degenerative diseases are enormous. However, the source of the cells is the source of the debate.

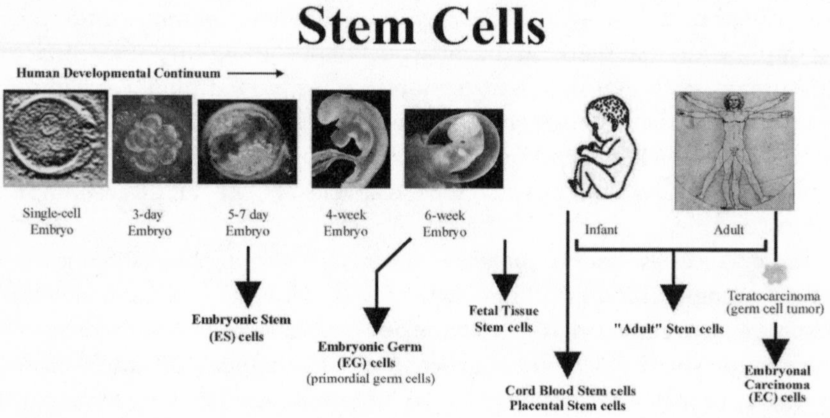

Stem Cells

Figure 1. Stem cell sources

Stem cells can be isolated from a wide array of tissues and from various stages during our human development. (See figure 1.) Historically, it was thought that only a few adult tissues contained stem cells and that they were very limited in the types of specialized cells that they could form: for example, bone marrow stem cells making blood cells and intestinal stem cells regenerating the intestinal lining. It is now known that stem cells can be isolated from early embryos, fetuses, umbilical cord blood, placenta, virtually all adult tissues and even from certain adult tumors.

Embryonic stem cells (ES cells) are one of the first cells formed during early development of the embryo, and they go on to form all of the tissues of the body. ES cells were first isolated from mouse embryos in 1981 and from human embryos in 1998.[1] In humans, embryonic stem cells form in the embryo about five to seven days after conception. At that point of our development, the human embryo (termed a *blastocyst*) looks like a hollow ball with a few cells inside. (See figure 1.) The outer layer, the *trophoblast*, goes on to form the placenta. The inner cells, or *inner cell mass*, are the embryonic stem cells that form body tissues.

ES cells are said to be *pluripotent*, meaning that they can form all of the tissues of the adult body. This is, of course, what they do during normal human development. ES cells are obtained by breaking open an embryo and removing the inner cells. Thus, obtaining ES cells requires the destruction of a human embryo, whether the embryo is a so-called leftover embryo (i.e., an embryo frozen at an IVF clinic) or an embryo freshly created for the express purpose of research.

A similar type of cell, termed an *embryonic germ cell* (EG cell), was also first isolated from humans in 1998. EG cells are derived from early fetal tissue (five to nine weeks after conception), specifically from the progenitor cells that will become germ cells (egg or sperm). When placed into laboratory culture, EG cells show many of the same characteristics found in ES cells. However, the fact that they come from aborted human fetuses also casts a pall over the use of these cells.

Human ES cells have been touted as a "master cell," with the potential to repair and rejuvenate any damaged tissue in the body. In theory this should be possible, because these are the cells that initially form all body tissues during embryonic development. The supposed advantages of embryonic stem cells are that they could be grown indefinitely in laboratory cultures, providing an almost limitless source of stem cells, and that they could form any body tissue. While there is published scientific evidence to back up the first claim (apparently limitless growth in the lab culture dish), there is precious little published evidence that laboratory-grown ES cells can be used successfully to treat disease. So far there is evidence that embryonic stem cells in the lab dish can form various cell types, including beating heart cells, muscle cells, blood cells and different types of nerve cells.

However, one problem with ES cells as a source of tissues for transplant is the artificial environment of the laboratory dish. The cells are taken out of the normal developmental context of the embryo, placed into laboratory culture and then expected to recapitulate normal developmental programs to form specific desired tissues. The situation is completely artificial, as has been noted in testimony to the President's Council on Bioethics: "It's a total tissue culture

---

[1]For an overview, see J. M. Jones and J. A. Thomson, "Human Embryonic Stem Cell Technology," *Seminars in Reproductive Medicine* 18, no. 2 (2000): 219-23.

artifact of those cells which can survive under the harsh tissue culture conditions. So I would argue ES cells have no counterpart in the normal animal model."[2] Given the artifactual nature of ES cells and the lack of a normal developmental context, it is not surprising that there is very little success at deriving specific specialized cells in the culture dish:

> Rarely have specific growth factors or culture conditions led to establishment of cultures containing a single cell type. . . . Furthermore, there is significant culture-to-culture variability in the development of a particular phenotype under identical growth factor conditions.[3]

In fact, ES cells seem to be largely uncontrollable in terms of forming specific desired cell types. As Douglas Melton of Harvard has said, "Normally, if you take an embryonic stem cell, it will make all kinds of things, sort of willy-nilly."[4]

Most of the differentiation reported for ES cells relies on identification and isolation of spontaneously differentiating cells within a mixture of ES cells in the lab dish. When transplanted into animals, there has been modest success at ameliorating damage from spinal cord injury, diabetes or Parkinson's disease in these experimental models. But even these results show problems. In many cases, the ES cells spontaneously differentiate into multiple tissues besides the desired cell type:

> Transplanted ES cells spontaneously differentiate into any of a variety of ectodermal, endodermal and mesodermal cell types—sometimes into a disorganized mass of neurons, cartilage and muscle; sometimes into teratomas containing an eye, hair or even teeth.[5]

There is also a question of whether ES cells actually secrete insulin or simply release insulin that they had stored during culture. And in animal studies on Parkinson's disease, injected ES cells killed one-fifth of the treated animals by forming tumors in their brains—not a very promising treatment.[6] This

---

[2]Rudolf Jaenisch, testifying on July 24, 2003, before the President's Council on Bioethics <http://www.bioethics.gov/transcripts/july03/session3.html>. (The URLs cited in this chapter were accessed on January 16, 2004.)

[3]J. S. Odorico, D. S. Kaufman and J. A. Thomson, "Multilineage Differentiation from Human Embryonic Stem Cell Lines," *Stem Cells* 19 (May 2001): 193-204.

[4]Douglas Melton, quoted by Jacqueline S. Mitchell in "Stem Cells 101," *Scientific American Frontiers*, May 28, 2002, PBS <http://www.pbs.org/saf/1209/features/stemcell.htm>.

[5]R. P. Lanza et al., "Human Therapeutic Cloning," *Nature Medicine* 5 (September 1999): 975-77.

[6]F. Nishimura et al., "Potential Use of Embryonic Stem Cells for the Treatment of Mouse Parkinsonian Models: Improved Behavior by Transplantation of In Vitro Differentiated Dopaminergic Neurons from Embryonic Stem Cells," *Stem Cells* 21 (March 2001): 171-80; L. M. Bjorklund et al., "Embryonic Stem Cells Develop into Functional Dopaminergic Neurons After Transplantation in a Parkinson Rat Model," *Proceedings of the National Academy of Sciences of the United States of America* 99 (February 19, 2002): 2344-49.

problem of tumor formation is a significant one that is an all-too-often occurrence with ES cells.[7] Injecting ES cells into a patient presents a serious and unacceptable risk of tumor formation. ES cells may show uncontrolled differentiation into unwanted tissues or uncontrolled growth into tumors due to their general instability in culture.[8] In one sense these problems are not unexpected: the "job description" of an ES cell is to grow as fast as possible and to make all tissues, essentially all at once. For an ES cell in culture to show controlled growth and make only one specific cell type is not its normal tendency.

Another problem for ES cell treatments is transplant rejection. To prevent rejection of transplanted cells and tissues, patients would have to be treated with strong antirejection drugs for their lifetime, as is currently done for most normal organ transplants. Proposals have been made for techniques that could possibly minimize the transplant rejection problem, including genetically engineering the implanted ES cells to match the patient's tissues, changing the patient's immune system itself by replacing it with a new immune system made from ES cells, or using ES cells made from an embryo that is a clone of the patient. However, at this point these techniques are only speculative.

It should also be mentioned that there is significant inefficiency in getting ES cells to start growing and keep growing in the laboratory. Only about one in ten of the embryos destroyed actually provides useable stem cells that will take hold in culture and grow, and the cells are difficult to maintain in the laboratory. The significance of this inefficiency in isolation should not be lost on us. Claims that only a few more ES cell lines or embryos would be needed to further research far underestimate the actual numbers of embryos that would be destroyed in the process. A recent story regarding isolation of human ES cells in the UK highlights the horrendous destruction of embryos: starting with fifty-eight human embryos, researchers could only get cells isolated from three embryos, and only one ES cell line was produced.[9] Yet despite the lack of published success using ES cells, proponents continue to clamor for additional embryo destruction, like Dickens's Oliver asking, "Please sir, can I have some more?" The human embryo is viewed as a source of raw materials for experiments, a piece of property, a commodity. Dr. Erwin Chargaff, renowned biochemist, characterizes this utilitarian attitude in the following way:

But there are some things you just don't do. If I suddenly decided to eat my

---

[7]S. Wakitani et al., "Embryonic Stem Cells Injected into the Mouse Knee Joint Form Teratomas and Subsequently Destroy the Joint," *Rheumatology* 42 (January 2003): 162-65.

[8]D. Humpherys et al., "Epigenetic Instability in ES Cells and Cloned Mice," *Science* 293 (July 6, 2001): 95-97.

[9]Steve Connor, "UK Scientists Grow Stem Cells from IVF Embryo," *The Independent* (UK), August 13, 2003 <http://news.independent.co.uk/uk/health/story.jsp?story=433110>.

mother, I wouldn't be able to say afterwards that she was tasty and therefore it was my perfect right to do so. We turned our backs on cannibalism, to a certain extent anyway. But now a kind of capitalist cannibalism prevails.[10]

Ethical Alternatives: Adult Stem Cells

In contrast to the exaggerations surrounding ES cells, little notice has been taken of ethical alternatives that do not involve destruction of human life to obtain stem cells. Indeed, most of the evidence regarding alternatives has accumulated over just a few years. Yet even those using a utilitarian calculus have recognized that ES cells are ethically tainted:

> In our judgment, the derivation of stem cells from embryos remaining following infertility treatments is justifiable only if no less morally problematic alternatives are available for advancing the research. . . . The claim that there are alternatives to using stem cells derived from embryos is not, at the present time, supported scientifically. *We recognize, however, that this is a matter that must be revisited continually as the demonstration of science advances.*[11]

What has been surprising is the recognition in recent years that even fully formed adult tissues also contain stem cells. The surprise has been that not only do a few tissues (such as bone marrow) contain stem cells, but most or all adult tissues contain stem cells. A further surprise was finding that many of these adult stem cells can form many more other types of tissue than was previously thought. Within just a few years, the possibility that the human body contains cells that can repair and regenerate damaged and diseased tissue has gone from an unlikely proposition to a virtual certainty. Adult stem cells have been isolated from numerous adult tissues, umbilical cord and other nonembryonic sources, and they have demonstrated a surprising ability to transform into other tissue and cell types and to repair damaged tissues.

The term *adult stem cell* is actually not completely correct, because these cells are present in organs and tissues from the moment we are born; and it is now recognized that similar stem cells are found in the placenta and in the umbilical cord. (See figure 1.) Since all of these stem cells are found in various body tissues at or after birth, some term them *tissue stem cells* or *nonembryonic stem cells*. However, the popular term *adult stem cells* has been used most widely to categorize these cells and to distinguish them from embryo-derived stem cells.

The published scientific literature is now full of reports on the abilities of adult stem cells with as much or more promise of treating disease as ES cells

---

[10]Quoted in Jordan Mejias, "Research Always Runs the Risk of Getting Out of Control," *Frankfurter Allgemeine Zeitung*, June 4, 2001.

[11]National Bioethics Advisory Commission, "Ethical Issues in Human Stem Cell Research," September 1999 (emphasis added).

have. Some of the past criticisms of adult stem cells have been that there was not a separate adult stem cell for each tissue; that they did not have the ability to make all body tissues; that they were difficult to isolate; and that they were present in the body in only small numbers and could not be kept growing indefinitely, so it would be difficult to get enough of these cells to actually treat a patient. Since 1999, all of those ideas have been disproved in the scientific literature.

In several studies it has been shown that adult stem cells from tissues such as bone marrow or the brain can form virtually any body tissue. The most noted example is that of multipotent adult progenitor cells (MAPC cells) from bone marrow—what some have called the "ultimate stem cell"—which can grow forever in culture and make all body tissues. By injecting the bone marrow stem cell into an early mouse embryo, researchers found evidence that the cell could help form all tissues of the body.[12] Another group has injected brain stem cells into an early mouse or chicken embryo (similar to experiments that have been done with ES cells) and demonstrated that the brain stem cell could help form many of the normal tissues of the animal.[13] In another experiment, scientists destroyed the bone marrow of mice and then injected into these same mice *one* bone marrow stem cell from another mouse. The recipients of this transplant would survive only if that one bone marrow stem cell lived and flourished. Not only did the single transplanted bone marrow stem cell survive and make bone marrow and blood cells, but it also could be found making liver, lung, digestive system, skin, heart and muscle cells.[14] And one research team has found cells in human blood that show pluripotent activity.[15]

Whereas just a few years ago it was believed that adult stem cells existed only in a few tissues of the body, it now appears that virtually every adult tissue contains stem cells, which either originate in that tissue or occupy the tissue as they pass through in the bloodstream. In short, whenever someone has taken the time to look at a tissue, they have found an adult stem cell there. Apart from being found in bone marrow, brain tissue, blood and umbilical cords, stem cells have been found in muscle tissue, liver tissue, amniotic fluid,

---

[12]Y. Jiang et al., "Pluripotency of Mesenchymal Stem Cells Derived from Adult Marrow," *Nature* 418 (July 4, 2002): 41-49.

[13]D. L. Clarke et al., "Generalized Potential of Adult Neural Stem Cells," *Science* 288 (June 2, 2000): 1660-63.

[14]D. S. Krause et al., "Multi-organ, Multi-lineage Engraftment by a Single Bone Marrow-Derived Stem Cell," *Cell* 105 (May 4, 2001): 369-77.

[15]Y. Zhao et al., "A Human Peripheral Blood Monocyte-Derived Subset Acts as Pluripotent Stem Cells," *Proceedings of the National Academy of Sciences of the United States of America* 100 (March 4, 2003): 2426-31.

hair follicles and even fat tissue.[16] Not a week goes by without some new report of the isolation of another adult stem cell or of the ability of an adult stem cell in one tissue to form a different tissue type. And while it might be more difficult to isolate a brain stem cell to make more nerve cells, it is relatively easy to isolate an adult stem cell from bone marrow, blood or skin, all of which have been shown capable of making nerve cells.

Even if there are very few adult stem cells available in the body to be isolated, the published scientific evidence now shows that some adult stem cells can be kept growing almost indefinitely in culture. Numerous other scientists have found key growth signals that can be added to cultures of adult stem cells to get them to multiply rapidly. So at least some adult stem cells do possess what are supposedly the two main advantages of embryonic stem cells: the ability to grow indefinitely so that many cells can be made for treatments, and the ability to form any adult body tissue.

The ability of an adult stem cell to grow in culture and form other tissues in the lab dish is interesting, but the real proof is not so much an adult stem cell's ability to keep growing or make different tissue in a dish, but its ability to actually repair damaged tissue and reverse the damage caused by disease. Adult stem cells have successfully shown their ability to do just that. Adult stem cells have been effective in experimental animals at repairing damage due to, for example, heart attack, stroke, liver disease, diabetes, Parkinson's disease and spinal cord injury.[17]

The most striking news regarding adult stem cells, however, is that they are already being used successfully in human patients. While it is still early in regards to human treatments, there are encouraging reports for repair of tissues using adult stem cells in patients suffering from conditions such as heart dam-

---

[16]For an extensive list of adult stem cell sources and references, see D. A. Prentice, "Adult Stem Cells," appendix K of *Monitoring Stem Cell Research: A Report of the President's Council on Bioethics* (Washington, D.C.: Government Printing Office, 2004), pp. 311-49 <http://bioethics.gov/reports/stemcell/appendix_k.html>.

[17]On heart attacks, see D. Orlic et al., "Mobilized Bone Marrow Cells Repair the Infarcted Heart, Improving Function and Survival," *Proceedings of the National Academy of Sciences of the United States of America* 98 (August 28, 2001): 10344-49. On strokes, see J. Chen et al., "Intravenous Administration of Human Umbilical Cord Blood Reduces Behavioral Deficits After Stroke in Rats," *Stroke* 32 (November 2001): 2682-88. On liver disease, see Eric Lagasse et al., "Purified Hematopoietic Stem Cells Can Differentiate into Hepatocytes in Vivo," *Nature Medicine* 6 (November 2000): 1229-34. On diabetes, see D. Hess et al., "Bone Marrow-Derived Stem Cells Initiate Pancreatic Regeneration," *Nature Biotechnology* 21 (July 2003): 763-70. On Parkinson's disease, see M. A. Liker et al., "Human Neural Stem Cell Transplantation in the MPTP-Lesioned Mouse," *Brain Research* 971 (May 2003): 168-77. On spinal cord injury, see C. P. Hofstetter et al., "Marrow Stromal Cells Form Guiding Strands in the Injured Spinal Cord and Promote Recovery," *Proceedings of the National Academy of Sciences of the United States of America* 99 (February 19, 2002): 2199-204.

age, Parkinson's disease, multiple sclerosis, corneal damage, a gangrenous
limb, sickle cell anemia and numerous other conditions.[18] In many cases, the
patient's own stem cells can be used. The obvious advantage of such treatments
is that there is no threat of immune rejection. Adult stem cells also show no evidence of tumor formation and appear to have a unique ability to "home in" on
damaged tissue to stimulate repair. Thus adult stem cells have all of the advantages needed for regenerative medicine without the clinical negatives associated with ES cells and without the necessity for destruction of human life.

Different Ways to Make an Embryo

In the continuing quest to use embryos for research and derive more ES cell
lines, proponents of embryo research have devised other methods for embryo
creation. In one sense these methods reflect attempts to decrease the controversy over embryo destruction; the thought is that embryos created via these
other methods are not truly embryos and hence their creation and destruction
for research will not arouse opposition. However, the ethical and biological
bases for such hopes are not well founded. In each case the entity created is biologically an embryo; if it is created using human cells and genetic material,
the entity is a human being, species *Homo sapiens;* and so each of these methods
entails research on, and destruction of, a human being.

One of the methods proposed for embryo and ES cell creation is *partheno-*

---

[18]On heart damage, see E. C. Perin et al., "Transendocardial, Autologous Bone Marrow Cell
Transplantation for Severe, Chronic Ischemic Heart Failure," *Circulation* 107 (May 13, 2003):
2294-302; C. Stamm et al., "Autologous Bone-Marrow Stem-Cell Transplantation for Myo-
cardial Regeneration," *Lancet* 361 (January 4, 2003): 45-46; H.-F. Tse et al., "Angiogenesis in
Ischaemic Myocardium by Intramyocardial Autologous Bone Marrow Mononuclear Cell
Implantation," *Lancet* 361 (January 4, 2003): 47-49; and B. E. Strauer et al., "Repair of Inf-
arcted Myocardium by Autologous Intracoronary Mononuclear Bone Marrow Cell Transplantation in Humans," *Circulation* 106 (October 8, 2002): 1913-18. On Parkinson's disease,
see M. Lévesque and T. Neuman, "Autologous Transplantation of Adult Human Neural
Stem Cells and Differentiated Dopaminergic Neurons for Parkinson Disease: One-Year
Postoperative Clinical and Functional Metabolic Result" (paper presented at the American
Association of Neurological Surgeons annual meeting, April 8, 2002). On multiple sclerosis,
see G. L. Mancardi et al., "Autologous Hematopoietic Stem Cell Transplantation Suppresses
Gd-Enhanced MRI Activity in MS," *Neurology* 57 (July 10, 2001): 62-68. On corneal damage,
see R. J.-F. Tsai et al., "Reconstruction of Damaged Corneas by Transplantation of Autologous Limbal Epithelial Cells," *New England Journal of Medicine* 343 (July 13, 2000): 86-93; and
I. R. Schwab et al., "Successful Transplantation of Bioengineered Tissue Replacements in Patients with Ocular Surface Disease," *Cornea* 19 (July 2000): 421-426. On gangrenous limbs,
see E. Tateishi-Yuyama et al., "Therapeutic Angiogenesis for Patients with Limb Ischaemia
by Autologous Transplantation of Bone-Marrow Cells: A Pilot Study and a Randomised
Controlled Trial," *Lancet* 360 (August 10, 2002): 427-35.On sickle cell anemia, see L. Gore et
al., "Successful Cord Blood Transplantation for Sickle Cell Anemia from a Sibling Who Is
Human Leukocyte Antigen-Identical: Implications for Comprehensive Care," *Journal of Pe-
diatric Hematology and Oncology* 22 (September-October 2000): 437-40.

genesis. In this method no sperm is required; the only thing needed is an egg. As it happens, before fertilization the human egg actually still has a full set of chromosomes: half will be used to merge with the chromosomes brought in by the sperm; upon fertilization the other half of the egg's chromosomes will be immediately ejected from the egg in what is called a *polar body*. For parthenogenesis to occur, the egg is induced to keep both sets of chromosomes using chemical treatments, resulting in a full number of chromosomes inside the egg. No parthenogenic mammals have yet been born, and no one is sure yet whether they would survive to birth. However, biologically the entity created is an embryo, and there remains the potential for its full development to birth. By analogy, before the birth of Dolly the cloned sheep, it was argued that mammals could never be cloned and brought to birth because as organisms they were too complex and the techniques to clone them were too complicated. In the end success at cloning mammals was simply a matter of determination and improvements in technique. Certainly a parthenogenic human embryo can be grown to the blastocyst stage, and ES cells have already been harvested from parthenogenic human embryos.[19] The embryo must still be destroyed to obtain these ES cells, and such cells still face the problems outlined above for ES cells obtained from embryos created by fertilization. A similar process called *androgenesis* might also be possible. For this technique the nuclear material from two sperm would be placed into an enucleated egg. However, this process so far does not seem to produce normal embryos that could be grown to the point where ES cells could be harvested.

Another proposal for production of ES cells has been creation of "crippled" embryos, though the proposals do not label the embryos as such. The idea behind such proposals is that if an embryo is unable to complete its development, then it does not truly qualify as an embryo and so can be used for research without ethical objection. Beyond the obvious absurdity that ES cells must come from embryos, these proposals equate being human with viability, especially viability to complete development to birth. However, in the end what is actually being created is, biologically, some form of intentionally crippled embryo, perhaps by mutation of a gene or genes such that the individual cannot implant into a womb.

Another way to produce new embryos is by reconstructing the parts of an embryo from ES cells. The ES cells are sandwiched between *tetraploid embryos*, which are created by fusing two-celled embryos. The sandwich leads to formation of a *trophoblast* layer derived from the tetraploid embryos, encapsulating the ES cells; essentially the ES cells are placed back into their original embry-

---

[19]H. Lin et al., "Multilineage Potential of Homozygous Stem Cells Derived from Metaphase II Oocytes," *Stem Cells* 21 (March 2003): 152-61.

onic position. Live born mice and cattle have been created in this way.

Cloning

When people talk about cloning, most mean creating a duplicate of an entire organism. Cloning simply means to make an identical or nearly identical copy. Molecules such as DNA can be cloned; individual cells such as a skin cell can be cloned. But cloning an organism does not immediately produce a full-grown adult. The clone starts as a one-celled embryo and must still go through embryonic and fetal stages of development before birth. Frogs were first cloned in the 1960s, but it was not until 1996 that the first mammal, Dolly the sheep, was cloned, with the announcement of her birth coming in 1997. Dolly started life as an embryo, the same as any other sheep. The difference for clones is that they are not produced by sexual reproduction (union of egg and sperm), so the process is termed *asexual reproduction*.

Human cloning is human asexual reproduction. There are various ways to accomplish this, including splitting an early embryo in half or breaking it apart into individual cells, each of which can continue development as an autonomous embryo; but these techniques start with a preexisting embryo. The technique most hotly debated regarding human cloning is somatic cell nuclear transfer (SCNT), in which the nuclear genetic material from one or more human somatic (body) cells is introduced into a fertilized or unfertilized egg cell whose nuclear genetic material has been removed or inactivated, producing a human embryo who is virtually genetically identical to an existing or previously existing human being. SCNT allows the cloning of an existing (or deceased) adult, recreating an individual who already exists (or existed).

Proponents of human cloning hold out two hopes for its use. First, in so-called reproductive cloning (or *live-birth cloning*), live-born children are created for infertile couples or those grieving over the loss of a loved one. Second, in the euphemistically termed *therapeutic cloning* (more properly termed *experimental cloning*), diseases might be cured with the medical miracle of harvesting ES cells from cloned embryos created from patients.

First let us be clear on the terms. All human cloning is reproductive, in that it creates, *reproduces,* a new developing human intended to be virtually identical to the cloned subject. In point of fact, both *reproductive* and *therapeutic* cloning use exactly the same technique to create the clone, and the cloned embryos are indistinguishable. The process, as well as the product, is identical. The only distinction is the purpose for which the embryo will be used. Either it will be transferred to a womb in the hopes of a live birth, or it will be destroyed in the hopes of a medical miracle.

The technique of cloning is finished once that first cell, the one-celled embryo *(zygote),* is formed. Anything beyond that step is simply growth and development. And despite the attempts to employ various euphemisms, scientifically and genetically what is created is a human being: its species is *Homo sapiens*; it is neither fish nor fowl, neither monkey nor cow. It is human. The use of disingenuous euphemisms to describe the process (e.g., "nuclear transfer to produce stem cells") or the embryo (e.g., "ovasome") as something other than what it is likewise are not scientific and diverge from the accepted definitions as put forth by the National Academy of Sciences, the National Institutes of Health and others, including well-known proponents of human cloning.

Cloning of human beings for whatever purpose constitutes unethical human experimentation. Reproductive cloning, for example, has an enormous failure rate: 95 to 99 percent of animal clones die before or soon after birth. In 1997, out of 277 cloned embryos, only one sheep—Dolly—was produced, and even this "successful" clone was beset with abnormalities.[20] (Dolly developed early onset arthritis and lung disease and was put down in February 2003.) In 2001 a group at the Whitehead Institute achieved five born mice from 613 cloned embryos, and all of the born mice showed abnormalities in their gene expression.[21] This "numbers problem" is seen in all species that have been cloned. There is also a question as to whether any clones are normal, even those that survive and grow to adulthood. Some experiments showed that Dolly was actually older than her birth age; she was cloned from a six-year-old sheep and may have aged rapidly. One indication of advanced age is that she developed early onset arthritis earlier than a normal sheep should. Another laboratory found that most of their cloned mice died early. While many surviving clones have gone on to reproduce normally, including Dolly, some experiments indicate there may be some fertility problems with cloned animals. To attempt to clone a human and bring the cloned human to birth would thus expose a large number of cloned human beings to certain death or disability as part of the experimentation. Ian Wilmut, creator of Dolly, has stated that there are no normal clones, and he notes that "there is abundant evidence that cloning can and does go wrong and no justification for believing that this will not happen with humans."[22] Given the results for all animal clones, we can expect that of those few cloned humans who survive to birth, most will die shortly thereafter and the others will be plagued by abnormalities due to the cloning process. In addition, the surrogate mothers of clones experience physiological problems. Because of the clone's abnormalities and large size, known

---

[20]I. Wilmut et al., "Viable Offspring Derived from Fetal and Adult Mammalian Cells," *Nature* 385 (February 1997): 810-13.

[21]D. Humpherys et al., "Epigenetic Instability."

[22]Ian Wilmut, quoted in Jonathan Leacke, "Gene Defects Emerge in All Animal Clones," *Sunday Times of London*, April 28, 2002.

as *large offspring syndrome*, carrying a clonal pregnancy to term will pose unique threats to the woman involved.

Therapeutic (experimental) cloning also constitutes unethical human experimentation, though in this case there is a 100 percent chance of death for the clone. In point of fact, no human cloning is "therapeutic" cloning. In medical ethics, "therapeutic research" is defined as research that could provide therapeutic benefit to the individual subjected to research risks. Thus "therapeutic cloning" is obviously not therapeutic for the embryo: the new human is created specifically to be destroyed as a source of cells or tissues.

> Moreover, because therapeutic cloning requires the creation and disaggregation ex utero of blastocyst stage embryos, this technique raises complex ethical questions. . . . Unlike much stem cell research, which can use spare embryos remaining from infertility procedures, CRNT [cell replacement through nuclear transfer, aka therapeutic cloning] requires the deliberate creation and disaggregation of a human embryo.[23]

Creating new human life solely to destroy it for the potential benefit of others is unethical. It turns human life into a commodity, creating a caste system of lesser humans for scientific sacrifice.

Human experimental cloning is also completely unnecessary for medical progress. *Theoretically,* the ES cells from the cloned human embryo might be used to generate matched tissues for transplant into the patient from whom the embryo was cloned. However, the theory is not supported by any of the scientific literature. In fact, the published evidence indicates the contrary: ES cells from cloned embryos do not produce matched tissues that evade immune rejection; rather they are still subject to transplant rejection as are ES cells from embryos created by fertilization. There has been only one published report of an attempt to show that so-called therapeutic cloning can actually succeed. While purported to show success of therapeutic cloning to treat a genetic defect in mice, the experiment actually was a failure in terms of the use of therapeutic cloning, for the mouse rejected the ES cells from the cloned embryo. The authors noted, in distinct understatement, "Our results raise the provocative possibility that even genetically matched cells derived by therapeutic cloning may still face barriers to effective transplantation for some disorders."[24] An independent review of the results was more blunt:

> Jaenisch addressed the possibility that ES clones derived by nuclear transfer technique could be used to correct genetic defects in the hematopoietic system. . . .

---

[23]R. P. Lanza et al., "The Ethical Validity of Using Nuclear Transfer in Human Transplantation," *Journal of the American Medical Association* 284 (December 27, 2000): 3175-79.

[24]W. M. Rideout et al., "Correction of a Genetic Defect by Nuclear Transplantation and Combined Cell and Gene Therapy," *Cell* 109 (April 5, 2002): 17-27.

However, the donor cells, although derived from the animals with the same genetic background, are rejected by the hosts.[25]

Indeed, the only real success in the experiment was achieved by bringing
cloned mice to birth and using bone marrow adult stem cells from the born
mouse to treat the disease. It should also be noted that the similar genetic defect
in humans—severe combined immunodeficiency syndrome (or SCID, known
as "the boy in the bubble disease")—has been cured in several infants since
2000 using gene therapy of the infants' own bone marrow adult stem cells.[26]

In 2002 another group claimed in the popular press that they had succeeded
with therapeutic cloning; but in the published scientific paper they admitted
that the experiment did not use ES cells at all, but rather tissue from cloned fetuses, which had been gestated for several months: "Because cloned cells were
derived from early-stage fetuses, this approach is not an example of therapeutic cloning."[27]

While there is some doubt over whether these tissues from cloned fetuses
were rejected by the host, if we assume that allowing natural development to
form the tissue provides better transplants, a logical extension of this principle
would be to grow clones to later and later stages of development—even to
birth—so that fully formed and functioning tissues could be "harvested" from
the clones for transplant.

Human cloning for any purpose poses potential significant health risks to
women. The National Academy of Sciences report on cloning in January 2002
spoke of the risk to women's health from cloning:

> Because many eggs are needed for human reproductive cloning attempts, human
> experimentation could subject more women to adverse health effects—either
> from high levels of hormones used to stimulate egg production or because more
> women overall would be sought to donate eggs, which involves surgery with its
> own inherent risks.[28]

But since the same procedure is used to create embryos for therapeutic cloning purposes, the same problem applies. In fact, the problem will be even
greater because the procedure used to create ES cell lines is itself inefficient. An

---

[25]R. Y. L. Tsai et al., "Plasticity, Niches and the Use of Stem Cells," *Developmental Cell* 2 (June
2002): 707-12.

[26]M. Cavazzana-Calvo et al., "Gene Therapy of Human Severe Combined Immunodeficiency
(SCID)-X1 Disease," *Science* 288 (2000): 669-72; and A. Hacein-Bey-Abina et al., "Sustained
Correction of X-Linked Severe Combined Immunodeficiency by Ex Vivo Gene Therapy,"
New England Journal of Medicine 346 (April 18, 2002): 1185-93.

[27]R. Lanza et al., "Generation of Histocompatible Tissue Using Nuclear Transplantation," *Nature Biotechnology* 20 (July 2002): 689-96.

[28]United States National Academy of Sciences, "Scientific and Medical Aspects of Human Reproductive Cloning," January 18, 2002.

enormous supply of human eggs will need to be made available to treat even a small group of patients, subjecting a large population of women of childbearing age to unethical health risks inherent in harvesting the necessary quantities of eggs for cloning. One calculation based on the published scientific literature for cloning of animals and derivation of ES cells, both of which are extremely inefficient procedures, reveals that to use therapeutic cloning to treat just one patient group—the 17 million diabetes patients in the United States—will require at least 850 million human eggs; approximately 85 million women of childbearing age would need to "donate" eggs. This is likely a minimum number of eggs necessary, assuming approximately fifty eggs could achieve one ES cell line. Another estimate published in the *Proceedings of the National Academy of Sciences* places the estimate closer to one hundred human eggs needed per successful cloning.[29] As the NAS panel points out, this will subject a large number of women to adverse health risks. The result will be that human eggs will also become a commodity, with the resultant exploitation of disadvantaged women in this country and abroad. Some have proposed using animal eggs instead, and one publication claims production of cloned human embryos using rabbit eggs.[30] However, the ES cells from these hybrid cloned embryos would have an even greater chance of transplant rejection. A recent report that eggs might be produced in large quantities directly from ES cells has also gained interest for manufacture of embryos, both through fertilization and through cloning.[31] At this point it is unknown whether such ES-derived eggs might function as true oocytes.

Normal development is an intricate dance of genes being expressed at the right time and in the right cells. The problem with getting normal clones probably has to do with gene reprogramming when the nucleus is transferred into the egg. In sexual reproduction the egg and sperm each have their genes programmed to start normal development. The way that genes are set to be expressed is called *gene imprinting*. The genes are set for expression as if they were a set of thirty thousand to seventy thousand on/off switches: different switches will be set off or on, depending on the particular cell type, tissue or stage of development. When the nucleus of an adult body cell is transferred into the enucleated egg to create a clone, many of the switches are set differently than they would be for the start of embryo development because the body cell has its programming set to do its job in a particular tissue. The cytoplasm in the egg must

---

[29]P. Mombaerts, "Therapeutic Cloning in the Mouse," *Proceedings of the National Academy of Sciences of the United States of America* 100 (September 30, 2003): S11924-25.

[30]Y. Chen et al., "Embryonic Stem Cells Generated by Nuclear Transfer of Human Somatic Nuclei into Rabbit Oocytes," *Cell Research* 13 (2003): 251-63.

[31]K. Hübner et al., "Generation of Oocytes from Mouse Embryonic Stem Cells," *Science* 300 (May 23, 2003): 1251-56.

reprogram the genes, resetting the switches so that normal development can occur. The failure of most cloning attempts likely is a result of not getting all of the switches set correctly.[32] It is also uncertain what such changes in the gene programming might mean later in the life of the clone.

Cloning as a technique, whether to produce live-born children or ES cells, is fraught with danger and unlikely to produce success. Even proponents of embryonic stem cell research have noted the unlikely chance of success: "The poor availability of human oocytes, the low efficiency of the nuclear transfer procedure, and the long population-doubling time of human ES cells make it difficult to envision this [therapeutic cloning] becoming a routine clinical procedure."[33]

Genetic Engineering

Genetic engineering can be subdivided into two main categories based on the type of cell targeted by the modification: *somatic genetic engineering* (also termed *noninheritable genetic modification*) and *germline genetic engineering* (also termed *inheritable genetic modification*). Somatic genetic engineering modifies or replaces genes within somatic cells (i.e., body cells); this excepts the sperm or egg cells or their immediate precursors (i.e., the germ cells). As such, this type of modification affects the treated individual only. Alterations of the genome of a particular cell or tissue are usually targeted toward correcting some genetic defect that causes disease in the treated individual (this is known as *genomic medicine*).[34] Germline genetic engineering alters the genes in sperm or egg cells (or their immediate precursors), in the zygote or in the early embryo. The usually stated goal of such genetic modifications is the same as that of somatic genetic engineering: to correct (or prevent) a disease state caused by a defective gene. However, germline genetic modifications affect *prospective* individuals, including not only the child who is engineered, but also all the descendents of the engineered child. Both techniques could be abused; either could be used for enhancements of genetically determined abilities as opposed to therapeutic treatments for disease. Because it alters a prospective individual, germline genetic engineering also can allow for the selection of genetic characteristics in a prospective child, producing a "designer baby" with desired traits.

Genetic engineering, whether somatic or germline, requires essentially two main components: the gene of interest and a vector to contain and control the

---

[32]W. Reik and W. Dean, "Silent Clones Speak Up," *Nature* 423 (May 22, 2003): 390-91.

[33]Odorico, Kaufman and Thomson, "Multilineage Differentiation," p. 201.

[34]For an overview see A. E. Guttmacher and F. S. Collins, "Genomic Medicine: A Primer," *New England Journal of Medicine* 347 (November 7, 2002): 1512-20.

gene and deliver (transfect) it into the cell(s) targeted for modification.[35] The gene of interest would be identified, characterized and copied multiple times. The identification and characterization of genes for possible genetic engineering have been greatly accelerated by the Human Genome Program. Already the number of identified genes that can be used for genetic screening purposes has multiplied, and these same genes can now be turned toward correcting or altering the genomes of individuals. The list of identified genetic components will soon include more complex, multigene disorders such as diabetes, Alzheimer's disease and perhaps elucidation of genetic predispositions to other conditions such as alcoholism.[36] One report now implicates the "short" form of a gene, when accompanied by stress, as associated with depression.[37] The "menu" from which to pick—whether for correction of genetic disorders, for selection of desired traits or, potentially, for enhancement of specific traits— will not be a limiting factor in genetic engineering. However, as the studies move forward, we should consider cautiously any reports that claim to have identified all gene factors for the control of complex behavioral phenomena. While genetics lays an important groundwork for who we become, we are much more than just the sum of our genes. Another significant point is the possibility that genes underling complex genetic traits may play more than one role. This has been noted for years regarding the single-gene trait for sickle cell anemia, where the heterozygous state is protective against malaria. A similar caution was noted for the previously mentioned depression-associated gene. Dr. Daniel Weinberger, chief of the Clinical Brain Disorders Branch of the National Institutes of Mental Health, warned against vilifying the short version of the gene because scientists do not know all the roles it plays. When a genetic variation is common in a population, it often provides some advantage, he said. "There may be other things that this [short variant] is good for."[38]

The vector that contains and delivers the DNA to the cell is a crucial component of the genetic engineering system. A vector is itself an engineered piece of DNA, designed to deliver the gene efficiently and precisely into a cell. The goals are, first, to insert the gene stably into the cell's genome so that as cell replication occurs the inserted gene is carried along as part of the genome and, second, to express the inserted gene in a normally regulated manner so as to restore (or

---

[35]E. H. Kaji and J. M. Leiden, "Gene and Stem Cell Therapies," *Journal of the American Medical Association* 285 (February 7, 2001): 545-50.

[36]Francis S. Collins and Victor A. McKusick, "Implications of the Human Genome Project for Medical Science," *Journal of the American Medical Association* 285 (February 7, 2001): 540-44.

[37]A. Caspi et al., "Influence of Life Stress on Depression: Moderation by a Polymorphism in the 5-HTT Gene," *Science* 301(July 18, 2003): 386-89.

[38]Quoted in R. Monastersky, "Scientists Find Genetic Link to Depression," *Chronicle of Higher Education*, July 18, 2003 <http://chronicle.com/prm/daily/2003/07/200307/1803n.htm>.

add) function to the cell. Most current vectors are engineered viruses.[39] The ideal vector—which targets the gene to the appropriate cells or tissues, stably trans-fects the cells and allows control of gene expression, all without causing an im-mune response or other adverse response—has yet to be achieved. A case in point is the successful genetic therapy for severe combined immunodeficiency syndrome.[40] While the patients were essentially cured of the immunodeficiency, a few of them subsequently developed a leukemia that may have been due to the vector integrating into the genome at an undesired location.[41] Design of an appropriate vector for target tissues is a matter of continuing development, in-cluding early work on a human artificial chromosome that could function as a sort of "super vector," containing multiple genes to be added to a cell, as well as any desired sequences for control of the individual genes.[42] The artificial chro-mosome could potentially also be constructed with the ability to be replicated along with other chromosomes and passed on to daughter cells as a discrete chromosome; it could also potentially turn off or remove the added genetic traits if they were no longer desired. The genetic transformation can be accomplished *in vivo* (in the patient's body) directly or *ex vivo* (in the laboratory using cells re-moved from the patient and then reinserted after genetic modification).

Questions regarding genetic engineering involve not only the safety and ef-ficacy of the technique, but also the intent and potential outcomes of the ge-netic modifications. Somatic genetic therapy seems straightforward enough as a therapeutic technique; yet not nearly enough is known about genetic inter-actions, or interactions between genes and the environment, to attempt more than simple therapies at this point. Somatic genetic enhancements (i.e., alter-ing the genome of a healthy individual to augment the person's normal func-tions or even to add additional genetic capabilities) are also highly question-able. Yet attempts at enhancement are likely. One need only look at the number of instances of physiological enhancement (e.g., steroid use, plastic surgery, human growth hormone usage and red-cell loading) to realize that individuals will be willing and eager to attempt enhancing their genetic constitution to gain an advantage. The possibilities also include formation of chimeras, hy-

[39]Kaji and Leiden, "Gene and Stem Cell Therapies." See also M. A. Kay et al., "Viral Vectors for Gene Therapy: The Art of Turning Infectious Agents into Vehicles of Therapeutics," *Nature Medicine* 7 (January 2001): 33-40.
[40]Cavazzana-Calvo et al., "Gene Therapy"; Hacein-Bey-Abina et al., "Sustained Correction."
[41]E. Marshall, "Gene Therapy a Suspect in Leukemia-Like Disease," *Science* 298 (October 4, 2002): 34-35.
[42]K. A. Henning et al., "Human Artificial Chromosomes Generated by Modification of a Yeast Artificial Chromosome Containing Both Human Alpha Satellite and Single-Copy DNA Se-quences," *Proceedings of the National Academy of Sciences of the United States of America* 96 (Jan-uary 19, 1999): 592-97; B. Grimes and H. Cooke, "Engineering Mammalian Chromosomes," *Human Molecular Genetics* 7, no. 10 (1998): 1635-40.

brids containing both human and nonhuman cells and genetics.

Germline genetic engineering raises many ·of the same questions as those raised by somatic genetic engineering, including the question of genetic enhancement; but because this is a heritable modification, genetic enhancement also has the added potential of actually reshaping humanity's future. The possibility of preventing development of a genetic disease is a powerful attraction, and the potential to pass on desirable traits is at least as powerful. But because this type of genetic modification alters not only the *prospective* individuals but all of the generations of progeny from that individual, there is a tremendous potential for abuse out of either willfulness or ignorance. Beyond our simple lack of knowledge regarding the complexity of the genome, its contents and its interactions, there is also a lack of perspective on what may constitute a disease versus what constitutes a good or bad trait. This attitude may be best exemplified in the statement of Nobel laureate James Watson at a 1998 symposium to discuss the possibilities of engineering the human germline: "I mean, if we could make better human beings by knowing how to add genes, why shouldn't we do it?"[43] However, the more pressing question is, who decides what's a *better* human being? In this scenario, which is becoming less a facet of science fiction and more a reality, parents could design their offspring. But in this future scenario the new human is the *created* property of another, designed and crafted to meet the maker's desires. We end up with humans making humans in their own image, without any higher standard to which the craftsperson is held. Given that the consequences of human germline genetic engineering are unpredictable and uncontrollable, it could lead to disastrous failures as well as to the creation of a genetic caste system (with those who are "gene-rich" or enhanced as opposed to the "normals"), the development of a manufacturer mentality for creation of children and the degradation of human dignity and individuality.

The scientific techniques that are here now and are coming soon raise challenges for us in terms of our attitude toward human life, human dignity and the future of the human species. Our attitudes revolve around the question posed earlier, what does it mean to be human? There is no need to degrade any human being or make use of any human as a source of raw materials, research fodder or a puzzle for design and manufacture. Indeed, good science continues to be ethical science. We can value human life, both the individual life as well as the human species, and all benefit.

---

[43]James Watson, comments made at the Engineering the Human Germline Symposium, University of California at Los Angeles, June 1998. (A partial transcript is available at <http://www.ess.ucla.edu/huge/report.html>.)

3

THE NEW GENETICS AND
THE DIGNITY OF HUMANKIND

C. BEN MITCHELL, Ph.D.

The hype that surrounded the initiation of the international Human Genome Project and the completion of the first mapping of the human genome has led to little in the way of clinical applications, despite immense hope and expectation. Yet genetics has already begun to play a crucial role in life-and-death decisions, and in this essay we review some of the techniques already in use (such as preimplantation genetic diagnosis, i.e., the screening of in vitro embryos) that will serve as the basis for what comes next, when the technology has become far more sophisticated. There is also a review of the underlying legal and ethical question of who owns our genes—indeed, whether they may be owned by anyone. The question of the use of patents is of increasing significance, since it is the key to corporate interest in biotech possibilities. Should people be able to "own" genes and even human organisms? These obscure issues of patent law are now central policy concerns for those who value the unique dignity of human life.

That draws stark attention to the fact that the current discussion of ethics and biotech is not being conducted within the walls of an ivory tower. Far from it, even the science professors who get drawn into the policy argument—and those who do not—have or hope to have substantial financial interest in the fruit of their research, since their intention is that it should leave the towers of academe and be applied and exploited in the marketplace. One commentator has suggested that the press should refer to them not as "scientists," since that term implies neutrality and detachment, but as "scientist-entrepreneurs." In this essay we look at recent discussion of the patenting of human genes, as corporate biotech seeks to gain "ownership" in the bodies and body parts of individuals.

Dr. Mitchell is well-placed to survey this field. In addition to his academic appointment in a graduate teaching position, he serves as bioethics consultant to the Ethics and Religious Liberty Commission of the Southern Baptist Convention, America's largest Protestant denomination. His doctoral work focused on gene patenting issues, and he has provided testimony and regular consultation on Capitol Hill.

NIGEL M. DE S. CAMERON

The genetic revolution has reached two significant milestones already in this young century. Not only has it been fifty years since the discovery of the double helical structure of the DNA molecule—that now ubiquitous twisted ladderlike emblem of twenty-first century science—but we now have a completed map of the human genetic blueprint. What these milestones may mean for the future of research science, medicine, social policy and our culture is the subject of this chapter.

Scientific and medical advances in genetics promise to be dazzling in the first half of this century. Some scientists and social commentators have a triumphalistic, almost utopian, attitude about the future. Others are less sanguine, seeing the benefits of genetic technology as contingent on the moral responsibility of both researchers and the larger culture. Still others view tampering with the molecular basis of our biological identity as dangerous and to be resisted at every level.

Will the future see the cure of genetically linked diseases or the redesign of human life? Will we see the dignity of every human person protected in our genetic future, or will we see human beings reduced to mere biological information? Will our genetic identities point toward something transcendent in us, or will they be used to discriminate against us? Will our children be valued because they are unique and "given," or will they be valued because they are designed and "chosen"? These are only a few of the questions presented to us in this new century.

Few question that genetic science is a double-edged sword. There are, and may yet be, wonderful benefits to enjoy through advances in genetics. At the same time, we are already finding that there may be both fiscal and social costs associated with our genetic future. Where will we go from here? Or, better, where *should* we go from here?

The Genetic Basis of Our Species

Human beings are very complex individuals. Like snowflakes, every one of us is unique in every way. We grew up in different families, with different ethnic backgrounds, in different socio-cultural-economic environments. We are different shapes, colors and sizes. Even so-called identical twins are not identical in every way.

Similarly, each of us is a unique individual genetically. Our genetic identity is uniquely our own. Having said that, there are sufficient molecular similarities that we can speak appropriately of the "human genome." That is, because we are all members of the same species, *Homo sapiens,* we share huge amounts of biological similarities. For instance, we are all carbon-based, upright, bipedal, psychophysical life forms. And the similarities go even deeper that that. We share most of our genetic information with other members of our species; and interestingly enough, we share much of our genetic information with other species. What is this genetic information and where is it found?

Inside each of the trillions of cells in our bodies there are chromosomes, threadlike units that contain our genes. We receive half of our chromosomes from our biological mothers and half from our biological fathers. So when egg and sperm unite successfully in fertilization, a genetically unique individual results (unless twinning occurs, in which case two genetically identical human beings result).

Genes are stretches of DNA (deoxyribonucleic acid) that contain the biological information for making a certain protein. Another way to think of the gene is to think of it as a sentence of information that gives the cell certain instructions. In this case, however, the alphabet has only four letters: A, T, C and G. These letters represent the various nucleotide bases that form the genes (adenine, thymine, cytocine and guanine), which combine in pairs to communicate with the cell. Since there are somewhere between thirty thousand and forty thousand genes in the human genetic blueprint, and since many of these genes have thousands of letters of information, the genetic information contained in every cell of the human body is over three billion base-pairs long. Deciphering the language of the genome (all the genetic information that constitutes a biological entity) is a huge task.

The Human Genome Project was begun in 1990 with the goal of creating a physical representation of the language of the human genetic catalogue, to map the human genetic code. The image of a map is useful conceptually because it points to the ways in which this information might be best used.

Imagine that you want to travel from Atlanta, Georgia, to Birmingham, Alabama, but you do not have a map. You do know, however, that Birmingham is somewhere between Atlanta and Los Angeles, California. And, in fact, you know that Dallas, Texas, is between Atlanta and Los Angeles. Thus Atlanta, Dallas and Los Angeles become "markers" to help you locate Birmingham. You discover that Birmingham is not between Dallas and Los Angeles. By "mapping" the distance between Atlanta and Dallas, you will have a better idea of where Birmingham is than if all you knew was that Birmingham was between Atlanta and Los Angeles. Similarly, by creating a physical map of the human genetic code, scientists have been able to identify genetic markers.

These genetic markers help scientists identify which genes inform our cells to make certain kinds of proteins. These proteins perform many tasks inside the cell to cause our cells to develop in specific ways. For instance, in some cases the genetic information in the cells instructs the cells to make a new human being a boy rather than a girl. In some cases our genetic information instructs the cells to make red hair or black hair. Thousands of genes for so-called genetic traits have been located on the genome. Likewise, many genes associated with diseases have been found. For instance, two genes associated with early onset breast cancer, BRCA1 and BRCA2, have been identified. Women with these genes have an increased risk of getting breast cancer.

The completion of the Human Genome Project is, in a very real sense, just the beginning. Francis Collins, the head of the National Human Genome Research Institute underscored this point when he said,

> So, to borrow from Winston Churchill, this is not the end of genomics. This is not even the beginning of the end. But it may be the end of the beginning. For me, as a physician, the true payoff from the HGP will be the ability to better diagnose, treat, and prevent disease, and most of those benefits to humanity still lie ahead. With these immense data sets of sequence and variation now in hand, we are now empowered to pursue those goals in ways undreamed of a few years ago. If research support continues at vigorous levels, it is hard to imagine that genomic science will not soon reveal the mysteries of hereditary factors in heart disease, cancer, diabetes, mental illness, and a host of other conditions; in fact, the public accessibility of the HGP data has already jump-started many of these endeavors. Working in effective partnerships with private industry, we can anticipate the application of these basic science efforts to the development of dramatic new therapies, although the pace of medical breakthroughs will always be slower than we wish. However, for this vision to come true, we must place as much emphasis on solving some of the ethical, legal, and social issues that accompany this rapid pace of genomic discovery as we do on the hard science—or we will face the likelihood that the public will be fearful of taking advantage of otherwise powerful and highly beneficial information. We must also work tirelessly to ensure that these medical advances provide benefits to all, and not just the privileged few.[1]

Curative Powers of Genetic Science

There is little doubt that the map of the human genome will be the medical textbook of this century. In fact, physicians are increasingly relying on genetic diagnosis to identify the cause of the symptoms their patients report when they come to the doctor's office or when they arrive at the hospital. Diseases such as cystic fibrosis, Duchenne's muscular dystrophy, Huntington's chorea, thalassemia, Down syndrome, heart disease and a host of cancers (including colon cancer, prostate cancer and breast cancer) may all be linked to our genes. In fact, over six thousand genetic and rare diseases, afflicting more than 25 mil-

---

[1]Francis S. Collins, "Contemplating the End of the Beginning," *Genome Research* 11 (May 2001): 643.

lion Americans, might be treatable through genetic interventions.[2] What is more, many diseases might be preventable through developments in genetic science. The potential for relieving human suffering and improving health is huge. The warrant for genetic medicine is clear.

In fact, we can safely say that we have a moral obligation to advance medical genetics. It is not enough to "crack the code"; we must now use this information's power to help those who are suffering from the burden of "bad genes."

Our genetic future may include the ability to treat genetic problems by "turning off" or "knocking out" the genes that are responsible for diseases like cystic fibrosis. Gene therapy might be offered to adults and children who are suffering from the symptoms of those genetic illnesses. Even more ideal would be genetic therapies that keep the disease gene from expressing itself in the first place. In this way individuals might never have to experience the symptoms and suffering associated with the diseases. Another genetic intervention might involve removing the bad gene from a person's reproductive cells (sperm or egg) and thereby preventing that person from passing on the bad gene to the next generation. If successful, this might mean eradicating certain diseases from entire families, clans or even the human species. Only extraordinary ethical, social and legal burdens should slow genetic research. As we will see, however, there are both real and potential problems with genetic research. These concerns ought to make us think carefully and critically about how these technologies may be developed in morally responsible ways. As Collins warns, "We must place as much emphasis on solving some of the ethical, legal and social issues that accompany this rapid pace of genomic discovery as we do on the hard science—or we will face the likelihood that the public will be fearful of taking advantage of otherwise powerful and highly beneficial information."[3]

The Diagnosis/Therapy Gap

The first problems in the ethics of genetic science are the problems associated with the diagnosis/therapy gap. For the foreseeable future we will have the ability to diagnose many genetic conditions long before we can offer any hope of treatment for these conditions. For instance, currently we can identify those who have the gene for Huntington's chorea, more commonly known as Huntington's disease. Huntington's is a fatal disease affecting the brain and central nervous system. The disease manifests itself in three types of symp-

---

[2]The National Human Genome Research Institute (NHGRI) maintains a website containing very helpful information at <http://www.genome.gov>. (The URLs cited in this chapter were accessed on January 16, 2004.)
[3]Collins, "Contemplating the End."

toms: movement disorders, including clumsiness, loss of coordination and loss of balance; cognitive problems, including difficulty remembering, keeping track of things and making decisions; and psychiatric problems, including irritability, depression and lethargy. Eventually, the disease results in increasingly severe dementia and progressive motor dysfunction. In late-onset Huntington's, these symptoms do not show up until a person is in his or her late forties or fifties.

Interestingly, we now know that the Huntington's mutation occurs on gene IT-15. The defective gene can be detected with a simple blood test, which can be administered to an adult, a child or even a fetus in the womb. Yet frighteningly we can offer no treatment or cure for Huntington's disease. No one knows whether or when a therapy will be available.

The diagnosis/therapy gap means individuals may live with the knowledge that they have a genetic anomaly for many years without being able to do anything about the problem. Sadly, they may even go to their grave having known for twenty or thirty years what the cause of their death would be. This gap has led to several moral, legal and social problems.

Discrimination. As we have seen, in some cases a person's genetic status can be known through a blood test. One's genetic status can also be established by taking a hair, tissue or fingernail sample. Likewise, one's genetic status may sometimes be known long before any symptoms develop. Furthermore, some genetic diseases are unlike Huntington's in that the presence of the gene does not guarantee that one will develop the symptoms of the disease. With some diseases individuals may only have an increased risk of getting the disease, even though they may have a given disease gene. For instance, though there are genes associated with atherosclerosis (or hardening of the arteries), dietary and lifestyle changes can impact the progression of the disease.

In an unscientific PBS online poll, only 62 percent of respondents said they would want themselves or a loved one to be tested for a gene that increases risk for a disease. Twenty-six percent said they would not want the test. A full 11 percent say they do not know whether or not they would want to be tested.[4] Not all people at risk for a genetic disease, then, wish to know whether or not they have the gene for that disease. They would rather live with the possibility than the proof. Clearly, others want to know. Spouses might want to know whether a husband or wife has a certain inheritable disease. Prospective parents might want to know their genetic status to determine whether they will risk having children with a particular genetic trait or disease. Siblings and children might want to know. But as long as the diagnosis/therapy gap exists, this knowledge comes with a high price.

---

[4]Survey results can be found at <http://www.pbs.org/wgbh/nova/genome/survey.html>.

No one knows exactly how many individuals have been subjected to job and insurance discrimination due to their genetic status, but the numbers will grow without adequate protections. In 1982 only 1.6 percent of companies reported that they were using genetic tests for employment purposes. By 1997 the American Management Association found that the number had grown to as many as 10 percent of companies. Increasing numbers of persons report genetic discrimination in the workplace. At the same time only about twenty-one states have enacted laws to prevent workplace genetic discrimination and only forty-two states have even minimal protections against insurance discrimination based on genetic conditions.

In the same survey cited above, 93 percent said they thought employers should *not* have access to their genetic information. Poll after poll shows that overwhelming numbers of Americans want genetic privacy protected. Yet to date no national comprehensive genetic privacy/antidiscrimination legislation has been passed. What will the future hold for those with genetic conditions? Will they be able to get jobs? Will they be able to secure insurance?

A group of policy experts convened by the American Association for the Advancement of Science made the following recommendations to resist insurance and job discrimination:

- Individuals should be able to gain information about their genetic makeup but should be able to protect themselves against discrimination by controlling access to such information.

- Genetic information should be used only to enhance, not undermine, an individual's quality of life. Society, therefore, in pursuit of the common good, has a responsibility to protect citizens against the misuse of genetic information.

- Policies should be adopted to ensure opportunities for people to participate in research studies and clinical trials without fear that their genetic information could adversely affect their health insurance status.[5]

Discrimination does not have to take the form of denied employment or canceled insurance. For instance, in her recent volume *Future Perfect: Confronting Decisions About Genetics*, Chicago-Kent School of Law professor Lori Andrews cites rabbi and bioethicist Elliot Dorff, who argues that "women with the defective BRCA1 [gene for breast cancer] have a duty to inform their prospective mates of the fact," apparently so the men could choose another

---

[5]American Association for the Advancement of Science, "Statement on Genetic Discrimination in Health Insurance," November 1999.

spouse with "better genes."[6] The future may also see women ostracized for bringing genetically "defective" children into the world.[7] Some law journals are even beginning to explore so-called wrongful-life suits in which children with genetic anomalies sue their parents for not aborting them. Not far behind will be charges of "genetic negligence" against parents who do not provide gene therapy for children with deleterious genes.

Preimplantation genetic screening and embryo destruction. Discrimination based on genetic diagnosis may take the form of deliberate embryo destruction. Through preimplantation genetic diagnosis, human embryos may be screened for desirable genetic traits or against undesirable genetic traits before being transferred to a woman's uterus. In this case embryos are created through in vitro fertilization, a procedure that unites sperm and egg in a Petri dish. Typically, as many as a dozen embryos are created at the same time. After the embryos develop to the six- to eight-cell stage, a cell is extracted from each embryo for biopsy. Only those embryos that are free of disease genes are transferred to the mother's uterus. The other embryos are either destroyed or used in destructive research.

Preimplantation genetic diagnosis is growing. As increasing numbers of genetic conditions become diagnosable, there is every reason to believe the numbers of embryos destroyed will grow as well. In one well-publicized case, the Nash family had a daughter with a rare genetic disorder known as Fanconi anemia, a condition that eventually leads to bone marrow failure. Because the gene for Fanconi anemia is a recessive gene, if both parents carry the mutation there is a twenty-five percent chance their offspring will inherit the gene. If the child inherits both copies of the gene, he or she will contract Fanconi anemia. Treatments for Fanconi anemia include a number of potential therapies, the most successful of which is bone marrow transplantation.

In the Nash case, Molly, their six-year-old daughter, had Fanconi anemia. The Nashes decided to try to conceive another child who would be both free of the FA gene and who could be a bone marrow donor for Molly. Because there was a one in four chance of having a child without the FA gene and a three out of sixteen chance of having a donor match, the likelihood of having a child who met both criteria was fairly low. The Nashes started with about thirty embryos, but only five had the right genetic blueprint for their purposes. In the fourth attempt at pregnancy, the last embryo implanted and was born. Little Adam Nash, as he is called, became a cord-blood donor for his sister. The

[6]Lori Andrews, *Future Perfect: Confronting Decisions About Genetics* (New York: Columbia University Press, 2001), p. 85.
[7]Mary B. Mahowald, Dana Levinson, Christine Cassel et al., "The New Genetics and Women," *Milbank Quarterly* 74, no. 2 (1996).

other embryos, his brothers and sisters, were either killed in attempts to get Mrs. Nash pregnant, discarded or used in research that led to their deaths.

In an even more bizarre case reported in the *Journal of the American Medical Association*, a thirty-year-old woman from a family with a history of early onset Alzheimer's disease decided to use preimplantation genetic diagnosis to try to have a child without the gene associated with her particular form of the disease.[8] Several members of her family began to show signs of the disease in their early forties. In fact, she had a sister who had the disease, and she had watched her sister decline mentally and physically to the point where she could no longer care for her children. Vowing not to let that happen to her, she chose to use preimplantation genetic diagnosis. In this case, not only were embryos destroyed in the effort to have a child free from the Alzheimer's mutation, but the child born to this woman will be sentenced to watch her own mother die from the disease, since if her mother's illness follows those in her family, the child will be about ten years old when her mother begins to develop symptoms of Alzheimer's. Even though the mother may have delivered her child from having one specific form of Alzheimer's, she may have sentenced her daughter to an extremely traumatic childhood, followed by the remainder of her life without her mother.

The New Eugenics

Eugenics is a compound word from two Greek words meaning "good" and "genes." The eugenics movement began at the turn of the last century in England and the United States. Under the leadership of social engineers such as Francis Galton and Charles Davenport, the eugenics movement became a powerful social force.

So-called Fitter Families contests were held across the United States in the 1920s and 1930s. Fitter Families were families with fewer incidences of physical and mental disability. Their ethnic heritage also had to remain intact. Racial intermarriage disqualified families. Thus the fitter families were exclusively Caucasian. Mary T. Watts, cofounder of the first contest at the 1920 Kansas Free Fair, said, "While the stock judges are testing the Holsteins, Jerseys, and whitefaces in the stock pavilion, we are judging the Joneses, Smiths, and Johns." Winners were given a medal inscribed with the slogan, "Yea, I Have a Goodly Heritage."

The eugenics movement tried to create "better humans through breeding." Yet breeding was not the only way to achieve the desired goals. In order to prevent "undesirables" from reproducing, mandatory sterilization laws were en-

---

[8]Yury Verlinsky et al., "Preimplantation Diagnosis for Early-Onset Alzheimer Disease Caused by V717L Mutation," *Journal of the American Medical Association* 287 (2002): 1018-21.

acted. Those deemed feeble-minded, indolent and licentious were sterilized either without their consent or against their wills. So-called eugenical sterilizations increased from around 3,000 in 1907 to over 22,000 in 1935. By the 1930s most states had mandatory sterilization laws. In one well-known case, a young mentally retarded girl named Carrie Buck was given the "choice" either to be sterilized or to be returned to her asylum. Because both her mother and grandmother had been mentally retarded, the famous jurist Oliver Wendell Holmes declared of Buck, "Three generations of imbeciles is enough" and mandated that she be sterilized.[9]

With the power of genetic technology, a new eugenics has emerged. A 1993 March of Dimes poll found that 11 percent of parents said they would abort a fetus whose genome was predisposed to obesity. Four out of five would abort a fetus if it would grow up with a disability. Forty-three percent said they would use genetic engineering if available simply to enhance their child's appearance.

Increasingly college-age women are being solicited for their donor eggs on the basis of their desirable genetic traits. In the summer of 2000 the *Minnesota Daily*, the student newspaper of the University of Minnesota, ran an ad for egg donors. Preferred donors were Caucasian women five-foot-six-inches or taller, with high ACT or SAT scores and with no genetic illnesses; extra compensation was offered to those with mathematical, musical or athletic abilities. The ad stated that acceptable donors would be offered as much as $80,000 for their eggs. This is eugenics with a vengeance.

Our culture's emphasis on the genetically "fit" and our difficulty in embracing those who are "less fit" fuels this new eugenics mindset. We must resist the new eugenicists if we are to preserve a truly human future.

Engineering Future Humans

Not only may genetic interventions be used to treat existing conditions, but the technology may be used in the future to alter our species. So-called germline engineering would be one way genetics could be used to alter future generations of our species. Simply put, there are two types of cells in our bodies: somatic cells and germ cells, or reproductive cells. The germ cells are sperm or eggs. All the other cells are somatic cells. Whatever manipulations are achieved in the somatic cell alters only the genome of the person whose cells they were.

One might want to alter the germ line to attempt to remove hereditary genetic problems from one's progeny. By removing or canceling out the gene in the germ cell, some disorders would be eradicated from a family, a clan or

---

[9]For information and hundreds of pictures from the American eugenics movement, see <http://www.eugenicsarchive.org/eugenics>.

(eventually perhaps) the human race. While on the surface this sounds like a very laudable goal, the risks of germline intervention make it unlikely that it will ever be morally acceptable. Why?

First, most genetic diseases are multifactorial. That is to say, they involve more than one gene and very complex environmental factors. There are relatively few single-gene traits or diseases. Single-gene traits include the ability to roll one's tongue, whether one has a widow's peak hairline and whether one has long or short earlobes. Single-gene disorders include sickle-cell anemia, cystic fibrosis, Duchenne's muscular dystrophy and Marfan syndrome. Multifactorial traits, like skin color and height, are contingent not only on the presence of several genes working together, but also on environmental factors like diet. Similarly, the expression of multifactorial disorders may require, in addition to multiple gene interactions, very unpredictable environmental conditions. For instance, certain forms of colon cancer are "genetically linked," but the link is not to a single gene. In order to get the cancer, one must be genetically predisposed and must have made dietary and lifestyle choices that realize the predisposition in the expression of the gene in the form of cancer.

All of that is to say that we humans are very complex organisms. We must also recall that we are at the very early stages of the genetic revolution. In terms of an analogy, we have just learned the genetic alphabet. We are a very long way from being able to compose grammatically correct sentences, much less compose great works of literature. In other words, because of the complexity of the organism and because of the relatively primitive nature of the science, our genuine attempts to help relieve suffering by manipulating the reproductive cells could cause a cascade of problems in our effort to help.

At the very least, germline manipulation would require a scientific genetic sophistication we simply do not possess and will not possess in the foreseeable future. If we permit germline experimentation in humans, we could cause great harm not only to one individual, but also to all the children and the children's children. The only way to control a failure in germline engineering would be to sterilize those whose reproductive cells had been altered. Mandatory sterilization of competent adults is not itself morally defensible.

Additionally, the same genetic technology used to treat disease can be used to alter future humans in order to "engineer in" desirable traits. So-called genetic enhancement technology applied to the germline might alter our species in terrible ways. If we could identify the genetic conditions required for increased IQ, should we engineer future humans to have a higher IQ? What would be the consequences of doing so? In our effort to do so, might we create a family or clan with other problems we could not foresee? Who decides how many IQ points are desirable? Is IQ an obviously good trait? Perhaps in altering IQ we would damage other traits. Once we had altered IQ, would it be ethical to reverse the procedure is something went wrong? If IQ were altered in the reproductive cells, would we create a family of geniuses or, if something went wrong, of imbeciles? Who would be responsible for the failure? Even if the venture were successful, who would have access to the relatively expensive IQ-enhancement technology? Would the fact that only the well-off could afford it create a genetic class system? These are all such insurmountable problems that it seems nearly impossible to imagine conditions under which germline manipulation could be morally responsible.

Who Owns Our Genes?

The answer to the question, who owns my genes? may seem obvious. "I own my genes," one might respond. But this is less than clear. Once our genes are removed from our bodies, they are up for grabs. Genes and other human tissues may become patentable property under the present patent system.

In an interesting state Supreme Court case, *Moore* v. *Regents of the University of California,* John Moore brought suit against physicians who patented a cell line from his diseased spleen. In October 1976, shortly after learning that he had hairy-cell leukemia, Moore consulted physicians at the University of California at Los Angeles Medical Center. The attending physician, David W. Golde, informed Moore that his condition could be fatal and that a spleenectomy was indicated. His spleen was removed October 20, 1976.

Using either Moore's diseased spleen or tissues retrieved during follow-up treatment, Golde established a cell line from Moore's T lymphocytes. Without the patient's knowledge or consent, Golde and his colleague Shirley G. Quan, applied for a patent on the cell line. Based on university policy, any royalties or profits arising out of patents obtained by employees in their function as employees would be shared by the university. Patent number 4,438,032 was issued on March 20, 1984, naming Golde and Quan as inventors.

Moore v. *Regents of the University of California* both demonstrates that patents are issued on human body parts and illustrates the ways the courts typically treat matters of biological ownership vis-à-vis patents.

Efforts of the National Institutes of Health, an agency of the United States government, to patent *expressed sequence tags* (ESTs) continued the dubious tradition of patenting human genes. ESTs are clones of small segments of DNA. These copies, called *complementary DNA* (or cDNA) may be useful in the production of therapeutic products such as human growth hormone and erythropoietin (EPO). In order to be used for therapeutic benefit, not only must the particular cDNA be identified, but also its function in the gene must be known. Once researchers have identified the function of cDNA, they can determine whether and how it may be used to treat illnesses.

NIH researchers developed a technique to rapidly sequence genes using cDNA, making it possible to identify thousands of ESTs in a very brief span of time. While the ESTs had been sequenced, their use remained unknown. That is, even though researchers at NIH had identified the ESTs, they did not know how to use them to produce therapeutic tools.

Craig Venter and his colleagues at NIH filed for patents on several thousand ESTs in 1991. In doing so NIH was presumably hoping to protect their investment in developing the technology to identify ESTs. Once the attempt to patent ESTs became known, another cloud of controversy surrounded the United States Patent and Trademark Office and the patenting process. In November 1991, the American Society of Human Genetics (a professional society of over 4,500 U.S. and Canadian physicians, scientists and genetic counselors) maintained that "the issuing of patents for ESTs is likely to do far more harm than good." Much of the controversy focused not so much on the fact that patenting ESTs of unknown biological function violated the utility requirement of the patent statutes, but on the patenting of human genes qua human genes. The debate made international headlines, leading to, for instance, an editorial in the *Financial Times of London* that called for the NIH to cease and desist in their efforts to patent ESTs. In that editorial the French minister of science, Hubert Curien, is quoted as saying, "A patent should not be granted for something that is part of our universal heritage." Bernadine Healy, at that time director of the NIH, said in response to Curien's comments,

> In fact, human and other genes have been patented by scientists of many countries. Indeed, most scientists and most governments of industrialized nations are arguing not against the patenting of genes, but rather against their being patented "prematurely"—that is, before their biologic function and commercial potential are adequately defined.

In December 1992 the Patent and Trademark Office rejected the NIH's patent claims on ESTs. The PTO did so on the basis of the utility and nonobvious requirements of the patent statutes. Since by definition ESTs had unknown biological function, the usefulness of ESTs could not be known. Moreover, since ESTs were identified by what amounts to a mechanical process, the identification of ESTs was deemed obvious to anyone skilled in the art.

The Human Genome Organization (HUGO), an international consortium of genetic scientists, issued its statement on patenting ESTs in January 1995. HUGO's position is that "the patenting of partial and uncharacterized cDNA sequences will reward those who make *routine* discoveries but penalize those who determine biological function or application."

The controversy over patenting human genes is hardly over. In March 1995 the Patent and Trademark Office granted a patent on a cell line derived from a member of the Hagahai tribe of Papua New Guinea. The cell line was thought to be useful in a similar manner as John Moore's cell line was. That is to say, the Hagahai cell line was derived from a man who was infected with human T cell leukemia. The man was not suffering from symptoms of leukemia, which gave researchers hope that his cell line would be helpful in treating the disease. The dispute over patenting the genetic materials of an indigenous tribe became so heated that on October 24, 1996, NIH filed paperwork to "disclaim" the patent. Opponents of patenting genetic materials of indigenous peoples worry over not only the patenting of human genes, but the commercial exploitation of people groups in the Southern Hemisphere by the industrialized nations of the Northern Hemisphere. The Rural Advancement Foundation International (RAFI) has labeled this and similar practices as a new form of "colonialism." RAFI charged that

> private ownership of human biological materials raises many profound social, ethical, and political issues. Industrialized nations are lobbying vigorously for "harmonization" of intellectual property laws worldwide with the ultimate goal of imposing patenting laws worldwide. In the South, issues of development and national sovereignty are at stake. Fundamental human rights are jeopardized everywhere.[10]

In another very surprising move, Utah-based pharmaceutical firm Myriad Genetics announced in 1998 that they had received patents on the breast cancer genes BRCA1 and BRCA2 and on a test to identify these genes. In order for a woman who suspects she has the gene to have the test, she must first pay Myriad Genetics more than $2,500 in fees. Furthermore, because Myriad holds the patent on the genes, they effectively have a monopoly on the test.

Finally, in May 2003, the science journal *Nature* published a story chronicling the efforts of the United States Centers for Disease Control and Prevention to patent the SARS virus. By patenting the virus preemptively, the CDC would be able prevent private researchers from patenting the virus and monopolizing it for financial benefits. Julie Gerberding, a spokesperson for the CDC, told reporters that "in private hands, a patent on the viral sequence might delay the development and refinement of tests and treatments for the contagious pneumonia that has already killed several hundred people."[11] This worry demonstrates the growing awareness that gene patents hinder research at the cost of risks to public health. Yet, to date, there is no patent-reform leg-

---

[10]Originally published in a 1994 issue of RAFI *Communique;* later included in Hope Shand, *Human Nature: Agricultural Biodiversity and Farm-Based Food Security* (Pittsboro, N.C.: Rural Advancement Foundation International, 1997). an independent study prepared for the Food and Agriculture Organization of the United Nations.

[11]"Gene Patents and the Public Good," *Nature* 423 (May 15, 2003): 207.

islation pending in the Congress or policy changes being undertaken by the PTO. The commodification of human genes persists despite the moral and practical problems. Money talks!

Preserving a Truly Human Future

Genetic technology may be used to relieve human suffering, treat human diseases and thereby protect human dignity; or it may be used in ways that erode our dignity and treat us as mere commodities or, even worse, refashion us in someone else's image. In both Jewish and Christian theology, humankind is understood to be the special creation of God, made in his own image and likeness (Gen 1:26-28; 9:1-6). Though fallen and corrupted, human beings remain image bearers of God.

Because we are fearfully and wonderfully made in God's image (Ps 139:14), we have every reason to seek greater knowledge of our biology as an expression of devotion to the God who made us. In fact, the impetus for modern science, including molecular biology, came from a Christian worldview. We should recall that one of the pioneers of genetics was a monk named Gregor Mendel.

Science does not operate in a moral vacuum, however. Ethically responsible genetics entails that we use the power of our understanding of the human genome in ways that protect ourselves and our neighbors from being harmed or manipulated for the sake of dubious visions of a posthuman future.

Research science, biomedicine and public policy must be underwritten by a robust view of human dignity, lest genetic science will become an enemy rather than a friend, a trafficker in human body parts rather than a remedy for human ailments, an idol rather than a servant of the Great Physician.

4

TECHNO SAPIENS

Nanotechnology, Cybernetics, Transhumanism and the Remaking of Humankind

C. CHRISTOPHER HOOK, M.D.

In parallel with the possibility that biology may enable us to manipulate human nature according to our own design lies the prospect that other technologies may be used for the same purpose. These technologies are at root two: nanotechnology (the engineering of very small devices, on a molecular scale) and cybernetics (artificial intelligence, the use of computers to generate aids, enhancements and replacements to the human mind). There are debates within the artificial intelligence community as to whether it will actually be possible to develop computers as powerful as the human brain. Some suggest that the human power of creativity is unduplicatable; others suggest that since it has been estimated that within thirty years our computing power will have advanced by a factor of one million, it is not possible to place such limits on the outcome of this technology.

Meanwhile, very substantial corporate funding is advancing these technologies, and already the federal government is spending in the region of one billion dollars each year on nanotech research.

These technologies have many benign applications. But as they grow in sophistication, they will increasingly have uses that may prove inimical to human dignity. And in parallel with these developments in technology, there is growing philosophical interest in the uses to which they may be put. So the terms posthumanism and transhumanism have been coined to suggest our development of capacities that may enable us to take control of the human species and move the species—or some of its members—into new forms of existence. And this kind of thinking is not being done only on the extremes. The federal government's National Nanotechnology Initiative's website already gives evidence of this kind of future vision, in which our vision of human dignity is undermined.

Few Christians have even begun to engage in these questions. Dr. Hook directs ethics education at the Mayo Graduate School of Medicine, has testified before the U.S. Congress and is a member of a key government advisory committee on human genetics. He may be unique among Christians in having followed these developments, both technical and philosophical, with critical acumen that avoids the opposite temptations of Luddism on the one hand and naive technophilia on the other.

NIGEL M. DE S. CAMERON

As we enter the twenty-first century, we are being confronted with significant ethical, scientific, medical and social challenges posed by our rapidly increasing knowledge. Much has been written and is still intensely discussed and debated about, for instance, the potential harms and benefits of our new knowledge about the human genome. Most controversial among the topics in the genetics/genomics field are the possibilities of genetic engineering. While there continue to be many concerns about the use of genetic information to pursue eugenic ideals, either corporately or by a "eugenics of the market place," the ability to manipulate genes directly to produce desired phenotypic expression opens new eugenic tools and potential. Thus one of the questions before us is, should we deliberately reengineer human beings by genetic manipulation?

Though these issues are critically important, other technologies are being rapidly developed that will enable human beings to reengineer themselves without the need to involve genetic and reproductive mechanisms. Rather the existing person will soon be offered an array of means to remake himself or herself via tissue reconstruction or prosthetic enhancement. The tools that will enable this type of reconfiguration are nanotechnology and cybernetics.

The first portion of this chapter will review the nature of nanotechnology and cybernetics, discuss where things stand presently in their development and provide a vision of what the scientists and engineers engaged in these areas of research hope to accomplish with their work. The next portion will address a growing philosophical, social and technical movement known as *transhumanism* or *posthumanism*, which actively promotes the reengineering of humankind, exploring its worldview and goals. The chapter will conclude with a critique, from both a secular and a biblical perspective, of the movement and its use of these technologies.

Cybernetics

Cybernetics in its purest definition is the science of "control and communication in the animal and the machine"; it was devised by Norbert Weiner in the 1940s. The word is derived from the Greek for steersman, *kybernetes*. Weiner wrote in *The Human Use of Human Beings,*

Society can only be understood through a study of the messages and the communication facilities which belong to it; and that in the future development of these messages and communication facilities, messages between man and machines, between machines and man, and between machine and machine, are destined to play an ever-increasing part.[1]

Ashby described the focus of this theory of machines as not on what a thing is, but on what it does, stating, "Cybernetics deals with all forms of behavior in so far as they are regular, or determinate, or reproducible. The materiality is irrelevant."[2] Recognizing that there are significant similarities in biological and mechanical systems, subsequent researchers have pursued the ideal of merging biological and mechanical/electrical systems into what Manfred Clynes and Nathan Kline termed *cyborgs* (*cyb*ernetic *org*anisms).[3] In this sense cybernetics has taken on the meaning of adding prostheses to the human or animal body to replace lost function or to augment biological activity.

Humans have long used tools to augment various functions, and they have for centuries also intimately attached some of these tools to their bodies. Filled or artificial teeth, glasses and contact lenses, hearing aids, pacemakers, and artificial limbs are all examples of this phenomenon. Recently there have been significant advances in the fields of neuroscience and computer technologies that allow the direct interface of animal or human nervous systems with electromechanical devices. A few examples of this evolving field are the creation of neural-silicon junctions involving transistors and neurons to prepare neuronal circuits, the remote control of mechanical manipulator arms by implants inserted into the motor cortex of owl monkeys, and the remote control of rats to move over a directed path via implanted electrodes and a computer moderated joystick.[4]

Peter Fromherz and colleagues at the Max Planck Institute for Biological Cybernetics in Tübingen, Germany, have successfully grown connections between the neurons of several species of animals and transistors allowing two-

[1]Norbert Weiner, *The Human Use of Human Beings* (New York: Da Capo, 1950), p. 16. See also Norbert Weiner, *Cybernetics: Or Control and Communication in the Animal and the Machine,* 2nd ed. (Cambridge, Mass.: MIT Press, 1948).

[2]W. Ross Ashby, *An Introduction to Cybernetics* (London: Chapman & Hall, 1957), p. 1.

[3]Manfred Clynes and Nathan S. Kline, "Cyborgs and Space," *Astronautics* (September 1960): 26-27, 74-75.

[4]On the creation of neural-silicon junctions, see Martin Jenker, Bernt Muller and Peter Fromhertz, "Interfacing a Silicon Chip to Pairs of Snail Neurons Connected by Electrical Synapses," *Biological Cybernetics* 84 (2001): 239-49. On motor cortex implants, see Johan Wessberg et al., "Real-Time Prediction of Hand Trajectory by Ensembles of Cortical Neurons in Primates," *Nature* 408, no. 6810 (2000): 361-65. On remote control via implanted electrodes, see Sanjiv Talwar et al., "Rat Navigation Guided by Remote Control" *Nature* 417, no. 6884 (2002): 37-38.

way communication through the silicon-neuronal junction.[5] More recently researchers at Infineon Technologies in Germany, working in collaboration with the Max Planck group, announced the development of the "neuro-chip." This device has more than sixteen thousand sensors per square millimeter and is able to record at least two thousand readings per second (or, in aggregate, 32 million information values per second). Neurons are kept alive in a special nutrient fluid that coats the chip's surface. The architecture of the chip ensures that each neuron in the matrix covers at least one sensor. Thus without the need to invade the structure of the neurons themselves, the chip can maintain prolonged undisturbed interactions between neurons, and measure and process the flow of information through the neuronal network.[6]

In 1999 Garrett Stanley and his colleagues at the University of California at Berkeley were able to measure the neuronal activity of the optical pathway of a cat via 177 electrical probes, process the information and re-create rough images of what the cat's eyes were viewing at the moment. While the images were of fairly poor resolution—similar to the degree of resolution of computed tomography (CT) scans in the early 1980s—with improved signal processing, one would to be able to produce more exact images.[7] The implication of this line of research is that if we can decode the visual images from their neural representations, we will in time be equally capable of directly transmitting "visual" images into a recipient's brain, bypassing the use or need of light-collecting visual organs. It could become the ultimate tool for virtual reality.

On a more practical note, a type of cybernetic technology is already being used to help the blind regain some degree of sight. Researchers at the Dobelle Institute have implanted electrodes connected to a digital camera and computer complex into the visual cortex of blind patients, restoring some degree of sight. In one case the patient was even able to drive around the parking lot of the hospital with the degree of restored vision.[8]

Investigators at Emory University have helped two patients with locked-in syndrome, a state in which the brain is conscious but cannot produce any movement of the patient's voluntary skeletal muscles. Someone with locked-

---

[5]Peter Fromherz and Alfred Stett, "Silicon-Neuron Junction: Capacitive Stimulation of an Individual Neuron of a Silicon Chip," *Physical Review Letters* 75 (1995): 1670-73; S. Vassanelli and Peter Fromhertz, "Neurons from Rat Brain Coupled to Transistors," *Applied Physics A: Materials Science and Processing* 65 (August 1997): 85-88.

[6]Press release accessed January 16, 2004, at <www.boise.com/vmw/03/articles/vmw/LVVM-04-03-25.html>.

[7]Garrett Stanley, F. Li Fei and Dan Yang, "Reconstruction of Natural Scenes from Ensemble Responses in the Lateral Geniculate Nucleus," *Journal of Neuroscience* 19 (September 1999): 8036-42.

[8]Steven Kotler, "Vision Quest: A Half Century of Artifical-Sight Research Has Succeeded and Now This Blind Man Can See," *Wired*, September 2002, pp. 95-101.

in syndrome is often thought to be in a persistent vegetative state. The two patients received brain implants into which their neurons grew, establishing a link with a computer. This enabled the patients to use their minds to control a cursor on a computer screen and thus communicate with others.[9]

Richard Hahnloser and his colleagues have reported the successful creation of a silicon chip that uses digital selection and analog amplification in mimicry of the nerve cells of the brain.[10] Ultimately such devices will allow easier integration of cybernetic prostheses with the brain as the means of processing, and relaying information will be similar between the silicon and organic components.

In Chicago in June 2000 the first artificial retinas made from silicon chips were implanted in the eyes of three blind patients suffering from retinitis pigmentosa. Each implant, which was two millimeters in diameter and 1/1000 of an inch thick, contained approximately 3,500 microphotodiodes that convert light energy into electrical impulses to stimulate the remaining functional nerve cells of the retina.[11]

A team at the University of Southern California is planning to replace part of the hippocampus of rats with a special silicon chip. The hippocampus is a crucial part of the brain where the laying down and retrieval of memories is coordinated. The implant would in effect be a memory chip. While designed as a treatment to replace damaged tissue in poststroke patients or those with Alzheimer's disease, it is not difficult to imagine such a device (which at the time of this writing is estimated to be at least ten years off) being used for memory augmentation for normal people as well.[12] While exciting on one level, devices such as this illustrate the significant technical and safety issues involved in developing and employing neuroprostheses. Even if such a device could communicate with the rest of the brain in storing memories, there are still very serious issues to be resolved. Not only does the hippocampus participate in memory, but it is also a significant component of the brain pathways that affect awareness, consciousness and emotions. Thus how such a device may affect other significant elements of brain function and personality is unknown.

While the above are examples of direct, internal interfaces between a nervous system and a cybernetic prosthesis, another approach to cybernetic augmentation is through the use of external or wearable computing devices. In this approach prosthetic enhancement is achieved by miniaturizing traditional

---

[9]Victor Chase, "Mind over Muscles" *Technology Review* 103 (March/April 2000): 39-45.

[10]Richard Hahnloser et al., "Digital Selection and Analogue Amplification Coexist in a Cortex-Inspired Silicon Circuit," *Nature* 405 (June 22, 2000): 947-51.

[11]For more, see <www.optobionics.com>.

[12]Duncan Graham-Rowe, "World's First Brain Prosthesis Revealed," *New Scientist*, March 12, 2003 <www.newscientist.com/news/news.jsp?id-ns99993488>.

computing devices, interface mechanisms and optical projection devices and incorporating them seamlessly into clothing, glasses and jewelry.[13]

Recently this form of cybernetic enhancement has moved from the academy to the commercial stage. Aside from allowing the user/wearer of such devices wireless access to the Internet and other databases on a continuous basis, they may also be used for so-called augmented reality. Augmented reality is the concept of supplementing traditional sensory input with augmented senses or even new types of sensory data. Examples include retrograde vision (seeing to one's rear), distant or projected hearing and infrared vision. Further visual input may be analyzed and correlated with other information, such as Global Positioning System (GPS) location identification. Thus buildings and streets could be labeled, hours of business accessed, and persons one encounters visually identified with demographic information provided, with all of this data directly projected onto the user's retina. A variety of companies have recently been peddling wearable computing products including, for example, those made by Hitachi (Xybernaut), Charmed Technologies and Interactive Imaging Systems.[14]

Nanotechnology

Another area of active development is the field of nanotechnology. Nanotechnology will be a major contributor to the development of cybernetic devices and other direct means of human modification.

As the name implies, nanotechnology is engineering or manipulating matter (and life) at nanometer scale, that is, one-billionth of a meter. Ten hydrogen atoms side by side span one nanometer. The DNA molecule is 2.3 nanometers across.[15] If such feats were possible, then it is conceivable that the structures of our bodies and our current tools could be significantly altered. In recent years many governments around the world, including the United States with its National Nanotechnology Initiative, and scores of academic centers and corporations have committed increasing support for developing nanotechnology programs.[16] For example, in December 2003 the president signed into law the Twenty-First Century Nanotechnology Research and De-

---

[13]See <http://wearcam.org> and <http://www.media.mit.edu/wearables/>.

[14]For more, see <http://www.xybernaut.com>, <http://www.charmed.com> and <http://www.iisvr.com>.

[15]National Science and Technology Council, *Nanotechnology: Shaping the World Atom by Atom* (December 1999) <http://www.wtec.org/loyola/nano/IWGN.Public.Brochure/ >. For extensive discussions of nanotechnology, see the National Nanotechnology Initiative site at <http://www.nano.gov > and the Foresight Institute site at <http://www.foresight.org >.

[16]Steven Glapa, *A Critical Investor's Guide to Nanotechnology* (Milpitas, Calif.: In Realis, 2002) <http://www.inrealis.com>.

velopment Act, authorizing that $2.36 billion be spent over three years on nanotechnology programs (starting in fiscal year 2005).[17]

The idea behind nanotechnology originated with Nobel laureate Richard Feynman in a speech given at an annual meeting of the American Physical Society.[18] He described the development of tools for molecular engineering, that is, for building materials molecule by molecule. His startling claim was that this sort of task would not require a new understanding of physics, but was completely compatible with what scientists already understood about the nature of fundamental forces and matter. Little was done in response to Feynman's challenge until the publication of works by Eric Drexler that both demonstrated the feasibility of such manipulation from an engineering perspective and provided a vision for the possible benefits of such technologies.[19]

The list of potential uses of nanotechnology continues to expand. The primary focus of research at this point concerns miniaturization of electronic components, but nanoscale materials may dramatically improve the durability of materials used in machinery and potentially create production methods that will be less polluting and more efficient.[20] The military, which has a significant interest in nanotechnology, has created the Center for Soldier Nanotechnologies (CSN). Among the initial aims of the CSN is to create stealth garments (and coatings) that are difficult to see or detect, that are highly durable, that may provide increased protection from penetrating objects, that will be lightweight (so as to significantly lessen the load an individual must carry onto the field of battle) and that can rapidly and accurately detect the presence of biological or chemical weapon attacks. The CSN is also interested in the use of such technology to help create the seamless interface of electronic devices with the human nervous system, engineering the cyborg soldier.[21]

Medical uses of microscopic, subcellular machines could potentially include the following:

• rational drug design

---

[17]See <http://www.access.gpo.gov/nara/publaw/108publ.html>.

[18]Richard Feynman, "There's Plenty of Room at the Bottom," *Engineering and Science* 23 (February 1960): 22-36 <http://www.zyvex.com/nanotech/feynman.html>.

[19]K. Eric Drexler, *Engines of Creation* (New York: Anchor, 1986); K. Eric Drexler and Christine Peterson, *Unbounding the Future: The Nanotechnology Revolution* (New York: William Morrow, 1991); K. Eric Drexler, *Nanosystems: Molecular Machinery, Manufacturing and Computation* (New York: John Wiley & Sons, 1992).

[20]On the miniaturization of electronic components, see Adrian Bachtold et al., "Logic Circuits with Carbon Nanotube Transistors," *Science* 294 (November 9, 2001): 1317-20; and D. J. Hornbaker et al., "Mapping the One-Dimensional Electronic States of Nanotube Peapod Structures," *Science* 295 (February 1, 2002): 828-31.

[21]See the Institute of Soldier Nanotechologies site at <http://www.aro.army.mil/soldiernano/>.

- devices specifically targeting and destroying tumor cells or infectious agents[22]

- in vivo devices for at-the-site-of-need drug manufacture and release

- tissue engineering or re-engineering

- early detection or monitoring devices

- in vitro lab-on-a-chip diagnostic tools[23]

- devices to clear existing atherosclerotic lesions in coronary or cerebral arteries

- biomimetic nanostructures to repair or replace DNA or other organelles

- artificial replacements for red blood cells and platelets[24]

- tools to augment or repair interaction between neurons in the brain

- devices to improve biocompatibility and the interface between brain tissue and cybernetic devices

- more durable prosthetic devices or implants[25]

Such tools have also been envisioned to provide new means of cosmetic enhancement, such as providing new forms of weight control, changing hair or skin color, removing unwanted hair or producing new hair simulations.[26]

The development of nanotechnology has taken two major pathways. The first is the so-called top-down approach, which attempts to directly manipulate matter atom by atom and molecule by molecule and which depends heavily on high technology machinery such as atomic force microscopy. Other top-down approaches pursue a more traditional chemistry-based approach, such as the production of carbon nanowires or carbon spheres, like buckminsterfullerene (or "buckyballs"). Carbon nanowires have proven to be excellent conductors and are being used in a variety of ways to develop

---

[22]Michael R. McDevitt et al., "Tumor Therapy with Targeted Atomic Nanogenerators," *Science* 294 (November 16, 2001): 1537-40.

[23]So-Jung Park, T. Andrew Taton and Chad A. Mirkin, "Array-Based Electrical Detection of DNA with Nanoparticle Probes," *Science* 295 (February 22, 2002): 1503-6.

[24]Robert A. Freitas Jr., "Respirocytes: A Mechanical Artificial Red Cell: Exploratory Design in Medical Nanotechnology," rev. vers., 1999, Foresight Institute <http://www.foresight.org/Nanomedicine/Respirocytes.html>.

[25]Robert A. Freitas Jr., *Basic Capabilities*, vol. 1 of *Nanomedicine* (Austin: Landes Bioscience, 2000); B. C. Crandell, ed., *Nanotechnology: Molecular Speculations on Global Abundance* (Cambridge: MIT Press, 1999); BECON (NIH Bioengineering Consortium), *Nanoscience and Nanotechnology: Shaping Biomedical Research; June 2000 Symposium Report* <www.becon.nih.gov/poster_abstracts_exhibits.pdf> and <www.becon.nih.gov/nanotechsympreport.pdf>.

[26]Richard Crawford, "Cosmetic Nanosurgery," in *Nanotechnology: Molecular Speculations on Global Abundance*, ed. B. C. Crandell (Cambridge: MIT Press, 1999), pp. 61-80.

new forms of transistors and microscopic circuitry, leading to significant gains in the miniaturization of electronic devices. Buckyballs are being evaluated as the base for a variety of drug delivery systems.

The second approach, the bottom-up approach, recognizes that the building blocks of life—all the enzymes and other components of each living cell—are already acting as little machines operating at the nanoscale. This approach then tries to use biological materials in new and different ways. For example, a group of researchers led by Carlo Montemagno recognized that one of the critical enzymes in each cell in our body—a protein that is involved in the storage of energy in a molecule called ATP—actually rotates around a central axis like a motor during its function. This same enzyme can work in reverse taking ATP, releasing its stored energy and producing rotary motion. The researchers developed a process to attach a small metal propeller to the central axis of this enzyme, ATP-ase. They then exposed the new "molecular motors" to an energy source in the form of a solution of ATP molecules, just like they might encounter in a living cell. Some of the motors spun the propellers around their axes. While only a minority of the engineered molecules were able to perform this function (e.g., sometimes the propeller would fall off), some of the motors worked for several hours.[27] Montemagno's team has now devised a way to couple these motors to photosynthetic molecules so that sunlight is converted into a steady source of ATP to fuel the molecular motors. His group is also working on ways of synthetically producing moving devices that propel themselves like amoebas.[28] Dan Shu and Peixuan Guo have described that certain forms of viral RNA also bind ATP, releasing its energy and powering a DNA packaging motor that enables the virus to be created with all the genetic material packed into the small capsule of each individual viron.[29] This system indicates the significant amount of force that can be applied at the molecular level.

Another bottom-up technique has been to use DNA and RNA molecules, the fundamental molecules in our genes and gene functioning, as tools for computation. In 1994 Dr. Leonard Adleman at the University of California at Los Angeles used DNA molecules to solve a complex mathematics problem

[27]Ricky Soong et al., "Powering an Inorganic Nanodevice with a Biomolecular Motor," *Science* 290 (November 24, 2000): 1555-58. See also Carlo Montemagno et al., "Constructing Biological Motor Powered Nanomechanical Devices," *Nanotechnology* 10 (1999): 225-31; a draft version of this paper can be found at <http://www.foresight.org/Conferences/MNT6/Papers/Montemagno/>.

[28]Accessed at <http://www.biomotors.ucla.edu>.

[29]Dan Shu and Peixuan Guo, "A Viral RNA that Binds ATP and Contains a Motif Similar to an ATP-Binding Aptamer from SELEX," *Journal of Biological Chemistry* 278 (February 28, 2003): 7119-25.

known as the "Hamiltonian path problem."[30] Laura Landweber of Princeton University reported in 2000 that her team had made an RNA computer to solve a chess problem.[31] Others have used enzymes—normally involved in the production, encoding and decoding of genetic material—to create analogs of digital logic devices, such as AND gates, OR gates and NOR gates, similar to those that are used in the chips of calculators and computers.

Ehud Shapiro and colleagues at the Weizmann Institute of Science have demonstrated that the DNA molecule also intrinsically stores sufficient energy to power calculations using these molecules. Thus the DNA provides not only the information, but also the power.[32] Shapiro believes that eventually (sometime in the next fifty years) biological devices will replace inorganic, silicon-based electronics. In another fascinating report, Adam Heller and his colleagues described the development of a biofuel cell that operates at body temperature and works off a body's normal physiologic fluids.[33] This would provide another intrinsic energy source of cybernetic devices, though eerily is reminiscent of *The Matrix*.[34]

Of further interest, our cells also regularly produce structures that integrate inorganic metals into proteins. It is thus quite feasible that DNA-controlled processes can be designed to construct molecules that will facilitate the biological-inorganic interface. This would allow, for example, more seamless integration of our nervous system with electronic devices, furthering cybernetic developments. A recent report illustrates other uses for such organic-inorganic melding: gold nanoparticles were attached to DNA molecules serving as antennae; radio-signal controls were then used to cause the DNA to unwind and start producing the protein encoded by the segment of DNA, producing in essence a radio-controlled switch for turning genes on and off.[35]

If many of the potential therapeutic uses listed above become reality—allowing more effective treatment of life's greatest killers, such as cancer, infectious disease and vascular disease—it should be clear that longevity could be greatly enhanced. In fact, there are those who predict that nanotechnology and

---

[30]Leonard M. Adleman, "Molecular Computation of Solutions to Combinatorial Problems," *Science* 266 (November 11, 1994): 1021-24.

[31]Dirk Faulhammer et al., "Molecular Computation: RNA Solutions to Chess Problems," *Proceedings of the National Academy of Sciences* 97 (February 2000): 1385-89.

[32]Yaakov Benenson et al., "DNA Molecule Provides a Computing Machine with Both Fuel and Data," *Proceedings of the National Academy of Sciences* 100 (March 4, 2003): 2191-96.

[33]Nicholas Mano, Fei Mao and Adam Heller, "A Miniature Biofuel Cell Operating in a Physiological Buffer," *Journal of the American Chemical Society* 124 (2002): 12962-63.

[34]In the 1999 movie *The Matrix* (written and directed by Andy and Larry Wachowski), humanity has become enslaved by a race of intelligent machines that humans had created. The AI machines keep the humans in chambers, confined in a world of virtual reality facilitated by brain implants, while the humans' bodies are used as a source of power for the machines.

[35]Otis Port, "Silicon Gets a Reprieve—By Way of Less Than a Hair," *Business Week*, December 23, 2002.

cybernetics together will enable humankind to pursue a form of technological "immortality." Others, while looking forward to increased lifespan, are more interested in enhanced function now. The pursuit of enhancing or extending life by technological augmentations is strongly supported by a growing philosophical and social movement known as *transhumanism*.

Transhumanism

Philosopher Nick Bostrom defines *transhumanism* as

> the study of the means and obstacles to humanity using technological and other rational means to becoming posthumans, and of the ethical issues that are involved in this. "Posthumans" is the term for the very much more advanced beings that humans may one day design themselves into if we manage to upgrade our current human nature and radically extend our capacities.[36]

Posthumans, as the name implies, are no longer human beings, having been so significantly altered as to no longer represent the human species. Underlying this "study" is a core belief that "the human species does not represent the end of our evolution but, rather, its beginning."[37]

While the names *transhumanism* and *posthumanism* have been coined recently, the ideas they represent are anything but new. The underlying philosophical ideals are fully those of the Enlightenment, imbued with a healthy dose of postmodern ethical relativism. From the Enlightenment comes a fully reductionistic view of human life characteristic of that movement's materialistic empiricism; add to that a triumphalistic, technoutopian replacement of God with worship at the alter of scientism. Julian Offrey de La Mettrie's statement from *L'Homme Machine* (*Man a Machine,* 1748) that humans "are, at bottom only animals and perpendicularly crawling machines," and de Condorcet's claim that "no bounds have been fixed to the improvement of faculties. . . . The perfectibility of man is absolutely indefinite" could be easily updated to recent transhumanist writings, such as those of Bart Kosko, who asserts, "Biology is not destiny. It was never more than tendency. It was just nature's first quick and dirty way to compute with meat. Chips are destiny."[38]

---

[36]Nick Bostrom, "What Is Transhumanism?" (2001) <http://www.nickbostrom.com/old/transhumanism.html >. See also the World Tranhumanist Association website <http://www.transhumanism.org>.

[37]Nick Bostrom, "The Transhumanist FAQ" (1999); vers. 2.0 of the FAQ <http://www.transhumanism.org/resources/faq.html>.

[38]Julian Offray de La Mettrie, *L'Homme Machine* (Leyden: Elie Luzac, 1748) <http://www.santafe.edu/~shalizi/LaMettrie/Machine/>; Marie Jean Antoine Nicholas Caritat, Marquis de Condorcet, *The Future Progress of the Human Mind,* 1795 <http://www.fordham.edu/halsall/mod/condorcet-progress.html>; Bart Kosko, *The Fuzzy Future: From Society and Science to Heaven in a Chip* (New York: Harmony, 1999), p. 256.

This sentiment is found also in Kevin Warwick's declaration, "I was born human. But this was an accident of fate—a condition merely of time and place. I believe it's something we have the power to change."[39] Derived from other enlightenment ideals is a fierce libertarianism, supported by postmodern ethical skepticism, which proclaims that each individual is the final arbiter of what is right and wrong and has total autonomous control over what is to be done with his or her life and body.[40]

As a named movement, transhumanism started in the 1980s with the writings of a futurist, who called himself FM-2030; the term *transhuman* is shorthand for *transitional human*.[41] Transhumans were "the earliest manifestation of new evolutionary beings, on their way to becoming posthumans."[42] In the early 1990s a whole series of groups emerged embracing transhumanist ideology, including the Extropians, the Transtopians and the Singularitarians, the latter group anticipating and working to bring about the "technological singularity" predicted by Vernor Vinge. Vinge claims that the exponential increase in scientific and technical knowledge, coupled with feedback loops from artificial intelligence systems, will soon lead to a massive destabilization and transformation of all social structures, technical devices and human beings to superior beings.[43] Ray Kurzweil, whose book *The Age of Spiritual Machines* could be seen as a manifesto for the transhumanist movement, is the most widely known of Vinge's disciples.[44] While technological singularity is the most extreme of the variety of transhumanist visions, the idea that humankind should engineer the next phase of its evolution—and that human beings should be augmented and altered, even to the point of losing their humanity—has captured the thinking of numerous academic faculty and leaders in the engineering and scientific establishment.

The first assertion of transhumanist thinking is a rejection of the assumption that human nature is a constant.[45] There is nothing sacrosanct about "nature" in general or "human nature" in particular. Criticisms of attempts to modify nature as "playing god" or as the ultimate human hubris are rejected

[39]Kevin Warwick, "Cyborg 1.0," *Wired*, February 2000, p. 145.
[40]Anders Sandberg, "Morphological Freedom: Why We Not Just Want It, but Need It," (based on a talk given at the TransVision 2001 conference in Berlin, June 22-24, 2001) <http://www.nada.kth.se/~asa/Texts/MorphologicalFreedom.htm>.
[41]Bostrom, "Transhumanist FAQ."
[42]FM-2030, *Are You a Transhuman?* (New York: Warner, 1989); cited in Bostrum, "Transhumanist FAQ."
[43]Vernor Vinge, "The Coming Technological Singularity," 1993 <http://www.rohan.sdsu.edu/faculty/vinge/misc/singularity.html>.
[44]Ray Kurzweil, *The Age of Spiritual Machines: When Computers Exceed Human Intelligence* (New York: Viking, 1999). Kurzweil also maintains a website at <http://www.kurzweilai.net>.
[45]Bostrom, "Transhumanist FAQ."

as inappropriate or irrelevant. In contrast, "human nature is a work-in-progress: a half-baked beginning that can be remolded in desirable ways through intelligent use of enhancement technologies."[46]

N. Katherine Hayles has described four characteristic posthuman, or transhuman, assumptions. First, information patterns are more important or essential to the nature of being than any "material instantiation, so that embodiment in a biological substrate is seen as an accident of history rather than an inevitability of life."[47] Second, consciousness is an epiphenomenon. There is no immaterial soul. Third, the body is simply a prosthesis, albeit the first one we learn to use and manipulate. Consequently, replacing or enhancing human function with other prostheses is only a natural extension of our fundamental relationship with our begotten bodies. Last, the posthuman views human being

> so that it can be seamlessly articulated with intelligent machines. In the posthuman, there are no essential differences or absolute demarcations between bodily existence and computer simulation, cybernetic mechanism and biological organism, robot technology and human goals.[48]

While it might be tempting to dismiss transhumanist thinking as the musings of a few extreme, yet isolated, technogeeks, it would be a grave mistake to do so. This is most evident in the degree to which the U.S. government has formally embraced transhumanist ideals and is actively supporting the development of transhumanist technologies. The U.S. National Science Foundation, together with the U.S. Department of Commerce, has initiated a major program (NBIC) for converging several technologies (including those from which the acronym is derived—nanotechnology, biotechnologies, information technologies and cognitive technologies, e.g., cybernetics and neurotechnologies) for the express purpose of enhancing human performance.[49] The NBIC program director, Mihail Roco, declared at the second public meeting of the project in February 2003 that the expenditure of financial and human capital to pursue the ends of reengineering humanity by the U.S. government will be second in equivalent value only to the moon landing program.[50]

One of the more distressing aspects of the NBIC project is the brazen assumption that citizens of the United States widely support the deliberate de-

---

[46]Bostrom, "What Is Transhumanism?"

[47]N. Katherine Hayles, *How We Became Posthuman: Virtual Bodies in Cybernetics, Literature and Informatics* (Chicago: University of Chicago Press, 1999), pp. 2-3.

[48]Ibid., pp. 2-3.

[49]Mihail Roco and William Sims Bainbridge, eds., *Converging Technologies for Improving Human Performance* (2002) <http://wtec.org/ConvergingTechnologies/>.

[50]I attended the conference at which Roco made this claim ("NBIC Convergence 2003: Converging Technologies for Improving Human Performance," February 5-7, 2003, University of California at Los Angeles).

velopment of technology for the reengineering of the human species; yet there has been little in the way of true public discussion of the project or these goals. When I have presented material on the NBIC project to various members of Congress, they have been shocked to learn of the project and its goals. Nothing is being hidden per se, for the proceedings of the meetings are available to the public. Yet it is troubling that such an immensely important—and controversial—project is proceeding without sufficient, informed public input.

Accidents, Abuses and Regulation

The possible medical uses of nanotechnology and cybernetics are exciting, and even if only a portion prove possible, many thousands of patients may benefit from them. As Christians we can applaud the development of new tools to help the lame to walk, the blind to see, the deaf to hear, those afflicted with cancer to be healed and so on. These uses are all in keeping with the classic goals of medicine and with the traditional Christian mission of compassionate healing. But these technologies are not entirely benign, and the risks are significant, even if we for the moment suspend consideration of the idea of creating the new species *Techno sapiens*.

In first considering some of the risks associated with nanotechnology, we must acknowledge that any device which can operate on the subcellular level, directly building and interacting with cellular components and functions, can just as easily be designed to destroy as to repair or heal. In fact, it will likely be far easier to develop destructive rather than constructive devices. One of the first applications of medical nanotechnology already in development involves a device that can target and destroy cancer cells. Similar devices could likewise be designed to attack normal cells, producing nanoscale weapons that could be borne on the winds or in the water and food supply. Devices with appropriate targeting or the ability to synthesize toxic substances once inside the host could prove to be lethal or disabling.

If self-replicating assemblers—such as Eric Drexler's lifelike, autonomous nanobot, which would be capable of replication using materials from its environment like a virus or bacterium—ever were created, then the level of personnel or environmental harm could be that much greater as the volume of destructive agents continued to increase. Some fear that autonomous, self-replicating assemblers could escape control or mutate in such a way as to destroy life and the environment on a massive, cataclysmic scale. This is Drexler's "gray goo" scenario.[51] Of the many possible negative consequences nanotechnology could have, this has been the most frequently covered in the lay press. Robert A. Freitas Jr., however, has calculated that this nightmarish scenario is unlikely because

---

[51]Drexler, *Engines of Creation*.

of our ability to detect early on the activity of such "biovorous" devices and neutralize them.[52] In the early days of recombinant DNA research, there were many similar concerns about releasing lethal plagues into the environment. Yet the scientific community responded strongly, prospectively and wisely to those challenges, establishing procedural safeguards that remain in use to this day, serving as a model for developing and containing potentially harmful technologies.[53]

More probable than the accidental "gray goo" scenario is the deliberate creation of specific nanoweapons. Concern over the potential military or terrorist use of such technology—which could ultimately be fairly cheap to produce and thus impossible to sufficiently regulate once in existence—has led some (even within the technology community, such as Bill Joy, cofounder and chief scientist of Sun Microsystems) to contend that the only safe way to proceed is to choose not to develop the tools and methods of nanotechnology at all.[54] In this view, the only way to prevent the potential devastating harms of a technology (or the consequences of malicious use of knowledge and technology) is not to develop the technology (or acquire the knowledge) in the first place. Arguments of this type, however, assume the burden of proving that, first, the projected abilities of the device in question are possible to achieve; second, the feared harms cannot be prevented, controlled or mitigated to an acceptable degree; third, it is feasible to achieve universal consensus that the area of technology or knowledge in question should not be pursued; and, fourth, such a prohibition can be sufficiently policed.

In the case of the first issue, it seems very likely that biological nanodevices will be developed as we have already noted. Therefore, it is morally imperative to prospectively evaluate the possible effect of these technologies as they are being developed, so as to implement appropriate safeguards to protect against accidents, unanticipated consequences or inappropriate use of the technology.

Although many disagree with Joy's conclusions, his concerns for the potential harms that autonomous technology could produce are legitimate. It is his response to the second issue—the likely ability or inability to control or protect against foreseeable or unforeseeable harms—that has led to the most dissent. Pursuing a similar course of prospective risk assessment and guideline development, the Foresight Institute (established by Drexler and his wife, Christine

---

[52]Robert A. Freitas Jr., "Some Limits to Global Ecophagy by Bivorous Nanoreplicators, with Public Policy Recommendations," April 2002, Foresight Institute <http://www.foresight.org/NanoRev/Ecophagy.html>.

[53]Sheldon Krimsky, *Genetic Alchemy: The Social History of the Recombinant DNA Controversy* (Cambridge: MIT Press, 1982); Donald S. Fredrickson, *The Recombinant DNA Controversy: A Memoir* (Washington, D.C.: ASM Press, 2001).

[54]Bill Joy, "Why the Future Doesn't Need Us," *Wired*, April 2000 <http://www.wired.com/wired/archive/8.04/joy.html>.

Peterson) has published the "Foresight Guidelines on Molecular Nanotechnology."[55] At the time of this writing, the guidelines remain recommendations, to be followed voluntarily, but they could be used as a framework for formal regulation and licensing of biologically or environmentally active nanodevices. Some of the recommended design principles include the following: ensuring dependence on a single fuel source or cofactor that does not exist in the natural environment; requiring constant signaling from an external source for function of the device; and programming termination times (similar to apoptosis, or programmed cell death, in living cells). While one might hope that all responsible researchers and engineers would embrace suggestions such as these, there will need to be formal regulation with serious economic, licensure and punitive penalties for failure to comply. While controversial and likely to receive significant opposition from industry, the granting of licenses and the approval to perform research in nonlaboratory settings or to market nanodevices should be contingent on proof of the developer's ability to detect and destroy the devices in both in vitro and in vivo settings.

Joining the Foresight Institute (which exists primarily for the promotion of nanotechnology) in pursuing the safe development of nanotechnology prospectively, Chris Phoenix and Mike Treder created in 2002 the Center for Responsible Technology (CRN), an organization with the goal of specifically encouraging the safe development and use of nanotechnology.[56] The CRN website lists numerous social, ethical and environmental challenges that will need to be adequately addressed if the current projections for nanotechnology come true, including the just distribution of technology, the impact on jobs and the economy and the effects created by increased longevity.

Probably the greatest weakness of Joy's argument is the idea that humankind could reach a universal, or even a substantial, agreement on limiting or forbidding certain areas of research, particularly when that field of knowledge may produce major benefits to health, life span, productivity, national economic and military security, and so on. Such agreement simply isn't going to happen. Even if we could reach a consensus (an event unique in human history), policing such restrictions will be essentially impossible. The force of curiosity, as well as the stubborn human heart's universal propensity to rebel against restriction, will ensure that the research and development will take place, perhaps just not as rapidly as it might have otherwise. Rather it will be wiser to direct the development of the technology in such a way as to simul-

---

[55]Foresight Institute, "Foresight Guidelines on Molecular Nanotechnology," rev. vers. 3.7 (draft), June 4, 2000 <http://www.foresight.org/guidelines/current.html>.

[56]For more, see the Center for Responsible Nanotechnology website <http://www .crnano.org >.

taneously prepare defenses while we create the devices themselves. It is only in this way that humankind and individual societies can be prepared to meet the threats of terrorism, accidents and other calamities resulting from the creation or abuse of a particular technology.

The Borgification of Humanity

Cybernetic developments raise their own questions and challenges. From an individual's perspective, the first questions should be concerned with the safety of cybernetic devices—with safety understood as including physical, emotional and cognitive safety. Today medical devices present the patient with risks for infection, local reaction, tissue injury, unexpected side effects and, in the case of pacemakers or other electrode dependent devices, undesired neural or muscular stimulation. These are local effects, contained to the specific environment of one person's body, and they are fixed by the intrinsic nature of the device itself. Cybernetic devices, on the other hand, will often be connected to a shifting network environment, dependent on software and the exchange of information, in addition to the hardware of the device. As such, risk is dynamic, changing with the larger environment. For example, viral computer code could potentially disrupt function of the device or possibly be induced to injure the user. Even wearable devices, as opposed to implanted ones, could potentially be turned into weapons or, at the least, significant irritants. Consequently, there will need to be strong regulation with software and hardware safeguards to protect against such mischief. Safeguards, though important, can only reduce the risk of such hazards, as the exploits of computer hackers continue to demonstrate.

Emotional and cognitive safety will be more challenging to understand and regulate. Already in the present era of the Internet there is a growing literature addressing problems of personality fragmentation, the breakdown of direct personal relationships in favor of cyber relationships, the encouragement of inauthentic behavior, increased dissatisfaction with reality, addiction to cybersex and online pornography, and other psychosocial concerns.[57] It would seem evident that these problems can only worsen when individuals are cybernetically connected most, if not all, of the time. Further, still unknown are the long-term consequences of prolonged exposure to virtual environments, but they could be substantial.

Then there is the issue of privacy. While cybernetic devices might be configured only for downloading purposes, even this one-way application could be closely monitored by others via relay devices and "cookies." What informa-

---

[57]See, e.g., Jeri Fink, *Cyberseduction: Reality in the Age of Psychotechnology* (Amherst, N.J.: Prometheus, 1999).

tion a given individual accesses can provide a powerful insight into that person's interests, values and personal information. While augmented reality systems may help the user locate herself or identify her immediate surroundings, these devices, which are often based on transponders, can also be used to locate and track the individual. For information-oriented cybernetic devices to be used to their full potential, however, two-way communication will be necessary, just as exists now with the Internet. If implanted devices allow the exchange of information between the biological substrate and the cybernetic device, what is to prevent the activity of the brain from being communicated through the machine to the outside world? Consider a brain chip implanted in the hippocampus to augment memory. This device would be intimately associated with the creation and recall of memories as well as with all the emotions inherent in that process. If this device were directly wired to a communication module to allow the importation of information from the Internet, could the device also allow the memories and thoughts of the individual to be downloaded or read by others? In essence, what is to prevent the brain itself from being hacked? Even if the device were not directly connected to a communication module, there will be devices that will allow external monitoring of the information being processed through the internal chip. Already work is being done to read brain activity indirectly via functional MRI and other devices. Cybernetic implants will only make the job easier. The last bastion of human privacy, the brain, will have been breached.

Let us assume for a moment that safety issues can be resolved to satisfaction—that we can assure users that adequate safeguards to prevent direct physical injury of the user are in place, that privacy can be protected, and that we can demonstrated that there are few if any long-term liabilities to at least the majority of users. There still remain significant ethical and social issues. While many transhumanists assert that individuals should have full free choice whether to pursue enhancing or augmenting technologies for themselves, the reality is that significant social forces may compel individuals to get "plugged in." Just as there is now a growing, unspoken laissez faire eugenics, there will soon be similar pressures surrounding the use of these technologies.

Imagine, for example, the field of medicine somewhere between twenty years and forty years from now. Brain chips or wearable computers now make it possible for a physician to have immediate, 24/7 access to databases that contain all standard medical knowledge, plus the latest medical information and practice guidelines. All ongoing clinical trials are immediately identifiable. So far this information might be obtainable via an external device, but this would require porting and might not be with the physician in the event of an emergency. Thus internal devices would be more efficient. Additionally, the device can rehearse procedures in the visual and motor cortex allowing physicians to maintain state-of-the-art proficiency in a vast array of surgical procedures. Indwelling nanodevices provide pharmacological or direct neural stimulation to maintain alertness and calm. With such a device the cyborg physician can also mobilize additional resources—such as colleagues in consultation or emergency teams—with a thought. If you, the patient, were given a choice, would you want a physician with capabilities like this, or would you want the standard nonaugmented model: a physician, probably deprived of sleep, with a biological brain dependent on a limited memory and personal experience? It is not difficult to imagine that physicians would be compelled by strong professional and social forces to undergo cybernetic and nanotechnological modification. This would be true for those in many other professions, including law, engineering, finance, the military and so on.

Consider further whether the military, after investing billions in the development of technologies to create the cyborg soldier (albeit with the noble intent of improving the survivability and force capability of each soldier), would allow individual soldiers to decline the enhancements because of religious or personal qualms. It is not likely. Individuals may indeed dissent and decline technological augmentation, but such dissenters will find job options increasingly scarce.

Because the network of cyborgs will require increasing levels of cooperation and harmonious coordination to further improve efficiency, the prostheses will continue to introduce means of controlling or modulating emotion to promote these values. Meanwhile, the network is increasingly controlled by central planning structures to facilitate harmony and efficiency. While everyone still considers themselves fully autonomous, in reality behavior is more and more tightly controlled. Each step moves those who are cybernetically augmented toward becoming like the Borg, the race of cybernetic organisms that inhabit the twenty-sixth century of the *Star Trek* mythology. The Borg, once fully human, became "assimilated" by the greater collective mind, losing individuality for the good of the whole.

Lest the reader think the past several paragraphs are a bit excessively paranoid, consider that a team at Los Alamos has been creating a new Internet structure designed to carefully monitor each user, constantly modifying its networked structure (similar to the way the brain modifies its synaptic connections) for the expressed purpose of creating a global brain.[58] NBIC director Mihail Roco, in the report of the first NBIC conference proceedings, wrote,

Humanity would become like a single, distributed and interconnected "brain" based in new core pathways in society. . . . A networked society of billions of hu-

---

[58]Michael Brooks, "Global Brain," *New Scientist* 166 (June 24, 2000): 22-27. See also the Principia Cybernetica website at <http://pespmc1.vub.ac.be/>.

man beings could be as complex compared to an individual being as a human being is to a single nerve cell. From local groups of linked enhanced individuals to a global collective intelligence, key new capacities would arise from relationships arising from NBIC technologies. . . . Far from unnatural, such a collective social system may be compared to a larger form of biological organism. . . . We envision the bond of humanity driven by an *interconnected virtual brain* of the Earth's communities searching for intellectual comprehension and conquest of nature.[59]

As the Borg would say, "Resistance is futile."

We live in a society that is motivated increasingly by competition and personal gain, and less by any idea such as what is best for human nature or our destiny, particularly as it relates to a nature as a created being responsible to a Creator. A significant number of individuals will actively pursue these enhancements, undergoing every upgrade. Those who refuse to be enhanced will find themselves considered Luddites and as backward and inferior. They may even be considered harmful to the larger collective in its goals of integration and control. Discrimination is unavoidable.

Healing Versus Enhancement

As I have stated earlier, despite significant concerns about cybernetic and nanotechnologies, there is much that we can happily anticipate, especially those new tools that can facilitate healing. An increasingly difficult issue will be, however, defining the distinction between *healing* and *enhancement*. The definition of disease is often shifting, frequently because of changes of social forces and opinion. With increasingly subjective standards for the definition of disease and the evaluation of "treatment" (primarily the consequence of the predominance of patient autonomy in contemporary medical ethics, at least in the United States), establishing clear lines of demarcation to guide groups of concerned patients, medical institutions and practitioners, and third-party payers will be quite difficult. Consequently, though in principle it is appropriate to support the therapeutic use of these technologies while denying enhancement, in practice it may be rather challenging. The best definition I have been able to formulate thus far to distinguish treatment from enhancement is to allow as healing that which may return a given function to a level normal for the species, not to exceed the capability of the fittest members of the species, trained in the most rigorous fashion. Yet even this definition is not static as norms continue to shift.

Probably the greatest social threat created by these technologies is the encouragement and empowerment of transhumanists to pursue their utopian delu-

---

[59]Mihail Roco, in *Converging Technologies for Improving Human Performance*, ed. Mihail Roco and William Sims Bainbridge (New York: Kluwer Academic, 2003). Emphasis in the original.

sions. The greatest flaw of any utopian dream of human perfection is the failure to understand, or even recognize, the darkness of the unredeemed human heart. Sin is not for them a real category; they think only of flaws that can be engineered out of the evolving species. Short of salvation and transformation through Jesus Christ, however, any human means of pursuing a supposed perfection will lead not only to failure, but to great misery along the way. The lesson of the twentieth century should have been to beware the power of utopian dreams to enslave, destroy and demean rather than produce the promised justice, freedom and human flourishing. Unfortunately as a culture we appear to have learned precious little. Yet again humankind seems ready to plunge headlong into another human, or demonic, contrivance promising salvation and eternal happiness for all. This time the Faustian bargain is being struck with technology, what John McDermott referred to as the "opiate of the intellectuals."[60]

Finally, even if we for a moment look at the world through the materialist assumptions of transhumanism, we should still sense trouble ahead. Death is a very natural part of the ecosystem human beings inhabit, a process that serves important functions for the overall preservation of the larger ecological order. In higher-level biological systems, mortal non-stem cells that try to become immortal develop into cancers. These cancers often have a high degree of internal necrosis, or death and degradation, as the process expands. As their numbers grow, they threaten the health or life of the larger whole. Many transhumanists see this disruption and the death of *Homo sapiens* as a natural part of the evolutionary process, culminating in the cataclysm they refer to as the "singularity." Despite whatever rhetoric transhumanists concoct to put a positive spin on the process, what actually transpires will be not evolution but destruction. At this time in human history, transhumanist philosophy is akin to a carcinogen, a toxin offered up as another fruit that promises god-like transformation but that in reality transforms healthy cells into cancerous neoplastic cells. It is a temptation we must avoid.

Biblical Considerations

While it is clear that many practical concerns regarding augmentation of human persons by cybernetic or nanotechnological tools are being raised—issues with which all individuals must be concerned, regardless of worldview—are there specific issues that confront those who claim the name of Jesus Christ? Are there objections that would specifically prevent Christians (if no one else) from undergoing such "enhancements" even if all social, technical and medical concerns could be dealt with satisfactorily? I believe that indeed there are.

---

[60]John McDermott, "Technology: The Opiate of the Intellectuals," *The New York Review of Books,* July 31, 1969.

In exploring this claim we first must step back as Christians and acknowledge two very important things: our nature in Christ and what is expected of us as we fulfill our command to be Christ to the world and to be his living body.

As those redeemed by God through the works of Christ Jesus and the Holy Spirit, our lives are not our own (1 Cor 6:19-20; 7:23). We are living sacrifices in the service of our heavenly Father (Rom 12:1). Thus we are not free to do with our bodies and our lives anything we may please. Our bodies are not just prostheses for our pleasure and manipulation, as the transhumanists assert. Rather we are to treat our bodies as the temples of the Holy Spirit, recognizing that our embodiment as *Homo sapiens* is important. Christ was incarnated as a human, not a posthuman. His way of perfection is one of the heart and soul, not of intelligence, strength or some other attribute that we tend to value above that which is truly important. His resurrected body, like the body we will one day have as well, is perfect; it is not some other form of degradable matter that will always decay, always fail, always be dependent on some kind of supplemental physical energy. If our relationship with God and, in God's love, our relationships with one another are the most important things in our lives (as many Christians claim), then pursuing attribute enhancement in these forms is a distraction and a delusion and is, frankly, idolatrous.

As Jesus emphasized, the two greatest commandments given to us are to love the Lord God with all our heart, mind, soul and strength and to love our neighbor as ourselves (Mk 12:28-31). In so doing, we are to spread the gospel to all the ends of the earth. Do we need to remodel our bodies and brains into some trans- or posthuman form to fulfill these commands? Not at all. In fact such transformation would be counterproductive. God loves us as we are in all our frailty. This does not mean that we cannot undergo healing procedures to address disease or handicap. Christ healed and is a model to us in this. But Christ did not enhance those whom he encountered—except to enhance them spiritually, which is completely a gift and not something we ourselves can accomplish. This is a critical observation, for we must ask, why did Jesus not make the apostles the most amazing of men, with towering intellect and bodies impervious to pain, illness and death? I would say he did not do so because they didn't need to be altered that way to accomplish their mission. And I believe Jesus also recognized that if they were so altered, they would probably soon strike out on using their own power and opinions, refusing to be dependent on the Holy Spirit and on God's provision and guidance. What they needed for success as disciples, and for their personal fulfillment, was a relationship with him and the gift of the Holy Spirit. That is all we need as well.

To promote some sort of human-engineered superbeing as necessary or desirable for human flourishing, or even to presume that such would be pleasing or acceptable to God, is to undermine the whole gospel message. It promotes the flawed views of humanly defined perfection that haunt each and every one of us and the world in which we live. Weakness is a valuable teacher, and it reminds us of our ultimate dependence on God. As Paul learned, God's "grace is sufficient for you, for [his] power is made perfect in weakness" (2 Cor 12:9). We do not need to have enhanced brains to stand and give testimony before even the most seemingly intelligent and powerful among the human race: "When you are brought before synagogues, rulers and authorities, do not worry about how you will defend yourselves or what you will say, for the Holy Spirit will teach you at that time what you should say" (Luke 12:11-12). Nonbelievers have a very hard time understanding this confidence, and it is difficult to accept when seen as an isolated statement. Yet the living witness of transformed members of the body of Christ demonstrates the truth of these claims more clearly than any argument can. For the witness to occur, however, Christians must be willing to live as Christians, foregoing the transhumanist temptation and demonstrating the real human flourishing, peace and happiness that only occur with the indwelling of the Holy Spirit and the true renewing of the human heart and mind.

The world has always needed a faithful witness from the church, but now as the battle for the human species intensifies, the church must more than ever before truly be the church. We must rouse ourselves from our narcissistic self-absorption, engage in truly loving community and be living sacrifices for the Truth. We must do more than simply say no to transhumanist augmentations; we must live and demonstrate the superior alternative. The reason transhumanism and other secular utopian dreams grow is that Christians have not demonstrated the life which should be ours in Christ. We embrace materialism just as much as our unbelieving neighbors do; we live without being transformed by the scripture, by our theology or by the Spirit, and we appear scarcely different in any way from our non-Christian peers. Yet all the while we take upon ourselves the name of Christ. Why shouldn't those who see little difference in us seek their own way?

Each of us as individual Christians, and as members of communities in the body of Christ, must diligently seek the face of the Lord and immerse ourselves in his Word. We must daily put on Christ. We must pray unceasingly for wisdom. We must demand that our leaders, both within and outside the church, confront these technological advances. And we must choose now to stand together as one *eternally transformed* body, today and in the challenging days to come.

May God grant us the wisdom, the strength and the love to accomplish these things. Amen.

5

PROMISE AND PERIL

Clinical Implications of the New Genetics

DAVID STEVENS, M.D.
EXECUTIVE DIRECTOR, CHRISTIAN MEDICAL ASSOCIATION

Clinical applications of human genetics have been slow to appear, much slower than we had been led to expect. Indeed, some recent clinical trials have been halted because patients receiving innovative medical treatment have died.

Dr. Stevens, who is qualified in both medicine and bioethics, gives a wide-ranging review of recent developments in genetics and their applications in fields as diverse as pharmacogenomics (intended to provide us with tailored medications that will work with our own unique genetic makeup), the forensic use of DNA testing and bioarcheology. His theme is that the promise and the potential perils are both great.

This clinical focus makes it clear that even though little of the vast store of new knowledge gained from the genome has so far yielded medical benefits, we will continue to see more applications of this knowledge, some of them excellent and others plainly evil or at best problematic in character. For the church, the issues raised will not be merely political; they will affect every individual and every family. It is therefore crucial for the church to be prepared to respond to them. As executive director of the Christian Medical Association, Dr. Stevens is in a vital position to ensure that Christian physicians take a lead in this response. On the policy level he argues that we must "put an ethical and scientific safety net around this rapidly developing but almost totally unregulated field."

NIGEL M. DE S. CAMERON

Beth was more than just scared. Fear and dread permeated her life. Her mother had been diagnosed with breast cancer in her thirties. The doctors had tried every weapon in their arsenal to defeat the creeping malignancy that was irresistibly growing inside her, but it was only a delaying action. Skin and bones, her abdomen bloated with fluid, her mother died two days before

Christmas, soon after the cancer reached her brain.

Beth's aunt had caught her first lump early. Fortunately, they got all the cancer with her first mastectomy. But they found another malignancy in the other breast three years later. She wasn't so fortunate with that one, and died six months later.

Then Beth's older sister Stephanie got the dreaded call about her biopsy on her thirty-fifth birthday. She opted for a lumpectomy followed by three months of nauseating chemotherapy. She was now hairless and enduring six weeks of daily radiation.

It was no wonder Beth couldn't sleep. Only thirty-two and sure she would be next to get the horrible news, she had gone for a breast exam and mammogram. Her tests were negative, but with her family history, her physician had advised a genetic test to see whether she had the gene mutation that caused familial breast cancer.

The test was a simple blood test but the result—positive for a mutation of her BRCA1 gene—turned her life upside down. She now continually replayed the statistics over and over in her mind. At age thirty she had a 3 percent risk, by age forty it went up to 20 percent, and by seventy she had an 85 percent chance of getting breast cancer.[1] If that wasn't bad enough, her mutation also gave her a much higher risk of ovarian cancer.[2] She was a walking malignancy time bomb.

Now what? The gene mutation couldn't be treated. She could be screened every six months with the hope of catching her cancer early. That was the way she would need to go if she and John were going to have a family, but there was a 50 percent chance that each child born to her would have the same gene mutation.[3] Could she put her child through the same terror she was experiencing?

The other option was to have both breasts and both ovaries removed, shattering her dream of having her own child.[4] Could she do that? If she did, would she be half a woman? Would John still look at her the same? And what about telling her brothers and sisters the awful news? If her brother tested positive for a mutation of the BRCA1 gene, his risk for prostate and colon cancer were much higher.[5] He might even get breast cancer.[6] Her sister Stephanie was

---

[1]S. A. Gayther et al., "Germline Mutations in the BRCA1 Gene in Breast and Ovarian Cancer Families Provide Evidence for a Genotype-Phenotype Correlation," *Nature Genetics* 11, no. 4 (1995): 428-33.

[2]Ibid.

[3]Stephanie Slon, "Breast Cancer," WebMD (1999) <http://my.webmd.com>. (The URLs cited in this chapter were accessed on January 16, 2004.)

[4]Ibid.

[5]"Do We Know What Causes Prostate Cancer?" American Cancer Society (2003) <http://www.cancer.org>.

[6]Ibid.

likely to have the mutation since she had breast cancer so young. If confirmed, she would need to have a bilateral mastectomy. And what about Stephanie's seven-year-old daughter? Should they have her tested?

In some ways Beth wished she never had gotten the gene test. Knowing what lay ahead was almost worse than being ignorant of it.

Beth's story is fictional, but it is an all-too-real scenario for women who have a positive BRCA1 analysis, and BRCA1 is only one of the more than two hundred gene mutations that can be clinically tested. Many more tests are being developed.[7] Ready or not, we are on the front edge of a genetic revolution in medicine that will profoundly affect you and your family. Through genetic testing, not only will doctors be able to diagnose when you have a specific disease, but they'll also be able to tell you the probability of getting it. And that is just the tip of the iceberg. The new genetics will permeate society far beyond the doctor's exam room. From the farm to the supermarket, from the court-room to the pharmaceutical company, and from the hazardous waste clean-up firm to the animal breeder's laboratory, the new genetics will profoundly affect every human being. This new frontier holds wonderful potential and significant dangers. To reap the benefits and avoid the dangers, you will need a roadmap. Let's start at the beginning, with you.

Your genome is the complete instruction manual that guided your development and that regulates your bodily functions. Half of your genome came from your mother's egg and half from your dad's sperm. When they united, all the information for developing you was in one cell that began to divide and multiply. Today, your genome —all your genetic information—is duplicated in each of the 100 trillion cells in your body.[8]

Your genome is made of DNA (deoxyribonucleic acid), a twisted ladder-like molecule about six feet long and fifty-trillionths of an inch wide. If you placed the DNA in all your cells end to end, its result would be a string that would stretch to the sun and back twenty times. Each rung of the DNA ladder is made up of one of four different pairs of nitrogen compounds, called *base pairs*. These base pairs form your genetic code, which controls the development of the structure and functions of the 210 different types of tissues in your body. This chemical code, similar to but more complex than any computer program, is contained in every cell of an adult human's body. Through poorly understood control mechanisms, your cellular genome only uses a small portion of the DNA in each cell. Each tissue is like a CD with many songs, playing only

---

[7]"Medicine and the New Genetics," U.S. Department of Energy Human Genome Program (2004) <http://www.ornl.gov/sci/techresources/Human_Genome/publicat/primer2001/6.shtml>.

[8]"Cracking the Code of Life," Nova Online, April 2003, PBS <http://www.pbs.org/wgbh/nova/genome/dna_sans.html>.

the track with the information that determines its design and function.[9]

The DNA in each cell is organized on forty-six chromosomes—twenty-three from your father and twenty-three from your mother. If a father gives an X-chromosome, a girl is born. If he gives a Y-chromosome, the child is a boy. The chromosomes contain around 30,000 genes, segments of around 3,000 rungs on the ladder that code for the over 100,000 proteins. Proteins are what constitute muscle, lungs, hormones, digestive enzymes and much more of what makes the body work. Genes make up only about 5 percent of chromosomes. The other 95 percent of DNA is part of the genome's regulatory mechanism or has a function unknown to us.[10]

Ready for some bad news? All people have missing or damaged genes. You were born with fifty to sixty abnormal genes.[11] The good news is that most malformed genes cause no visible effects; the bad news is that some can cause an increased risk of cancer, diabetes or other diseases. Some abnormal genes (like BRCA1) are passed down from parents. That is why some diseases run in families. For example, in cystic fibrosis there is a familial component due to a defect of only three base pairs (three rungs out of three billion pairs on the DNA ladder) that cause children to have abnormally thick secretions, resulting in pneumonia and an early death.[12] A small aberrancy in the genetic code at a critical point can lead to devastating effects.

Other genetic defects happen through mutations. When the DNA divides and duplicates itself to produce a new cell, sometimes a mistake is passed on to each new cell. Other mutations can occur due to damage from radiation, carcinogens, infections or other environmental factors.[13] Skin cancers often result from genome that has been damaged by ultraviolet radiation from sunlight.[14] Many cervical cancers are caused by genetic malformations resulting from an infection with human papillomavirus, a sexually transmitted disease.

Genetics, the branch of biology dealing with heredity and genetic variations, is not a new field. It goes back to before Gregor Mendel (1822-1884) and his

---

[9]Dinesh C. Sharma, "Fifty Years of DNA Discovery: Controversies Old and New," Press Information Bureau Government of India (March 12, 2003) <http://pib.nic.in/feature/feyr2003/fmar2003/f120320031.html>.

[10]Denise Casey, "Primer on Molecular Genetics," U.S. Department of Energy (1992) <http://www.ornl.gov/TechResources/Human_Genome/publicat/primer/toc.html>.

[11]Ibid.

[12]Cystic Fibrosis Foundation, "What Is Cystic Fibrosis?" (May 2003) <http://www.cff.org/about_cf/>.

[13]"Health or Disease?" U.S. Department of Energy Human Genome Program <http://www.ornl.gov/hgmis>.

[14]D. E. Brash et al., "A Role for Sunlight in Skin Cancer: UV-Induced p53 Mutations in Squamous Cell Carcinoma," *Proceedings of the National Academy of Sciences USA* 88, no. 22 (1999): 10124-28.

study of plant genetics. Its big entrance into medicine came with James Watson and Francis Crick's discovery of the double helix of DNA in 1953. By 1959 the additional chromosome that causes most cases of Down syndrome was identified. In 1966 it became possible to perform prenatal diagnosis for this condition by analyzing amniotic fluid. (Unfortunately there is no treatment for this genetic defect, so many parents opt to abort babies with Down syndrome.)[15]

A medical team at Harvard isolated the first gene in 1969. The biotech company Genentech cloned the gene for insulin in 1978, which led to the first genetically engineered drug, human insulin, in 1982. Gene mapping began in earnest around 1980. By 1985 over 700 genes had been located.[16]

In 1990 the Human Genome Project was undertaken with the goals of accurately mapping the three billion base pairs of the DNA ladder and of identifying each gene. This required the development of faster and more accurate mapping technologies and ways to store this vast amount of information in public databases for scientists to use. The $3 billion project involved two hundred principal investigators located in eighteen countries.[17]

The announcement that this enormous project, led by Dr. Francis Collins, was 90 percent complete was made at the White House in June 2000 with enormous media hype. It was likened in significance to the moon landing and the Manhattan Project. The public was given the impression that most diseases would soon be cured using this new knowledge.[18] Some even claimed that since scientists knew the map of the human genome, it was proof that there was no God, that humankind was just the product of the evolutionary development of the genetic code. Phillip Johnson, an expert on intelligent design, had a great retort for that claim in a CNN interview when he said, "Just because we can read the complete works of Shakespeare doesn't mean that there was no author."[19]

Three years later, in 2003—fifty years after Watson and Crick's announcement—the human genome map was completed.[20] What does that mean for

---

[15]Victor A. McKusick, "The Anatomy of the Human Genome," *Journal of the American Medical Association* 286 (November 14, 2001): 2289-91.

[16]Ibid.

[17]"What Is the Human Genome Project?" U.S. Department of Energy Human Genome Program (October 29, 2003) <http://www.ornl.gov/TechResources/Human_Genome/project/about.html>.

[18]"Human Genome Project Milestones Celebrated at White House," *Human Genome News* 11 (November 2000) <http://www.ornl.gov/TechResources/Human_Genome/publicat/hgn/v11n1/04draft.html>.

[19]Personal communication, June 26, 2000.

[20]"International Consortium Completes Human Genome Project," U.S. Department of Energy Human Genome Program (April 14, 2003) <http://www.ornl.gov/sci/techresources/Human_Genome/project/50yr/press4_2003.shtml>.

you and me now, and what are its implications for the future? Will this $3 billion (which came from our taxes) pay dividends in our life and health?

Undoubtedly the map of the human genome has incredible potential. Yet we must do the difficult job of harnessing its amazing power before its potential can be realized. When Columbus arrived in the Americas, he knew he had found something significant. But he had no concept of its resources or of the cities and industries that would rise on its soil. Likewise the human genome is an uncharted world we are only beginning to understand. Its exploration will consume medicine for generations to come. Like most pioneers, some scientists will make important discoveries while others will invest their lives on laboratory benches with little results. Some paths that will lead to benefits for humankind are visible, but many will only be discovered long after the journey is underway. Let's look down the paths visible now to see both the potential and the perils ahead.

Patients are benefiting from the early diagnoses made possible by genetic technology. Infants are routinely screened at birth for phenylketonuria (PKU), a genetic inability to break down a specific protein found in many foods. If diagnosed early, the child with PKU can be put on a special diet to significantly reduce the severity of the disease and to prevent mental retardation and other organ damage.[21] Newborn genetic testing differs from state to state but often includes tests for sickle cell disease, galactosemia and maple syrup urine disease, among others. Though these conditions can't be cured, their ill effects can be limited through early diagnosis. Adults can be tested as well for gene related conditions like Tay-Sachs disease, hereditary hemochromatosis and other diseases. Already four million genetic tests are done each year in the United States.[22]

Until recently most doctors learned about a few of the major genetic diseases in training but rarely saw them. These severe inborn diseases were uncommon, and when found, they were dealt with by superspecialists in major medical centers. Obstetricians and pediatricians simply referred the one percent of newborns that had a genetic problem to a specialist for evaluation.[23] There were no cures for these conditions, and their management was complex.

As knowledge of genetics has grown rapidly in the last few decades, scientists have radically changed their thinking. Doctors now believe that most individuals die of genetic disease. People just don't know it. Genes, along with

---

[21]"Phenylketonuria (PKU)," Save Babies Through Screening (July 10, 2003) <http://www.savebabies.org/diseasedescriptions/pku.htm>

[22]Sharon Begley, "Decoding the Human Body," *Newsweek*, April 10, 2000 <http://www.facstaff.bucknell.edu/pagana/mg312/humangenomeproject.html>.

[23]Steve Jones, "Genetics in Medicine: Real Promises, Unreal Expectations," *Milbank Reports* (June 2000) <http://www.milbank.org/000712genetics.html>.

other factors, cause many common diseases, from colon cancer to heart disease. The number of genes found with one or more disease-related mutations is now over a 1,400 and still climbing. These mutations result in over 1,600 recognizable diseases.[24]

In Beth's story a defect in the BRCA1, a cancer suppression gene, markedly increased her chance of a breast carcinoma, but only 5 percent of women with breast cancer have this mutation.[25] Most women with breast cancer (and a host of other common diseases) have poorly understood genetic factors in which a number of genes interact to increase their risk of disease. Unraveling these multifactorial genetic puzzles is a daunting challenge, but this is where scientists are focusing much of their efforts; for these diseases, unlike the single-gene malformations, affect a large number of people.

Every man and woman should, when they reach a certain age, begin regular screening for breast, uterine, prostate, colon and other cancers—despite the expense and discomfort of these examinations. But what if one's genetic predisposition to these cancers could be determined? Millions of people who don't have a genetic risk could be excluded from regular screening, and those with gene malformations could be screened more intensely to catch their disease early. The result would be the saving of both lives and money. For example, those with a higher risk for colon cancer could, starting at an early age, eat a high fiber diet and have more frequent colonoscopies.

The great benefit of genetic risk management will carry a price. Like Beth, some patients will have to spend more time and money for frequent screening. They will have to decide whether to pursue prophylactic treatment or surgery. They will need to inform their children and siblings that they too need testing.

If a person's increased risk for disease is known, he could lose his insurance or pay higher premiums than others his age, even though he as yet has no history of illness. There are not yet adequate laws to protect individuals' genetic privacy. Individuals with damaged genes could be discriminated against by employers. Why hire or promote someone who is going to degrade the company's insurance ratings, be out sick more frequently or die prematurely?

This risk is not hypothetical. African-Americans with sickle cell disease have been discriminated against in employment, the military and the workplace.[26] Some people have been fired when their employers found out that

---

[24]Francis S. Collins and Victor A. McKusick, "Implications of the Human Genome Project for Medical Science," *Journal of the American Medical Association* 285 (February 7, 2001): 540-44.

[25]Gayther et al., "Germline Mutations," p. 429.

[26]R. H. Kenen and R. M. Schmidt, "Stigmatization of Carrier Status: Social Implications of Heterozygote Genetic Screening Programs," *American Journal of Public Health* 68 (1978): 1116-20 <http://www.ajph.org>.

their sibling had Huntington's disease, a genetic condition that leads to a difficult death at mid-age.[27]

A person's most difficult burden may be living with the knowledge that her life may be cut short. A patient who knows she may die prematurely may suffer emotionally and psychologically.[28] She may become depressed and even suicidal before she even becomes ill. Even with good pre- and post-test counseling, it is hard to predict how each person will deal with the genetic information they receive. Some patients have had affairs, have gotten divorced, have recklessly spent money and have even hurt others after getting their diagnosis.[29]

The new genetics will not only enable doctors to better assess a patient's predisposition to disease in the future. It is already helping physicians to diagnose diseases quicker and more accurately using what are called *genetic probes.*

Every living organism has a unique genetic code. DNA probes are short segments of DNA that bind specifically to the unique sequence of DNA in the organism to be detected. Scientists can design these probes to be completely specific for detecting a certain organism. It is this high degree of accuracy for one species that is the genetic probe's greatest advantage over other available tests.[30]

For example, diagnosing tuberculosis in the past took eight weeks—while the patient's sputum or other body fluid culture grew in the laboratory. If the culture was positive, the doctor had a firm diagnosis; but a negative culture did not rule out the disease. Other cultures had to be obtained and the whole time-consuming process repeated. It could take many months to arrive at a diagnosis. In 1995 the company Gen-Probe developed a rapid test that was a more sensitive and accurate way to diagnose TB and only took four hours to complete. Their gene probe quickly and accurately detected a unique segment of the tubercle bacillus even if only very few of the bacteria were present in the specimen. This highly sensitive and specific test revolutionized the diagnosis of TB overnight.[31]

Hundreds of similar gene probes have been developed to screen blood do-

---

[27]P. R. Billings et al., "Discrimination as a Consequence of Genetic Testing," *American Journal of Human Genetics* 50 (1992): 476-82.

[28]M. R. Hayden, M. Bloch and S. Wiggins, "Psychological Effects of Predictive Testing for Huntington's Disease," in *Behavioral Neurology of Movement Disorders,* ed. W. J. Weiner and A. E. Lang, vol. 65 of *Advances in Neurology* (New York: Raven, 1995), pp. 201-10.

[29]T. D. Bird, "Outrageous Fortune: The Risk of Suicide in Genetic Testing for Huntington Disease," *American Journal of Human Genetics* 64 (1999): 1289-92.

[30]Dictionary of Genetic Terms, "probe," *Human Genome Project* (July 8, 2003) <http://www.ornl.gov/TechResources/Human_Genome/publicat/primer2001/glossary.html>.

[31]"Gen-Probe Rapid Tuberculosis Test Wins FDA Approval; Test Uses Genetic Probe Technology to Dramatically Cut Detection Time," *Business Wire,* December 18, 1995 <http://www.aegis.com/news/bw/1995/BW951208.html>.

nations for HIV and hepatitis and to diagnose sexually transmitted diseases and respiratory infectious agents. The government of India even developed a probe to identify rhino poachers, who sell the horn for its medicinal uses; the probe detects traces of the animal's horn after it has been crushed and mixed with other substances by traditional medicine practitioners.[32]

Companies are now turning their attention to developing gene probes for diagnosing cancers from a few cells shed in the bloodstream or in body secretions.[33] In vitro fertilization specialists are using probes to test embryos that have been created in the lab for genetic diseases.[34] If they find an abnormality, they destroy the embryo, essentially doing preimplantation eugenics. With the same technology, they can also use genetic probes to ensure that the embryo implanted will result in a baby who will be a tissue match for a sibling that needs a bone marrow or organ transplant.[35]

The use of genetic probes is becoming cheaper, more automated and more widespread. Many new probes are in development, and probes are even beginning to show up in home health self-test kits.[36] New technology will allow hundreds of probes to be incorporated onto a glass slide in a space the size of a thumbnail. Automation will allow scientists to screen hundreds of slides an hour, quickly diagnosing disease or identifying those with genetic abnormalities.[37]

The new genetics is also allowing scientists to better understand normal and abnormal cell mechanisms. When a normal cell turns into a cancerous one, what has gone wrong genetically? What triggers can be identified and removed? Why does a cell begin to replicate uncontrollably and then shed into the blood and lymph systems as it metastasizes to distant parts of the body? What genetic mechanism got turned off when this happens, and how can that mechanism be turned back on? Can we design a cancer therapy that will cause therapeutic agents to recognize the genetic makeup of a cancer cell, selectively bind to those cells and then destroy them without disturbing normal cells in the body? Some of these questions are already being answered.

---

[32]"Rhino Conservation," Government of West Bengal, Wildlife Wing <http://education.vsnl.com/bengaltiger/>.

[33]Uwe Bicker, "Changing Diagnostic Approaches to Disease: The Promise of Genetic Testing," *Medical Device and Diagnostic Industry* (May 1998) <http://www.devicelink.com/mddi/archive/98/05/015.html>.

[34]"Preimplanation Genetic Diagnosis," Genetics and IVF Institute (2003) <http://www.givf.com/pgt_sepv.cfm>.

[35]"Bringing Up Baby to Save a Sibling: How Far Should Preimplantation Go?" *Medical Ethics Advisor* (November 2000) <http://www.ahcpub.com/ahc_root_html/hot/archive/mea112000.html>.

[36]Rachel Newcombe, "Are Home Gene Test Kits Helpful?" BUPA (January 27, 2003) <http://www.bupa.co.uk/health_information/html/health_news/270103genetests.html>.

[37]Laura DeFranscesco, "MicroArrays in the New Millennium," pt. 1, BioResearch Online (2003) <http://www.bioresearchonline.com>.

Understanding each cell's normal and abnormal cell mechanisms will enable better disease prevention, earlier diagnosis of disease and more specific and potent treatments. But understanding the genome is only part of the puzzle to be solved. Scientists will need to understand how only 35,000 genes can code for more than twice that many proteins and how those proteins interrelate with each other in normal and abnormal metabolisms.

The genetic age will have a profound effect on pharmacology, the science related to drugs and their use. Scientists will be able to rationally design new drugs instead of discovering them, as they have done for hundreds of years.[38] Traditionally, drug companies screened ten thousand naturally occurring compounds to find five hundred that were "bioactive." Those were tested to find the one hundred that held promise for patient therapy. Further testing in animals might lead to ten that had enough potential to be tested in humans. Ultimately one drug might make it to market. This expensive and long process is similar to finding a needle in a haystack. As scientists better understand the genome and the proteins they code for, they can make a computer model of the actual chemical target site they want to reach. They then design a drug, molecule by molecule, that will attach at that critical site and block the disease mechanism. [39]

For example, some breast cancer patients have a receptor site on their tumor that binds to a growth promotion protein. This results in very rapid enlargement of the cancer. When scientists discovered this site, they designed an antibody that would bind to this specific area and block the effect of the stimulator protein. This HER-2 site acts like a lock, and the drug developed, Herceptin, acts as a key broken off in that lock. It prevents another key from being placed in the lock, slows cancer growth and has already saved many lives.[40]

Rational drug design will lead to drugs that are cheaper, more effective and more specifically targeted. It will also increase the number of classes of drugs on the market. It is estimated that by 2020 we will move from five hundred drug targets to over two thousand. Drugs will move from conception to development and actual clinical use much faster. Today it costs more than $500 million and takes an average of ten years to bring new drug to market.[41]

Many of these new drugs will be manufactured in a different way, using what is called *recombinant DNA technology*. In this process scientists build a

---

[38]"Inside Rational Drug Design," Accelrys (2001-2003) <http://www.accelrys.com/pharma/lead/rdd/>.

[39]"Our Science," Concurrent Pharmaceuticals (2004) <http://www.concurrentpharma.com/science.html>.

[40]Andrew Holz, "Herceptin: An Entirely New Weapon Against Cancer," Sapient Health Network (1998) <http://nasw.org/users/holtza/SHNASCOHerceptin.htm>.

[41]"Medicine and the New Genetics," U.S. DOE.

piece of DNA in the laboratory that codes for the protein that is desired for therapeutic purposes. It is spliced into the DNA of a harmless virus or bacteria. These organisms then become mini-drug factories that produce the protein desired. Already this technique is used to produce extremely pure human insulin and growth hormone. Many more drugs in the future will be "brewed" in large culture vats, purified and packaged. The products will be cheaper, higher quality therapeutic substances.[42]

And this is only part of what is on the horizon. Scientists want to personalize your treatment even further by tailoring your drugs and the dosage you are given to your individual genetic makeup. This new branch of science is called *pharmacogenomics*.[43] For years doctors have known that some patients metabolize drugs in a different manner from others. For instance, many drugs used for depression, high blood pressure, heart disease and even attention deficit hyperactivity disorder (ADHD) are metabolized in the liver by the cytochrome P450 enzyme system. This system breaks down the drugs into components that can be secreted from the body. Roughly 10 percent of Caucasians and 20 percent of Asians are poor P450 enzyme system metabolizers. A smaller number of people actually have a revved up enzyme system, which means they metabolize drugs affected by this system much faster than normal. Both groups of people are at risk if given standard doses of drugs that depend on this enzyme. Poor metabolizers will get toxic levels of their drug when given a standard dose, for it is not removed at a normal rate and therefore accumulates. Fast metabolizers have the opposite problem. Their drug is removed so fast that they don't have a therapeutic level around long enough to have any helpful effect. This cytochrome P450 enzyme system is involved in the metabolism of 20 to 25 percent of the drugs given by doctors.[44]

New genetic technology has solved these problems. The AmpliChip CYP450, introduced in July 2003, enables clinical diagnostic laboratories to accurately and quickly identify the makeup of two genes that code for these variations in metabolism in patients. Doctors are now able to identify how an individual will metabolize a drug before they ever get it and to lower doses for the slow metabolizers. They can also give higher doses to those who break down the drug at a faster rate.[45]

---

[42]"The Benefits of Recombinant DNA Technology in Today's Medicine," Poets Pharmacy (2000) <http://www.fertilityrx.com/rdna/recombinant.html>.

[43]"Pharmacogenomics," U.S. Department of Energy Human Genome Program (May 23, 2003) <http://www.ornl.gov/TechResources/Human_Genome/medicine/pharma.html>.

[44]Ibid.

[45]"Roche Diagnostics Launches the AmpliChip CYP450 in the U.S., the World's First Pharmacogenomic Microarray for Clinical Application," F. Hoffman-La Roche (June 25, 2003) <http://www.roche.com/med-corp-detail-2003?id=999&media-language=e>.

Pharmacogenomics will make treatment not only more personalized but much safer. Today, 100,000 people die each year from adverse drug reactions, and millions of others suffer uncomfortable or dangerous side effects. Some scientists are already predicting that in ten to fifteen years, every baby born will have his genome mapped and recorded on a CD before he leaves the hospital. That information will guide his future treatment by letting doctors check drugs they are considering giving him against the patient's own genetic profile to find out which drug is likely to work best, which has the fewest side effects and what the proper dosage is.[46]

Geneticists dream not only of diagnosing genetic malformations, but also of being able to treat patients with gene therapy. The goal is to remove or replace damaged genes with new ones.[47]

Progress is already being made. In 2002 there were six hundred clinical gene therapy trials underway, involving 3,500 patients worldwide. Four out of five of these studies took place in the United States.[48] Scientists can easily build new genes in the laboratory. The main obstacle in gene therapy is finding a safe and accurate mechanism to insert the new gene into the genome at the right place. Does the created gene need to be inserted into the nucleus of each the 100 trillion cells in the human body or just certain ones? What are the risks? These and many other unknowns are being explored.

Traditionally scientists have used viruses to carry genes into human cells. A virus causes disease by inserting a piece of its own DNA into the genomes of human cells and thus taking them over in a coup d'état. It turns that cell into a factory that makes more viruses to infect other cells. Scientists have used relatively harmless viruses, like the retrovirus, to splice DNA into the human genome. This modified virus is grown in culture (to multiply it) and then used to carry the desired gene into human cells.

The success of this technique was highly publicized when scientists used it to cure children with severe combined immunodeficiency syndrome (SCID). Gene therapy for SCID (often dubbed "bubble-boy syndrome" because it requires children to live in a sterile environment) involves a number of steps. First, the children treated had some of their genetically defective bone marrow aspirated. The bone marrow was grown in the laboratory and then infected with a virus containing the needed gene that would cause them to produce an immune response. The genetically altered bone marrow was then transplanted back into each child's bone marrow. Within a short time each child

---

[46]"Pharmacogenomics," U.S. DOE.
[47]"Gene Therapy," U.S. Department of Energy Human Genome Program (June 30, 2003) <http://www.ornl.gov/TechResources/Human_Genome/medicine/genetherapy.html>.
[48]"Medicine and the New Genetics," U.S. DOE.

was able to fight off infection and for the first time start living a normal life.[49]

This early success—the only genetic disease ever cured by gene therapy—was tempered in 2003 when two treated SCID children were diagnosed with leukemia. Apparently the retrovirus used to insert the needed gene put it in or near a gene that promotes cancer, turning that gene on. With the publication of these cases, scientists halted gene therapy trials around the world until a better understanding of what went wrong could be determined. Ideally scientists would like to find a vehicle to deliver new genes that is more predictable and less risky than viruses are.[50]

Not only can gene therapy be used to cure genetic defects, it also has the potential to be used for genetic enhancement or even for making "designer" children. With more predictable and safer gene therapy, parents could use in vitro fertilization with preimplantation genetic manipulation of the embryo to select their child's hair and eye color, height and other physical characteristics. Defective genes could be removed and replaced to ensure a healthier and longer life. Genes for higher intelligence, athletic ability or beauty could be inserted. If parents wanted their child to be of a race different from their own, that could be arranged as well. Via genetic manipulation, parents could change the sex of an embryo to the one they desire or even, as one scientist recently did, create a embryo that was half female and half male. Whatever the embryo owner decides would be "perfect" could be designed.[51]

Thus a "perfect" child could grow into an adult, marry a "perfect" spouse and populate the world with more "perfect" children. Of course making such a "perfect" child would come at a financial cost that most people could not afford. Ultimately over time the human species would have two classes of individuals: the enhanced and the unenhanced. The difference between the haves and have-nots would widen.

The genetic revolution affects human beings in many other ways. It is already helping law enforcement officials to absolutely identify criminals using DNA analysis of semen, skin cells, saliva, blood and other biological materials left at crime scenes. The home secretary of Great Britain recently announced that his country's five-year-old national crime database now contains more than 2 million DNA profiles:

Every week our national DNA database matches over 1,000 DNA profiles taken

---

[49]Marina Cavazzana-Calvo et al., "Gene Therapy of Human Severe Combined Immunodeficiency (SCID)-X1 Disease," *Science* 288 (April 28, 2000): 669-72.
[50]Jeffrey L. Fox, "U.S. Authorities Uphold Suspension of SCID Gene Therapy," *Nature Biotechnology* 21 (March 2003) <http://www.nature.com/nbt>.
[51]Kevin Bonsor, "How Designer Children Will Work," How Stuff Works (2003) <http://www.howstuffworks.com/designer-children.htm>.

from crime scenes with names on the database. Around forty-two percent of those matches are turned into detections within an average of fourteen days. That is a huge achievement.[52]

Not only are the guilty caught, but the innocent can be exonerated. By 2001 seventy-five prisoners were released after genetic tests on old biological evidence showed that they had not committed the crime for which they had been convicted.[53]

DNA analysis is also used for paternity and family identification. It can show whether a person is the genetic or biological father or mother of a child, and it can identify a child years after she has been abducted. It is available commercially for home testing for under $1,000.[54]

DNA analysis has been used for years to match organ donors with the recipients who desperately need them, minimizing the effects of tissue rejection. With the mapping of the human genome, scientists are extensively adding to the list of compatible and incompatibility markers. Better tissue matching means fewer cases of organ rejection.[55]

The application of the new genetics in agriculture is already in widespread use, and many more interventions are on the way. Scientists no longer need to crossbreed plants for generations to come up with a variety that gives greater produce yields or more effectively resists disease. They can manipulate a plant's genome in the lab before a seed ever touches the dirt. These genetically enhanced fruits and vegetables are already finding their way to the dinner table—but not without controversy. Fearing unknown effects, countries in Europe have banned their importation.[56]

Scientists are also working on designing produce that is more nutritious. One goal that is drawing a lot of attention is the attempt to splice the genetic material from childhood vaccines into plant genomes. If successful, developing countries with poor preventive health care could simply plant a vaccine-producing tree in the center of each village. Generations of children would be immunized by eating the tree's fruit. Recently a rabies vaccine was developed using spinach.[57]

---

[52]"Police Have Two Million People's DNA on Database," Ananova (June 25, 2003) <http://www.ananova.com/news/story/sm_793808.html>.

[53]Kathy Barks Hoffman, "Prisoner to Try State's DNA Evidence Law," *Detroit Free Press*, March 12, 2001 <http://www.freep.com/news/mich/dn12_20010312.htm>.

[54]DNA Diagnostics Center (2003) <http://www.dnacenter.com>.

[55]Christian Velten, "Genome News," *Scitari*, December 1999 <http://www.bionews.net/5/2/i9e33c66-001.htm!ArcEntryInfo=0004.5.I9E33C66>.

[56]"Genetic Engineering Applications, Impacts and Implications," Ag Biotech InfoNet, June 11, 2003 <http://www.biotech-info.net/>.

[57]"Plant-Based Vaccines Show Promise Against Infectious Diseases," AMA Science News (October 4, 2001) <http://www.ama-assn.org/ama/pub/article/4197-5329.html>.

Scientists also hope to design bacteria and viruses that could kill or limit the growth of agriculture pests but that would be harmless to humans. These bio-pesticides would markedly decrease the need for toxic pesticides, which end up in the food chain and on the dinner table.[58]

Those involved in animal husbandry desire to genetically engineer more productive and disease-resistant farm animals. Attempts to clone highly productive animals have met with limited success. A more fruitful avenue of research may be to manipulate the genome of animals at the one-cell stage, grow the embryo to a few days of age, conduct embryo splitting to create dozens of identical embryos and then implant those embryos to create a super herd of animals.[59]

Microbial genomics has enormous potential as well. Bacteria are the most common organisms on Earth. Scientists estimate that there are five million trillion trillion bacteria. (That is a five followed by thirty zeroes.) Over four thousand species of bacteria live in a single gram of soil, but only 0.01 percent of all the bacteria in the world have been studied. Many of them live and multiply in very hostile environments, use unusual sources of nourishment or make usable byproducts. By splicing genes in different bacterial genomes, scientists hope to design bacteria that can do useful things. Because of the limited amount of DNA or RNA in bacteria, modification can be done more easily.[60]

Possible uses include designing a bacterium that produces an unlimited supply of carbon fuels to power engines in automobiles, planes and power plants. Work is underway to discover or design microbes that indicate (e.g., by becoming fluorescent) when they detect an oil spill or pollutants in the environment. Better yet would be a nonpathological strain of bacteria that could be let loose in toxic waste sites to digest the offending material and excrete nontoxic and even useful byproducts. Scientists are especially interested in discovering a bacterium that can clean up oil spills.[61]

With the heightened concern about terrorism, scientists are attempting to genetically design better vaccines that would protect people from biological agents and that would have few adverse side effects when administered to the

---

[58]"Biopesticides," U.S. Environmental Protection Agency, April 1, 2003 <http://www.epa.gov/agriculture/tbio.html#Genetic>.

[59]Darryl R. J. Macer, "Shaping Genes: Ethics, Law and Science of Using New Genetic Technology in Medicine and Agriculture," in *Shaping Genes: Ethics, Law and Science of Using New Genetic Technology in Medicine and Agriculture* (Tsukuba Science City: Eubios Ethics Institute, 1990), pp. 109-26 <http://www.biol.tsukuba.ac.jp/~macer/sg/SG7.html>.

[60]"Microbial Genomics Gateway," Microbial Genomics, November 17, 2003 <http://www.microbialgenome.org>.

[61]"DOE Biological and Environmental Research Helps Fuel 'Biology Century,' " *Human Genome News* 10 (February 1999) <http://www.ornl.gov/TechResources/Human_Genome/publicat/hgn/v10n1/09doe.html>.

entire population. Scientists at Massachusetts Institute of Technology recently spliced a jellyfish gene for luminescence into rat B lymphocyte cells that had been sensitized to bacteria and viruses used in bioterrorism. This biosensor lights up when it comes in contact with even small amounts of these agents, providing a cheap, portable and accurate detection system that works in less than three minutes.[62]

Interestingly, the Human Genome Project grew out of the Department of Energy's congressional mandate to study the risk of genetic mutations from radiation, environmental toxins and drugs. Understanding what triggers mutations can better help people to avoid them. It is thought that most, if not all, of the cancers we suffer from are caused by genetic mutations.

Another application of genetic research is in bioarcheology, a growing field of study where scientists, through the study of genetic markers, can determine what people groups are related to or descended from each other. For thousands of years the Bantu-speaking Lemba tribe of South Africa has passed on the oral history that they are descendents of Jews from the Middle East. Fathers have told their sons that they came from a group of Jews that settled in Yemen and later migrated to Ethiopia, Tanzania, Kenya, Mozambique, Zimbabwe and South Africa. The Lemba believe in the god Nwali, and they worship on a holy day each week. Their elders circumcise Lemba boys at age eight, and the whole tribe eats neither pork nor other creatures prohibited in the Old Testament. There are over seventy thousand Lemba people in Africa.

Through genetic testing a team of bioarcheologists found that Lemba men carry a DNA sequence that is distinctive to a hereditary set of Jewish priests. In other words, geneticists demonstrated that about 2,700 years ago, descendents of Aaron (Moses' brother) left Israel and migrated south and are known now as the Lemba. Genetics support what the Lemba believed all along. They are indeed Jewish and are perhaps one of the lost tribes of Israel.[63]

Every day a new gene or genetic discovery is heralded in the news. Today it was the discovery of the malfunctioning version of the GATA4 gene, which causes a birth defect in the formation of the walls that separate the chambers of the heart. It is the fourth gene to be linked to a congenital heart defect.[64] Who knows what the headlines will read tomorrow—but there is no doubt that in the biotech century, the new genetics will affect you, your children and your grandchildren.

---

[62]Deborah Halber, "MIT Sensor Detects Pathogens Quickly and Acurately," MIT News, July 10, 2003 <http://web.mit.edu/newsoffice/nr/2003/sensors.html >.

[63]"Africans Have Jewish Ancestry," The Lemba, July 14, 2003 <http://www.haruth.com/LembaAfricansJewishAncestry.html >.

[64]"Specific Gene Mutations Cause Congenital Heart Defect," *Daily Times Monitor,* July 7, 2003 <http://www.dailytimes.com.pk/default.asp?page=story_14-7-2003_pg6_16>.

Much of what is happening with the new genetics will be good, but as with every new technology, there is an new power to do evil. The mastery of the genome is an incredible power. With it scientists can cure diseases, enhance the makeup of the human race or wipe the human race out entirely. A microbiologist could accidentally create a lethal bacteria or virus that is much more virulent and untreatable than the headline-grabbing SARS virus. This superbug could unleash an uncontrollable epidemic. A terrorist government could genetically modify a dangerous bacteria to increase its virulence and its resistance to all known forms of treatment. A gene modified to improve agriculture or animal husbandry could have an unforeseen effect on human beings.

Yet we cannot halt or ban genetic research. Its potential for good is too great. What we must do is put an ethical and scientific safety net around this rapidly developing but almost totally unregulated field. With adequate safeguards we can prevent most mishaps, while still reaping the benefits that will be lifesaving for many people.

What can you do? First educate yourself and then others about the new genetics.[65] Once you understand the basics, you can advocate for the safeguards that need to be put in place by government and scientific research organizations to protect us all. Working together we can move with confidence into the frontiers of biotechnology.

---

[65]Check out <http://www.standards4life.org >.

6

THE HUMAN EMBRYO
IN DEBATE

WILLIAM L. SAUNDERS, J.D.

The question of the nature of the human embryo lies at the heart of much biotech debate because the focus of current new technology is on the beginning of human life—the cloning of embryos for use in experiments and the culling of stem cells from embryos thus manufactured. In this essay Bill Saunders, who directs the bioethics project of the Family Research Council and has wide experience in bioethics and policy issues, takes the discussion back to the classic iteration of human dignity in the face of science and technology in the Nuremberg Code, formulated by the war crimes court that tried Nazi physicians and scientists.

Saunders explores the horrors of Nazi medicine that lay behind the code and the fundamental parallels between the Nazis' abuse of human beings for research purposes and the current abuse of human embryos. He also reports on the fundamental irrationality of those who seek to distinguish between an embryo in vivo (in the womb) and one in vitro (in a Petri dish), or between an embryo resulting from in vitro fertilization and one manufactured by cloning.

The Nazis derived their eugenic program from views—widely held in the United States and elsewhere in the early part of the twentieth century—that supported the compulsory sterilization of the "feeble-minded." So, Saunders concludes, "the debate about the embryo is not about the embryo at all." It is about "our culture, about our ethics." How do we treat the weak and disposable? Do we recognize them as bearing the image of God?

NIGEL M. DE S. CAMERON

The question of the moral status of the human embryo is the single most important issue in bioethics.[1] The resolution of the question depends on an examination of ethical standards, historical circumstances, scientific facts and theo-

---

[1] The author gratefully acknowledges the assistance of Yuri Mantilla, John Henry Crosby and Daniel Sullivan in the preparation of this article.

logical sources. However, the importance of the issues involved may be indicated by way of an example.

Regularly over the past several decades the United States has received reports from China that prisoners are being executed in order to harvest their organs, which are sold chiefly to wealthy non-Chinese residents in need of organ transplants. The timing and manner of executions are varied to suit the needs of the one purchasing the organ. In 2001 Chinese physician Wang Guoqi testified in gruesome detail about these practices before a committee of the U.S. House of Representatives, and included descriptions of his own participation in harvesting skin tissue from prisoners who had been shot but who were not always dead.[2]

These practices have been rightly condemned on several grounds, such as coercion, commodification of human body parts and so on. However, they have also been condemned because the practice kills one human being in order to transplant her organs into another human being. This is a clear violation of the doctor's responsibility to the patient. Understandably, the practices followed by the Chinese government have been condemned by the World Medical Association: "The physician's interest in advancing scientific knowledge must always be secondary to his primary concern for the patient."[3]

Yet I will attempt to show in this essay that certain current practices in some segments of the scientific and medical research community in the United States differ little in their ethical essence from the organ-harvesting practices of the Chinese government. In sum, if the embryo is a human being, its dismemberment (or "disaggregation") in order to procure stem cells that will then be either transplanted into another person or used in research aimed at helping others is subject to the same ethical standards that govern the treatment of the Chinese prisoners.

A Universal Ethical Standard

On February 13, 2002, the principal author of the National Academy of Sciences' report on cloning, Professor Irving L. Weissman, testified before the second meeting of the President's Council on Bioethics, which was established by President George W. Bush to provide him with advice on emerging issues in bioethics.[4] The report Weissman defended before the council held that it was ethically *impermissible* to proceed with "reproductive cloning" (i.e., cloning

---

[2]Wang Guoqi, testifying on June 27, 2001, before the House Subcommittee on International Operations and Human Rights; reprinted in *Laogai Report* 9 (Fall-Winter 2002): 8.

[3]Statement of the World Medical Association, 1987, quoted in ibid., p. 7.

[4]National Academy of Sciences Committee on Science, Engineering and Public Policy, *Scientific and Medical Aspects of Human Cloning* (Washington, D.C.: National Academy Press, 2002).

that brings the clone to birth), while it was ethically *permissible* to proceed with "therapeutic cloning."[5]

By what standard did Weissman and his NAS colleagues judge "reproductive cloning" to be impermissible? "Reproductive cloning," they maintain, is simply too dangerous. The risk to the cloned human subject is too great. The actual cloning process is difficult to manage: most animal clones are defective or, indeed, die unexpectedly. Ian Wilmut, the scientist who cloned the first mammal, Dolly the sheep, has stated that only 1 to 5 percent of embryos eventually result in the live birth of animals; and those that are born are plagued with obesity, lung and kidney problems, immune system failure, and so on.[6] Thus the magnitude of the risk to the cloned human subject being brought to birth is quite high. But how did Weissman *know* that this was an *impermissible* risk? In other words, despite the risk, were other considerations that made it a risk worth taking? What was it that, in Weissman's opinion, barred anyone from undertaking that risk despite the potential gains (such as producing a child for an infertile couple or trying to replicate someone with the mental ability of Albert Einstein)? Weissman's standard was the Nuremberg Code.[7] He deferred to it as setting the authoritative test by which cloning research (and all other research) is to be judged.[8]

Nazi Germany and the Nuremberg Code

In essence the Nuremberg Code sums up the ethical tradition of Western civilization regarding experimentation on human subjects.[9] One article of that

---

[5]Ibid. I will examine in detail the two terms *reproductive cloning* and *therapeutic cloning* later in this essay. However, as both terms will be found to be misleading, I will refer to them in the text in quotation marks (thus, "reproductive" cloning and "therapeutic" cloning). The President's Council on Bioethics prefers the terms *cloning for live birth* and *cloning for biomedical research*, respectively. I prefer the terms, *live birth cloning* and *research cloning*.

[6]Ian Wilmut and Harry Griffin, "Why No One Should Be Attempting to Clone a Child," in *Roslin Institute Annual Report*, April 2000-March 2001 <http://www.roslin.ac.uk/publications/0001annrep/child.html>. (The URLs cited in this chapter were accessed on January 16, 2004.)

[7]Weissman said, "What we are reporting to you is that human reproductive cloning is dangerous. It is a dangerous medical practice. It contravenes the Nuremberg Code clearly." For a transcript of the second meeting of the President's Council on Bioethics, on February 13, 2002, see <http://www.bioethics.gov/meetings >.

[8]Again, Weissman testified that "the Nuremberg Code, with which I am in full agreement, outlines those sorts of things you would not simply [do] for the sake of knowledge that involve human subjects. I personally believe it is one of the most elegantly written documents I have ever seen and I adhere to it completely" (ibid.).

[9]While the Nuremberg Code is not binding international law as such, its force as the ethical standard by which to judge research involving human subjects is universally acknowledged. The Nuremberg Code has also significantly influenced ethical codes developed since it enunciation. See "The Role of Codes in International and U.S. Law," part 3 of *The Nazi Doctors and the Nuremberg Code: Human Rights in Human Experimentation*, ed. George J. Annas

code states that there shall be no experimentation on a human subject when it is clear that it will result in death or disabling injury to the subject.[10]

The Nuremberg Code was announced by the Nuremberg Tribunal, which was convened by the Allied forces to judge the atrocities committed by the Nazis and the other Axis powers during World War II.[11] In other words, the Nuremberg Code was born (if one may use that term) in the civilized world's outrage at the genocide and other crimes against humanity committed by the Nazi regime. As such it is the acknowledged standard today.[12]

As we know, the Nazis killed between six and nine million people in the concentration or death camps, most of them Jews. Nazi laws had redefined Jews and other "undesirables" as nonpersons.[13] Eventually these "undesirables" were herded into the camps for extermination. But before the death camps were ever constructed, the Nazis had engaged in an extensive campaign of euthanasia against the sick and handicapped. However, the roots of that campaign reach back far before the Nazis.

Germany Before the Nazis

The crucial work justifying the extermination of "undesirables" was a book titled *The Permission to Destroy Life Unworthy of Life.* It was written by two emi-

---

and Michael A. Grodin (Oxford: Oxford University Press, 1992). Of course, Christians may prefer other articulations of the fundamental ethic, such as the golden rule ("do unto others as you would have them do unto you") and the Pauline principle ("do not do evil that good may come from it"). It is also true that such Christian ethical proscriptions have been decisive in shaping Western ethics. Further, the Nuremberg Code itself reflects Christianity's emphasis on the dignity, worth and inviolability of *each* human being. Thus, given the almost universal acceptance of the Nuremberg Code by all protagonists in the debate over the human embryo, that standard will be used primarily in this paper.

[10]Nuremberg Code, principle 5: "No experiment should be conducted where there is an a priori reason to believe that death or disabling injury will occur; except, perhaps, in those experiments where the experimental physicians also serve as subjects." <www.cirp.org/library/ethics/nuremberg/>.

[11]*Trials of War Criminals Before the Nuremberg Military Tribunals Under Control Council Law* (Washington, D.C.: U.S. Government Printing Office, 1949).

[12]Another widely respected source, one that builds on the Nuremberg Code, is the World Medical Association's Declaration of Helsinki. As amended through October 2000, the declaration contains several provisions relevant here: "In medical research on human subjects, considerations related to the well-being of the human subject should take precedence over the interests of science and society" (principle 5); "Medical research is subject to ethical standards that promote respect for all human beings and protect their health and rights. Some research populations are vulnerable and need special protection. . . . Special attention is also required for those who cannot give or refuse consent for themselves . . . [and] for those who will not benefit personally from the research"(principle 8); "It is the duty of the physician in medical research to protect the life, health, privacy and dignity of the human subject" (principle 10). <http://www.wma.net/e/ethicunit/helsinki.htm>.

[13]For example, the 1935 Nuremberg Laws prevented Jews from intermarrying with Germans and deprived them of German citizenship.

nent German professors, Alfred Hoche, a psychiatrist, and Karl Binding, a jurist. As discussed by Robert Jay Lifton in his book *The Nazi Doctors*, the incurably ill, the mentally ill, the feeble-minded, the retarded and the deformed were all regarded as "lives unworthy of life."[14] The destruction of these "unworthy lives" was "medicalized" by the authors: this was a "healing treatment" or "healing work."

It should be noted that the publication date of this book was 1920. The Nazi Party, though formed from the German Workers Party in 1920-1921, did not gain widespread support until 1929. Adolf Hitler did not come to power until 1933, when he was elected chancellor. Thus this book preceded by many years the rise to power of the Nazi regime. It was produced during the days of the Weimar Republic. It reflected—but in turn crucially helped to shape—cultural currents that were at work well before the Nazi regime but that, again, helped to bring that regime to power.

At the end of the nineteenth century, German social Darwinists, fearing a general "degeneration" of the human race, set about to establish a new kind of hygiene—racial hygiene. They believed that

> racial hygiene would provide long-run preventive medicine for the "German germ plasm" by combating the disproportionate breeding of "inferiors." . . . Medical scientists [not the Nazis] were the ones who invented racial hygiene in the first place. Most of the 20-odd university institutes for racial hygiene were established at German universities before the Nazi rise to power. . . . Racial hygienists were convinced that many human behaviors were at root genetic—crime, alcoholism, wanderlust, even divorce. Studies of how twins behave in different environments were supposed to prove the ultimate genetic origins of racial and social differences.[15]

As the Christian novelist Walker Percy noted, it is unlikely that Hitler ever read *The Permission to Destroy Life Unworthy of Life*: "He didn't have to."

> The point is that the ideas expressed in the book and the policies advocated were not the product of Nazi ideology but rather of the best minds of the pre-Nazi Weimar Republic—physicians, social scientists, jurists and the like who with the best secular intentions wished to improve the lot, socially and genetically, of the German people—by getting rid of the unfit and the unwanted.[16]

---

[14]Robert Jay Lifton, *The Nazi Doctors: Medical Killing and the Psychology of Genocide* (New York: Basic, 1986), p. 46.

[15]Robert N. Proctor, "Nazi Doctors, Racial Medicine and Human Experimentation," in *The Nazi Doctors and the Nuremberg Code: Human Rights in Human Experimentation*, ed. George J. Annas and Michael A. Grodin (Oxford: Oxford University Press, 1992), pp. 18-20.

[16]Walker Percy, unpublished letter to the *New York Times*, January 22, 1988; reprinted in appendix 1 of *Human Life Review* 114 (Winter 1996).

Germany Under the Nazis

Once the Nazis took power, the elimination of those who were "genetically inferior" proceeded in the following steps: first, the forcible sterilization law of 1933 (which was passed to keep the unfit from breeding); next, the marriage law of 1935 (which required proof the couple's offspring would not be afflicted with disabling hereditary disease); and finally, euthanasia.[17]

According to the United States Holocaust Museum, "fearful of public reaction, the Nazi regime never proposed a formal 'euthanasia' law. Unlike the forced sterilizations, the killing of patients in mental asylums and other institutions was carried out in secrecy. The code name was 'Operation T4.' "[18] The first Children's Specialty Psychiatric Department was established in 1940, under which "all therapeutic possibilities will be administered according to the latest scientific knowledge." A network of thirty killing areas within existing institutions was set up throughout Germany, Austria and Poland.[19]

In 1940 Hitler also decided to kill "undesirables" by carbon monoxide poisoning rather than by lethal injection. Gassing took place in chambers disguised as showers, complete with fake nozzles. The bodies were cremated. When the secrecy surrounding Operation T4 broke down, the program was discontinued—but not before 70,273 people had been killed by gassing at six centers between January 1940 and August 1941.

> Gas chambers from some of the euthanasia killing centers were dismantled and shipped to extermination camps. . . . The "euthanasia" killings continued, however, under a decentralized form. . . . In all [across Europe], between 200,000 and 250,000 people with mental and physical disabilities were murdered [by the Nazis] from 1939 to 1945 under T4 and other euthanasia programs.[20]

In the extermination camps, of course, mass murder took place.[21] In addition, Nazi doctors engaged in what now seem to us inexplicably cruel experiments on the Jews, Gypsies, Poles and others. They exposed them to extreme cold or immersed them in freezing water to see at what temperature death would occur. They injected them with poisons to see how quickly certain elements moved through the circulatory system. They took twins and subjected them to all manner of terrible conditions to see how genetically identical per-

---

[17]I will discuss forced sterilization below.

[18]United States Holocaust Museum, *Handicapped* (pamphlet) <http://www.holocaust-trc.org/hndcp.htm>.

[19]Lifton, *Nazi Doctors*, p. 54.

[20]United States Holocaust Museum, *Handicapped* (pamphlet).

[21]"Historians exploring the origins of the Nazi destruction of lives not worth living have only in recent years begun to stress the link between the euthanasia operation, on the one hand, and the 'final solution,' on the other. And yet the two programs were linked in both theory and practice." Proctor, "Nazi Doctors," p. 25.

sons reacted to different conditions. People in these concentration camps were "marked for death"; their lives had no future possibilities. They were "lives unworthy of life." If these people were going to be killed anyway, why not use them for research?

I called these experiments "inexplicable." But were they? Certainly, it is clear that many of them were simply sadistic and cruel. Anesthesia was withheld from the subjects. They were treated worse than are animals in contemporary scientific research.

But some of the experiments were designed to *preserve* life—albeit not the subjects'.

> The experiments chronicled in the Nuremberg trials were carried out for various reasons. Physicians forced people to drink seawater to find out how long a man might survive without fresh water. At Dachau, Russian prisoners of war were immersed in icy water to see how long a pilot might survive when shot down over the English Channel and to find out what kinds of protective gear or rewarming techniques were most effective. Prisoners were placed in vacuum chambers to find out how the human body responds when pilots are forced to bail out at high altitudes. . . . At Fort Ney, near Strasbourg, 52 prisoners were exposed to phosgene gas (a biowarfare agent) in 1943 and 1944 to test possible antidotes; at Auschwitz, physicians experimented with new ways to sterilize or castrate people as part of the plan to repopulate Eastern Europe with Germans. Physicians performed limb and bone transplants (on persons with no medical need) and, in at least one instance, injected prisoner's eyes with dyes to see if eye color could be permanently changed. At Buchenwald, Gerhard Rose infected prisoners with spotted fever to test experimental vaccines against the disease; at Dachau, Ernst Grawitz infected prisoners with a broad range of pathogens to test homeopathic preparations. Nazi military authorities were worried about exotic diseases German troop could contract in Africa or Eastern Europe; physicians in the camps reasoned that the "human materials" at their disposal could be used to develop remedies.[22]

The experiments were not conducted by mad Nazi doctors, but were often directed by, or affiliated with, renowned institutes.

> Neuropathologist Julius Hallervorden from the Kaiser Wilhelm Institute for Brain Research in Berlin-Bach . . . is known . . . as the discoverer of the Hallervorden-Spatz disease, a rare congenital brain disease. In the early 1940s, he ordered hundreds of brains of the victims of euthanasia from the killing hospital in Brandenburg-Gorden for his neuropathological studies. . . . The director of the prestigious Kaiser Wilhelm Institute for Anthropology, . . . Otmar von Verschuer, . . . directed [Josef] Mengele's research on twins in Auschwitz. To this

---

[22]Ibid., pp. 25-26.

day, Verschuer's twin studies are still cited by many of the world's leading geneticists.[23]

As can be seen, the ultimate aim of *some* of these experiments was to yield
a human good—to gain knowledge that would preserve human life or alleviate suffering. There was, in other words, allegedly a "greater good" involved.

Human Embryonic Stem Cell Research

If embryos are human beings, then conducting stem cell research on them
(during which their stem cells are extracted and they are killed) violates the
Nuremberg Code.[24] If, through therapeutic cloning, embryos are created to be
used in experiments that would likewise be lethal to them, that too violates the
Nuremberg Code. Would it matter if the extravagant claims of cloning and embryonic stem cell research advocates—cures for *every* human disease and *every*
human aliment—could actually be realized?[25] I will answer that question with
another question. Would our judgment of the Nazis have been affected if they

---

[23]Christian Pross, "Nazi Doctors, German Medicine and Historical Truth," in *The Nazi Doctors
and the Nuremberg Code: Human Rights in Human Experimentation,* ed. George J. Annas and
Michael A. Grodin (Oxford: Oxford University Press, 1992), pp. 36, 44. Verschuer and Hall-
ervorden are examples of physicians and scientists who were *not* "indicted at Nuremberg.
They represent not the extremes, but rather the attitude, thinking, and daily routine of a
large part of the average physician population. They were not fanatic Nazis or high-ranking
SS physicians. But they profited from the unique opportunity to experiment on living humans, and they supported the Nazi utopian view of a society cleansed of everything sick,
alien, and disturbing" (p. 38).

[24]Though the primary violation of the code is of principle 5, cited above, such research also
violates principle 7: "Proper preparations should be made and adequate facilities provided
to protect the experimental subject against even remote possibilities of injury, disability, or
death." Since the extraction of the stem cells always results in the death of the human embryo, it is impossible to protect it from "even remote possibilities of injury, disability, or
death." Principle 7 would be more directly relevant if a procedure could be developed to
extract some of the stem cells without necessarily killing the embryo. However, given that
stem cells are being extracted before implantation, when the stem cells are few in number
and the role of each in the development of the human embryo is quite important, it appears
likely that even if the certain death of the embryo could be avoided, the procedure would
still pose a significant risk of injury or disability and would, hence, remain prohibited by
principle 7.

[25]It is important to note that experiments on human embryos appear to violate another provision of the code, principle 2: "The experiment should be such as to yield fruitful results
for the good of society, unprocurable by other methods or means of study, and not random
and unnecessary in nature." Stem cells from sources other than human embryos have
yielded very promising results and appear to offer at least as great promise. See, e.g., C. M.
Verfaille et al., "Pluripotency of Mesenchymal Stem Cells Derived from Adult Marrow," *Nature* 419 (July 4, 2002): pp. 41-49. Since human embryonic stem cell research destroys the human embryo, surely the Nuremberg Code requires that such research be held in abeyance
at least until it has been determined whether the results being sought are truly "unprocurable by other means."

had found such cures? I do not think so. Surely everyone would agree that the imperative to conduct scientific research to "help people" must yield to the fundamental ethical norm expressed in the Nuremberg Code. Regardless of the good that might be produced by such experiments, the experiments are of their very nature an immoral use of human beings. In short, the end does not justify the means.

The analysis we have just completed should have demonstrated that it is a mistake to separate *being* from *personhood*. Though some, such as Princeton professor Peter Singer, argue that a human being earns her personhood (i.e., her dignity and rights) by her attainment of certain functions or abilities (cognition or sentience), such a position seems to me to be decisively rebutted by the example we have just considered.[26] After all it was the Nazis who were willing to find some lives "unworthy of life." And certainly, if the measure of a life worthy of life were cognitive or sentient ability, many of those executed by the Nazis would fail to qualify as a "worthy" life because they were mentally handicapped or paralyzed. The Nazis made a distinction between *a human being* and *a person entitled to the protection of the law*.

The idea of "racial hygiene" is discredited today, and I doubt any reader would defend such views. However, notice what the corollary is: Assuming that embryos are human beings, there is no morally significant difference between the people killed by the Nazis in their euthanasia centers and extermination camps and those embryonic human beings being destroyed currently.[27] If each is a human being, *each is a life worthy of life*. Thus, the same ethical standard must be used to judge actions by third parties that affect their well-being.

Thus, the question to be asked is, *are* human embryos *human beings?* The only morally relevant basis by which Professor Weissman and the National Academy of Sciences can distinguish "therapeutic cloning" (or human embryonic stem cell research) from Nazi experimentation is to maintain that, unlike Nazi experimentation, "therapeutic cloning" does not involve human beings.

---

[26]See, e.g., "Dangerous Words: An Interview with Peter Singer," *Princeton Alumni Weekly*, January 26, 2000, p. 18.

[27]This is not to deny that nonembryonic human beings (including fetuses) experience pain in ways that the embryo, apparently, cannot. Thus, it is certainly true that anyone who conducts unethical experiments on nonembryos does so knowing that this causes great suffering to the subject. It is also true that many of the Nazi doctors in the concentration camps were sadistic and cruel. And it is quite true that today's researchers have no intention to cause pain and suffering to the embryo when they dismember it. However, the ethical question—is this an unethical taking of human life?—does not change depending on the ability of that human being to experience pain.

The Scientific Facts of Human Embryology

Human life begins normally upon conception, that is, upon the fertilization of a female egg cell (or oocyte) by a male sperm cell.[28] It begins abnormally or asexually upon the activation by an electrical charge of an egg cell from which the original nucleus has been replaced by one taken from a "somatic" or body cell.[29] The cloning procedure supplies the oocyte with a complete set of chromosomes, all of which are contained in the nucleus, which is transferred into the denucleated ooctye. With sexual reproduction, however, half of the chromosomes are supplied by the sperm and half by the ooctye.

From that moment forward, we have a new human organism. The new organism, if the product of sexual reproduction, is genetically distinct from all other human beings. Unless it subsequently twins or is cloned, it is, and forever remains, genetically unique.[30] If the new human being is a clone, it is genetically (nearly) identical to one other human being but is, nonetheless, itself a distinct living human being.

From that first moment, armed with its complete set of chromosomes, the new single-cell organism directs its own integral functioning and development. It proceeds, unless death intervenes, through every stage of human development until one day it reaches the adult stage, as we have done. It will grow and develop and change its appearance, but it will never undergo a change in its basic *nature*. It will never grow up to be a cow or a fish. It is a *human* being—its nature is determined—from the first moment of its existence. As the great Christian ethicist Paul Ramsey noted, "The embryo's subsequent development may be described as a process of becoming what he already is from the moment of conception."[31]

---

[28]For more information on the beginning of human life, see William L. Saunders and Charles A. Donovan, *The Whole Truth About Stem Cell Research* (Washington, D.C.: Family Research Council, 2001).

[29]There have been recent claims to create an embryo by *parthenogenesis*. Parthenogenesis involves immersing an egg in a chemical bath. This "fools" the egg into "thinking" it has been fertilized, and growth and development begin. While it is uncertain that parthenogenesis can be successfully performed, if it can, it may best be understood as another kind of cloning. Cloning is the replication of a genetic duplicate. What parthenogenesis would accomplish is the creation of a genetic duplicate of the egg-donor.

[30]Twinning should be understood as *natural* cloning. As with cloning, where once there was one human being, there now exists a genetic duplicate of the first. There is nothing about the possibility of cloning, natural or artificial, that suggests the original human being was anything other than a complete, unified organism. See Robert P. George, "The Ethics of Embryonic Stem Cell Research and Human Cloning," *At the Podium* 87 (Washington, D.C.: Family Research Council, 2002).

[31]Paul Ramsey, *Fabricated Man: The Ethics of Genetic Control* (New Haven: Yale University Press, 1970), p. 11.

The Christian Perspective

Certainly, these scientific facts are confirmed by Scripture (which is no surprise, for truth cannot contradict truth), though without, perhaps, all the precision of the twenty-first century. In the Old Testament it seems clear the human being is present from the beginning embryonic stage, although it undergoes subsequent development in the fetal stage.[32] Of course, in the New Testament, we know that the Holy Spirit overshadowed Mary and she conceived (Lk 1:34-35). Our Lord's human life began *from that moment.* Let us remember that *Jesus Christ, God made man, was himself once a zygote.*

Still, some Christians wonder whether there is something about *the way* in which a *cloned* human being is created that makes it less than human. Rather than being a human being, it is, they believe, a human artifact, a thing made of biological material but not truly a human being.

I find it difficult to see the merit in this objection. After all, thousands of human beings have been created by in vitro fertilization (IVF); yet no one, Christian or atheist (so far as I am aware) contends that these are not fully human beings in the same sense as are those conceived by sexual intercourse.

Similarly, some Christians believe cloned human beings lack a soul and, thus, are not truly human beings. They believe that humanity cannot force God's hand, so to speak. God has ordained one way in which human beings are created, and if that is violated, whatever is created is not a human being.

Again, I do not find this objection persuasive. Obviously, the point that God ordained one way to create a human being cannot be pressed too far, else it would exclude the virgin birth of our Lord. Further, humans, to speak metaphorically, force God's hand all the time—whenever they engage in rape or incest or bigamy or polygamy or fornication or adultery. Yet Christian theologians do not speculate, nor does the church teach, that the beings that were born as a consequence of these sinful actions lack souls or are in any way different from human beings conceived normally.

In this area, as in all others, it seems to me that we must wrestle with the reality of sin. Sin distorts God's plan. While God intended that human beings be conceived within the realm of married love, sinful humankind has devised other ways to create human life. Once created, however, that life is as full of dignity, and is due as much respect, as is any other human life. God loves every human being and does not punish him for the sins of his earthly creators. That, it seems to me, is the heart of the gospel.

---

[32]Compare Jer 1:4-5 ("The word of the LORD came to me, saying, 'Before I formed you in the womb I knew you'") with Ps 139:13-16 ("For you created my inmost being; you knit me together in my mother's womb. . . . When I was woven together in the depths of the earth, your eyes saw my unformed body.")

Human Embryos Are Human Beings

Every human being begins as a single-cell zygote, develops through the embryonic stage and then the fetal stage, is born and then grows through the infant stage, through childhood, and through adulthood, until death. The human being was the same human being at every stage,[33] though it looks different at each stage.[34] Change is the very essence of life. Dr. John Harvey of Georgetown University's Center for Clinical Bioethics has noted that "a human being is unchangeable and complete only at the moment of death"![35] Consider photographs from your own infancy. If you compared one to a contemporary photograph, the two would look quite different. Yet each is a photograph of the *same* human being.

This is the fundamental scientific truth on which all our moral analysis must be built. If we obscure this fact, it is simply impossible to think clearly about these issues. Remember, the Nuremberg Code applies only to human beings. If "it" (the "thing" being discussed) is something else, then the ethical norm about killing human beings during research does not apply.[36]

---

[33]Under the questioning of the President's Council on Bioethics member Robert P. George, Weissman was forced to admit this. When asked by George whether the council chairman (Leon Kass) himself "had been in the blastocyst stage" before the adult, adolescent and fetal stages, Weissman answered in the affirmative, thereby establishing that the same entity—Leon Kass—had passed through successive stages of growth and development: embryonic, fetal, infantile, adult.

[34]At the blastocyst stage, when the embryo implants in the womb, it has been described as looking like a raspberry! John Collins Harvey, "Distinctly Human: The When, Where and How of Life's Beginnings," *Commonweal*, February 8, 2002.

[35]Ibid.

[36]It has been alleged that if the "thing" is produced by parthenogenesis and if it fails to progress beyond the blastocyst stage (whether because of introduced or inherent defects), it is not an embryo. This is important, because if it is not an embryo (i.e., an embryonic human being), killing it to extract its stem cells does not violate the Nuremberg Code. However, the contention that the "thing" produced by parthenogenesis is not an embryo must be rejected on its face. As noted, an embryo is simply the first stage of human development. It begins at the single-cell stage and continues for the next two months. Of course, there is no guarantee that any embryo will live that entire two months and enter into the fetal stage. But whether it lives or dies, it is an embryo from the first. It is, of course, true that sometimes there are defective fertilizations, resulting in the formation of hydatidiform moles (i.e., human tissue). It might be that parthenogenesis always results in the formation of a mole or a tumor. However, assuming that the "thing" produces stem cells (and the question only arises if it does), the morally relevant fact is that there appears to be no way of knowing that it is a mole and not an embryo. Thus, destroying it *might* be killing a human being. To put it another way, if it could be shown that parthenogenesis produces a mole and not an embryo and that the mole produces stem cells, the destruction of the mole (and the extraction of the stem cells) would not pose an ethical problem. However, it must be noted that since what scientists are seeking are *embryonic* stem cells, *not* alternative kinds of stem cells, it will be hard to show that the "thing" from which *embryonic* stem cells are not being extracted is not an *embryo*.

But again, "it" isn't something else. "It" *is* a human being. Every human being was once a zygote (or a single-cell embryo). Human life begins from that first moment. Embryologists are united on this point: Keith L. Moore and T. V. N. Persaud write, "Human development begins at fertilization. . . . This highly specialized, totipotent cell marked the beginning of each of us as a unique individual."[37] Bruce M. Carlson says, "Almost all higher animals start their lives from a single cell, the fertilized ovum (zygote). . . . The time of fertilization represents the starting point in the life history, or ontogeny, of the individual."[38] And Ronan O'Rahilly and Fabiola Muller assert that "although life is a continuous process, fertilization is a critical landmark because, under ordinary circumstances, a new, genetically distinct human organism is thereby formed. . . . The embryo now exists as a genetic unity."[39]

Denying the Facts of Science

Nevertheless, Weissman and others want to pretend that the embryo prior to implantation in the mother's womb is somehow fundamentally different, different in its very nature, from the embryo afterward. In doing so they continue a long and unhappy chapter of Western medicine.

The first step in denying "what everyone really knows" was taken in 1970, when *California Medicine*, the journal of the California Medical Association, invited its members to play a new game, "semantic gymnastics." The rules of this new game were the "avoidance of the scientific fact, which everyone really knows, that human life begins at conception and is continuous whether intra- or extra-uterine until death."[40] The purpose of this new game was to replace "the traditional Western ethic" respecting "the intrinsic worth and equal value of every human life regardless of its state or condition" with "a new ethic for medicine and society" in order "to separate the idea of abortion from the idea of killing."[41]

During the 1970s, the dehumanization of the unborn was taken a step further. Richard McCormick and others promoted the idea of the "pre-embryo," the embryo before it implanted in the womb. Certainly the embryo at this point is "preimplantation," that is, it has not yet implanted in the uterus. Implantation is a highly significant event: unless it implants, the

---

[37]Keith L. Moore and T. V. N. Persaud, *The Developing Human: Clinically Oriented Embryology*, 6th ed. (Philadelphia: W. B. Saunders, 1998), p. 18.

[38]Bruce M. Carlson, *Patten's Foundations of Embryology*, 6th ed. (New York: McGraw-Hill, 1996), p. 3.

[39]Ronan O'Rahilly and Fabiola Muller, *Human Embryology and Teratology*, 2nd ed. (New York: Wiley-Liss, 1996), pp. 8, 29.

[40]Editorial, *California Medicine: The Western Journal of Medicine*, September 1970, p. 67.

[41]Ibid.

embryo dies; if it implants, it receives nutrition and a safe environment in which to live, grow and develop.[42] But the critical question is, does implantation effect a change in the *nature* of the thing that implants? Embryologists are united in asserting that it does not.[43] In the 2001 edition of his leading textbook on embryology, O'Rahilly states, "The term 'pre-embryo' is not used here for the following reasons. . . . It may convey the erroneous idea that a new human organism is formed at only some considerable time after fertilization . . . [and] it was introduced in 1986 largely for public policy reasons."[44]

For what public policy reasons was the term *pre-embryo* invented? Princeton biology professor (and noted advocate for all the new biotechnologies) Lee Silver supplies the answer:

> I'll let you in on a secret. The term pre-embryo has been embraced wholeheartedly by IVF practitioners for reasons that are political, not scientific. The new term is used to provide the illusion that there is something profoundly different between a six-day old embryo and a 16-day old embryo. The term is useful in the political arena—where decisions are made about whether to allow early embryo experimentation—as well as in the confines of a doctor's office where it can be used to allay moral concerns that might be expressed by IVF patients.[45]

As Christian ethicist Gilbert Meilaender has noted, the pre-embryo is merely the *unimplanted* embryo. In other words, it is already an embryo, and all embryos are at first "unimplanted." Embryos subsequently implant unless something (or someone) interferes or the embryo is defective. The term *pre-embryo* was developed to avoid something everyone really knows—that life is continuous from the first moment (whether through fertilization or cloning) until death. The term *pre-embryo* was developed and used largely, if not exclusively, to mislead; to hide scientific facts about the beginnings and unity of human life; to bolster support for a new reproductive technology; and to obtain funding for experiments on human embryos. It has also had a life beyond these areas and has been adopted by some American courts. The

---

[42]All human beings—whether embryo, fetus, infant, adolescent or adult—need precisely the same things: nutrition and a safe environment. Without them, a woman, hale and hearty, intelligent and virtuous, will die, just as the embryo will.

[43]It is an embryo from the first moment. See, e.g., *The Harper Collins Illustrated Medical Dictionary* (New York: Harper Perennial, 1993), p. 146: "Embryo: an organism in the earliest stage of development: in a man, from the time of conception to the end of the second month in the uterus."

[44]Ronan O'Rahilly and Fabiola Muller, *Human Embryology and Teratology*, 3rd ed. (New York: Wiley-Liss. 2001), p. 88.

[45]Lee M. Silver, *Remaking Eden: Cloning and Beyond in a Brave New World* (New York: Avon, 1997), p. 39.

result has been that the embryo is treated more like property than like a human being.[46]

Dishonesty in the Debate About Cloning

Though the term *pre-embryo* has been rejected in science, the central idea behind it—the dehumanizing of the early embryo in order to justify its destruction—lives on.[47] In May 2003 it was part of the debate over the banning of human cloning just as it was present, a few months earlier, in the debate over the funding of human embryonic stem cell research.

In the cloning debate, the desire to "deny what everyone really knows" (per the strategy of *California Medicine* above) by finding language that would hide the facts about human life has been so convoluted that it would be amusing if lives were not at stake. First, proponents of cloning tried to deny that cloning created a human embryo. Since, they argued, the new entity did not result from sexual reproduction, it was not an "embryo." For reasons I have indicated (the nature of the thing as a living, genetically complete, unified, self-integrating human organism in the first stage of development), few have been taken in by that ploy. Even prominent advocates of embryonic stem cell research, such as Dr. John Gearhart of Johns Hopkins University, have acknowledged that the "thing" created by cloning is an embryo.[48]

Some have asserted that the *location* of the thing in a Petri dish or in an IVF clinic (i.e., outside a woman's womb) means it is not an embryo. They assert that since it will never be implanted in a womb, but will instead be used in research, it can never be a human being. For reasons discussed above, this is scientifically ridiculous. The argument is a variation on the theme of "potentiality." In other words, since the thing lacks the potential to be born, it is not a human being. However, it is disingenuous for those who would deprive the embryo of the chance to be born to claim that *their action* changes the status of the thing considered. This is like the Nazis claiming that concentration camp

---

[46]In *Davis* v. *Davis*, 842 S.W.2d 588 (1992), the Tennessee Supreme Court held that the "pre-embryo" occupied an intermediate position between property and humanity. The opinion was cited as authority in several other cases, such as *J.B.* v. *M.B.*, 2001 W.L. 909294 (N.J. 2001), which held that an ex-wife could not be forced by her ex-husband to "procreate" through having the IVF-produced "pre-embryos" implanted in someone else, with the consequence that the "pre-embryos" could be destroyed. If there is a properly executed document, these cases permit frozen but living embryonic human beings to be destroyed, effectively treating them as any other "personal property" to be disposed of per the will of the parties. It should be noted that it is ordinarily against public policy for two individuals to contract to kill a third.

[47] For a good overview of the linguistic distortions, see Neil Munro, "Cloning: The Language of Biotech—It's No Science," *National Journal*, December 17, 2001.

[48]See the testimony of Dr. John Gearhart on April 25, 2002, at the third meeting of the President's Council on Bioethics <http://www.bioethics.gov/meetings >.

inmates are not human beings *because* the Nazis intend to destroy them during lethal experiments.[49] Every human being, by virtue of that fact, is full of inherent potential. That potential may never be realized, or it may be impeded in particular cases in some intrinsic way. But that potential—to live, to grow and to develop—is part of what it means to be a human being.

Next, cloning advocates posited a distinction between "reproductive cloning" and "therapeutic cloning." But such a distinction collapses under its own weight. Once you have created a living human zygote, the *reproduction* of a member of the human species has occurred, *regardless* of the purpose (birth or experiment) for which the clone was created. Thus, *all* human cloning is reproductive.

Likewise, "therapeutic cloning" cannot be therapeutic.[50] For a treatment to be therapeutic, it must be so for the *subject*, not for someone else. Medical ethics have always insisted that there be greater protection for the subject when the subject is not himself benefited by the procedure.[51] Yet "therapeutic cloning" kills the subject (the embryo) every time (in order to get stem cells). Thus, it is clearly *nontherapeutic*. Given that the distinction between therapeutic and nontherapeutic procedures is so well established, with greater protection accorded to subjects in nontherapeutic experiments, the cloning proponents' decision to use the term *therapeutic* is even more troubling.[52] It is difficult to imagine that this was not an intentional effort to confuse the issue.

After opinion polls revealed that Americans did not like any kind of clon-

---

[49]Just as some of those inmates did survive the camps, so too some frozen embryos have been implanted and brought to live birth. See Mona Charen, "Another Kind of Adoption," *Jewish World Review,* February 29, 2001 <http://www.jewishworldreview.com/cols/charen022801.asp>.

[50]This is not to deny that the aim of the experiment is to identify cures for sick or injured people. But it is to assert that such an aim is wholly irrelevant to whether the experiment is "therapeutic."

[51]"In regard to pure or nontherapeutic research, the Nuremberg Code is as vital a document today as it was when it was created." Leonard H. Glantz, "The Influence of the Nuremberg Code on U.S. Statutes and Regulations," in *The Nazi Doctors and the Nuremberg Code: Human Rights in Human Experimentation*, ed. George J. Annas and Michael A. Grodin (Oxford: Oxford University Press, 1992), p. 199.

[52]"Concern for the individual subject's welfare and autonomy must take precedence over the interests of science and society. All enlightened codes and regulations, beginning with the Nuremberg Code and including the Helsinki declarations and the U.S. federal regulations, appeal to and buttress this principle. In a therapeutic trial, particularly one in which subjects stand to gain greatly, they may be willing to take proportionately greater risks, and this may be ethically permitted. In a nontherapeutic trial, however, where no benefit is expected for the subjects themselves, the risks should be vanishingly small, or 'minimal,' in the words of the federal regulations." Marcia Angell, "Editorial Responsibility: Protecting Human Rights by Restricting Publication of Unethical Research," in *The Nazi Doctors and the Nuremberg Code: Human Rights in Human Experimentation*, ed. George J. Annas and Michael A. Grodin (Oxford: Oxford University Press, 1992), p. 277.

ing, whatever the adjectival modifier,[53] the biotech industry took a breathtakingly bold gamble: they simply decided to *rename* the procedure. It would now be called *somatic cell nuclear transfer* or *nuclear transplantation to produce stem cells*. This is breathtakingly simple and utterly dishonest, for both phrases are simply the *definition* of cloning itself. In other words, when one speaks about cloning, one is speaking about a laboratory procedure in which the *nucleus* from a *somatic* (body) cell is *transferred* or *transplanted* into an egg cell from which the original nucleus has been removed—that's what *cloning* means. To substitute the definition of the term for the term and then to pretend the two connote different things is plainly dishonest.

Even worse, with the phrase *nuclear transplantation to produce stem cells*, cloning advocates obscured the fact that the procedure does *not* produce stem cells but rather produces an *embryo* that is later killed so its stem cells can be removed.[54] We would not describe the murder of inmates in the Nazi camps as "experiments to preserve the life of pilots who crash into freezing water." Nor can we permit the *purpose* of the embryo creation (i.e., to harvest stem cells) to be used to disguise the fact that *embryos* are being created, killed and "disaggregated."

These "semantic gymnastics" are in reality not a new game but an old game, a game in which human lives are sacrificed for the sake of ideology, while everyone purports not to know what is really going on. George Orwell, the author of *1984* and *Animal Farm*, observed in his essay "Politics and the English Language" the game being played in his day:

> In our time, political speech and writing are largely the defense of the indefensible. . . . Political language has to consist largely of euphemism, question-begging, and sheer cloudy vagueness. Defenseless villages are bombarded from the air, the inhabitants driven out into the countryside, the cattle machine-gunned, the huts set on fire with incendiary bullets: this is called pacification. Millions of peasants are robbed of their farms and sent trudging along the roads with no

---

[53]Complete Gallup poll analysis accessed at
<www.gallup.com/poll/content/default.asp?ci=6022&pg=1>.

[54]Sadly, this obfuscation continues in one of the "cloning" bills pending before the U.S. Senate in May 2003. S. 303, the "Human Cloning Ban and Stem Cell Research Protection Act of 2003," defines "human cloning" as follows: "The term 'human cloning' means implanting or attempting to implant the product of nuclear transplantation into a uterus or the functional equivalent of a uterus." And it defines "nuclear transplantation" as follows: "The term 'nuclear transplantation' means transferring the nucleus of a human somatic cell into an ooctye from which the nucleus or all chromosomes have been or will be removed or rendered inert." Thus, S. 303 confuses cloning with the transfer of the cloned human being into a uterus. It bans the transfer, not the cloning, of the embryo. For criticism of the bill along these lines, see the testimony of Leon Kass (chairman of the President's Council on Bioethics) on March 19, 2003, before the Senate Judiciary Committee. In light of the undisputed facts of science discussed herein, it is difficult to believe these errors were not intentional.

more than they can carry: this is called transfer of population or rectification of frontiers. People are imprisoned for years without trial, or shot in the back of the neck, or sent to die of scurvy in Arctic lumber camps: this is called elimination of unreliable elements. Such phraseology is needed if one wants to name things without calling up mental pictures of them.[55]

Christians, however, have not the option of "political euphemism." Our task—our reason for being—is to tell truth. The prophet thunders, "Woe to those who call evil good and good evil, who put darkness for light and light for darkness" (Is 5:20).

Christians know there is power in the name.[56] The name carries the essence of the reality it signifies. Peter and John, for instance, healed in the temple "in the name of Jesus Christ of Nazareth" (Acts 3:6). Paul exorcised demons "in the name of Jesus" (Acts 16:18). John writes "to you who believe in the name of the son of God" (1 Jn 5:13). Paul writes that "God has highly exalted him and bestowed on him the name which is above every name, that at the name of Jesus every knee should bow, in heaven and on earth and under the earth, and every tongue confess that Jesus Christ is Lord" (Phil 2:9-11 RSV).[57] The name of Jesus, because it carries (and because it is) truth, has power. [58] Woe to us, indeed, if we do not call things by their proper names.

America's Historical Role in Unethical Research

While failing to tell the truth about the human embryo is one error the proponents of cloning make, they make another, and it is perhaps even more fundamental. Weissman and other advocates of cloning and of stem cell research, who adhere to the Nuremberg Code in word but are unable to analyze their

---

[55]For the complete text of George Orwell's essay "Politics and the English Language," please see <http://www.resort.com/~prime8/Orwell/patee.html>.

[56]"Throughout the Bible, names are full of meaning. Scholars have long recognized that both for ancient Israel and the ancient Near East as well as for early Judaism and Christianity, the name of a person, place, or thing was somehow connected to and descriptive of its essence and/or personality. Thus names of individuals expressed their personality and status or nature." See "Names and Namegiving," *Oxford Companion to the Bible*, ed. Bruce M. Metzger and Michael D. Coogan (Oxford: Oxford University Press, 1993), p. 545. See also "Name of Jesus," *Oxford Dictionary of the Christian Church*, ed. F. L. Cross and E. A. Livingstone, 3rd ed. (Oxford: Oxford University Press, 1997): "In consequence of the close relation between name and person, the Name of Jesus is used in the NT as a synonym for Jesus Himself, denoting His character and authority. . . . This reverence for, and confidence in, the Name of Jesus has found expression in the Church from early times."

[57]See also Heb 1:4, noting that Jesus has become "as much superior to angels as the name he has inherited is more superior to theirs."

[58]This is, of course, as true for the Father as for the Son. See, e.g., Dan 2:20 ("Praise be to the name of God for ever and ever; wisdom and power are his") and 1 Chron 29:13 ("Now, our God, we give you thanks, and praise your glorious name").

own actions in its light, appear to believe it applies to some "others"—to Nazis, presumably, and other bad persons, but not to themselves. They seem to think the world is divided into two types of people: "bad" people, like Nazis, who have to be constrained by the Nuremberg Code, and "good" people, like themselves. Because of the enormity of their crimes, it is easy to think of the Nazis as evil by nature and as demonic and fundamentally different from ourselves. It is easy to do so, but it is wrong.

We saw above that it was not Nazi ideology (in the sense that such views originated with the Nazis) that lead to the unethical experiments on human beings. Rather it was a shared social milieu in which some human beings were seen as unworthy of respect and in which some human lives were judged fundamentally inferior to others.

For Americans, the parallel to slavery is obvious. In each case classes of human beings were defined in important ways as nonhuman and were treated accordingly. However, just as Jews sometimes understand the Holocaust in a way that limits its application to other instances of injustice, so too Americans sometimes see slavery as a unique evil, rendering it of little help in understanding our contemporary challenges. Perhaps if we reflect on the historical record of unethical medical and scientific practices in the American past, we will be better able to guard against it in the present.

On May 2, 2002, Virginia Governor Mark R. Warner issued a public apology for Virginia's campaign of forced sterilization.[59] In the years from 1924 to 1979, 7,450 sterilizations were conducted in Virginia as part of the eugenics movement, which sought to improve the genetic stock by rendering the "unfit" unable to reproduce. The governor's apology was issued on the seventy-fifth anniversary of the Supreme Court's decision in *Buck* v. *Bell*, which upheld Virginia's eugenics law. In that decision renowned jurist Oliver Wendell Holmes, in justifying forcible sterilizations of the "unfit," noted, "Three generations of imbeciles is enough."[60]

Virginia's eugenics program was scarcely unique. There were such programs throughout the United States, in every region—in the West, Midwest, South and Northeast.[61] There were 20,108 sterilizations in California alone. There were more sterilizations in Vermont than in Alabama; more in Michigan than in Georgia. In total more than 60,000 people were sterilized nationwide.

Social Darwinism, the "survival of the fittest" theory as applied to human communal life, was widely accepted and practiced around the world. How-

---

[59]Bill Baskerville, "Virginia Governor Apologizes for Eugenics Law," Associated Press, May 2, 2002.

[60]*Buck* v. *Bell*, 274 U.S. 200, 207 (1927).

[61]Philip R. Reilly, *The Surgical Solution: A History of Involuntary Sterilization in the United States* (Baltimore: Johns Hopkins University Press, 1991).

ever, "before Hitler, the United States led the world in forced sterilizations."[62] We should realize, too, that

> it was the United States that provided the most important model for German sterilization laws. . . . German racial hygienists during the Weimar period expressed their envy of American achievements in this area, warning that unless the Germans made progress in this field, America would become the world's racial leader.[63]

America's role in forcible sterilizations, in the name of eugenics, should demonstrate that it was hardly only Nazis, or Germans, or people alive in the first part of the twentieth century, who were disposed to engage in research and experimentation on human subjects that would be universally condemned today. Rather it is possible for anyone, from any country, to do so.

> It is important to understand the atmosphere that can give rise to ethical violations in human studies. In biomedical research, the competition for funding is growing increasingly intense. An important criterion for funding is evidence of past productivity. To receive a grant from the National Institutes of Health, the source of most funding, a researcher must submit a proposal that includes an account of past work, with a list of prior publications. Thus, there is a strong incentive to complete and publish as many studies as possible. In addition, status and promotion at the researcher's institution depend on a strong record of past work, in particular on a long list of publications—the tangible measures of past work. In this atmosphere, there is an understandable desire to do studies that are both scientifically rigorous and capable of being completed quickly. Unfortunately, it is often easier and more efficient to get answers to scientific questions if the rights of human subjects are violated.[64]

The Line Between Good and Evil

"The line separating good and evil," Aleksandr Solzhenitsyn reminds us, "passes . . . through every human heart. . . . [And] this line shifts [back and forth]."[65] Solzhenitsyn chronicled and suffered under an ideology, and a regime embodying that ideology, that denied the dignity of each and every human being. Communist Russia killed perhaps as many innocent people as did Nazi Germany. However, Solzhenitsyn did not regard the perpetrators as inhuman monsters. Rather, he saw the essential truth: they were human beings engaged in immoral acts. They engaged in those acts by dehumanizing the persons on whom they inflicted their brutality, and they did so in the name of

---

[62]United States Holocaust Museum, *Handicapped* (pamphlet).

[63]Proctor, "Nazi Doctors," p. 21.

[64]Angell, "Editorial Responsibility," p. 279.

[65]Aleksandr Solzhenitsyn, *The Gulag Archipelago,* trans. Thomas P. Whitney (New York: Harper & Row, 1973), p. 168 <http://www.spartacus.schoolnet.co.uk/Russolzhenitsyn.htm>.

(and while perhaps passionately believing in) a greater good. Solzhenitsyn reminds us that unless we are willing to admit that we are also capable of inhuman acts, for the best as well for the worst motives, we will have no guard against committing them.

This is the lesson to be drawn from the gulags and the concentration camps: No one is safe from brutality so long as we think that it is only others who are capable of inhuman acts. Rather we will be secure only when we are willing to look honestly at the objective reality of our acts, realizing that we, too, are capable of acts that violate the inherent dignity of another. This is the reality of original sin. Wisdom begins in the recognition of our own human weakness. We will be secure only when we refuse to engage in unethical acts despite the good we believe would result from doing otherwise.

In the end, then, the debate about the embryo is not about the embryo at all. Rather it is about us, about our culture, about our ethics. How will we treat the stranger among us? Will we treat her as a nonhuman, as a nonperson? Will we use her and exploit her? Or will we recognize that every person, at whatever stage of development, is stamped with the imago Dei—the very image of God (Gen 1:26)?

It is time to end the debate about the human embryo. This "debate" merely cloaks an ideological and political agenda. The human embryo *is* a human being. As such, he is entitled to our complete respect. He may not be sacrificed on the altar of scientific progress or on the altar of "compassion" (for others).

In light of this, we must heed the admonition of Scripture. "If you say, 'But we knew nothing about this,' does not he who weighs the heart perceive it? Does not he who guards your life know it? Will he not repay each person according to what he has done?" (Prov 24:12).

As Christians, this is a truth we know. It is our job to never cease reminding our culture of that truth.

7

LEARNING FROM OUR MISTAKES

The Pro-life Cause and the New Bioethics

PAIGE COMSTOCK CUNNINGHAM, J.D.

From her perspective as former president and board chair of America's oldest national pro-life organization, Paige Cunningham reviews the history of the pro-life movement, seeking lessons for our engagement in debate on biotechnology. She deplores the slow pace of evangelical engagement in the pro-life cause and notes the extraordinary speed with which biotech developments are announced.

Seeing the issues of abortion and biotech as "fraternal twins," she pleads for an urgent pro-life engagement in the wider biotech agenda in which the self-same sanctity and dignity of human life are under attack. She notes that one of the features of the debate about human cloning has been a coming together of pro-life and pro-choice leaders in joint activity. Suggesting that this may be costly for those whose own constituencies do not grasp the significance of collaboration, she urges those on both sides of the abortion debate to work together on these new questions—despite their conscientious and vigorous disagreement on abortion.

This is an important assessment of the current situation, since most of the political and cultural energy available to address the biotech agenda is presently locked up in the pro-life movement. The cloning question has drawn the pro-life organizations into their first engagement with the biotech agenda, and the patenting of embryos is another area where they have a plain commitment. However, the pro-life community's focus on abortion needs to be balanced by a parallel commitment to the broader, unfolding agenda in which the defense of human dignity is needed just as much.

NIGEL M. DE S. CAMERON

After more than two decades of experience in the pro-life movement, I am alarmed at the likelihood that history is about to repeat itself. We—the evangelical church—were slow to comprehend the corrosive effects of legalized abortion and even slower to claim a personal stake in tempering its devastation of future generations. The "it doesn't happen here" attitude was replaced by "it's happening here so I must be careful not to offend the women in my congregation" attitude.

So it is with the tidal wave of biotech issues racing toward us from the horizon. In our near-idolatry of children, we've moved from acquiescing in AIH (artificial insemination by husband) to acquiescing in AID (artificial insemination by donor) for single would-be moms; from accepting the obstetrician's "you're young, let this one die and try again for a healthy baby," to accepting prenatal testing for fetal anomalies whose only "cure" is abortion. How readily we comfort ourselves by denying that biotech issues have anything to do with the church or by throwing up our hands in despair at the impossibility of stopping the unstoppable.

We have time for neither denial nor despair.

The pro-life movement measures its generations by decades. I joined the pro-life movement as a law student over twenty years ago and am now part of the "second" generation. Some of my mentors—the founding fathers and mothers, if you will—have died. Former students of mine and other third-generation enthusiasts are now working on pro-life issues for members of Congress and state legislators. The fourth generation sits in the classrooms and pews. The cataclysmic "thud" of *Roe* v. *Wade* has reverberated for thirty years. Wave after wave of court battles have succeeded in securing some regulation of abortion. Yet abortion on demand is still the law of the land.

Meanwhile, biotechnology is developing at lightning speed. Its generations are measured in months, not years. Public policy, public opinion and moral insights are not keeping pace. Many of us are overwhelmed by biotech's promises of longer lives, good health and outstanding children. But are all these innovations right? The dazzling potential of corporate profits and private health benefits threatens to sweep these ethical concerns aside.

Nigel Cameron has helpfully organized the three generations of bioethics. The first generation—Bioethics 1, if you will—is the one most familiar to the pro-life movement. It includes abortion, infanticide, euthanasia, assisted suicide and assisted reproduction.[1] These primarily involve *taking life*. Bioethics 2 is about embryonic stem cell research (ESCR), human cloning, genetic engineering (both somatic and germline), gene patenting, genetic testing and genetic discrimination: *making life*. Bioethics 3 issues include cybernetics, nanotechnology, neurological manipulation and transgenics. These are about *faking life*, that is, "dis-integrating" the biological human and melding him with other species or machines.

---

[1] Assisted reproduction includes in vitro fertilization, artificial insemination by donor, gamete intrafallopian transfer, posthumous reproduction, surrogate motherhood and other collaborative reproduction.

The pro-life movement is primarily devoted to Bioethics 1 issues, and almost exclusively to abortion. The deaths of more than forty million young humans in the United States alone are ample justification for single-minded passion. But assaults against the value of the individual human being, and ultimately against the human race, are unrelenting. Stopping abortion today will not stop the exploitation, experimentation and extermination of future generations of nascent human beings. Children in the infertility clinic and biotech laboratory are at greater risk than are children in the womb, who have at least a three-out-of-four chance of survival until birth.

Can the pro-life movement see the connections? Can we learn any lessons from the abortion debate? Can we permeate our culture with ethical policies—policies that reject those biotechnologies that threaten the human future?

The Abortion Legal Strategy: From Challenging *Roe* to Changing the Culture

With the ever-growing number of postabortive women and those in relationship with them, abortion is becoming so common that it is in danger of becoming commonplace. The strategy to fight abortion in the courts was intended to reverse an abhorrent legal doctrine, to establish life-affirming public policies and to affect private attitudes and behavior so that abortion would not become culturally acceptable. For the first two decades of abortion on demand, the legal strategy was designed to respond to the Supreme Court's ill-founded creation of abortion rights. Then we were stunned by the Court's dismissal of constitutional arguments in favor of its perception that our society relies on abortion. We learned the lesson that *our courts both dictate cultural change and respond to it.*

Roe's Three-Legged Stool

Privacy. The *Roe* v. *Wade* decision relied on three central legal doctrines. The first is that abortion is a species of *privacy* right, protected in the "penumbras" emanating from various constitutional provisions.[2] Building on its decisions in two contraception cases, the Court found that one's privacy right to *prevent*

---

[2]In cases dating back to the early twentieth century, an implicit notion of familial privacy was deemed to protect matters such as the choice of a mate, freedom from involuntary sterilization, freedom to direct the education and religious upbringing of one's children, and freedom to use contraceptives in the marital bedroom. However, in a pivotal shift, the Court decided in the 1972 case of *Eisenstadt* v. *Baird* that constitutional privacy was not about marriage and family after all: "If the right of privacy means anything, it is the right of the *individual,* married or single, to be free from unwarranted governmental intrusion into matters so fundamentally affecting a person as the decision whether to bear or beget a child." *Eisenstadt* v. *Baird,* 405 U.S. 438, 453 (1972), emphasis in original.

a pregnancy also included the right to *terminate* a pregnancy. Subsequent cases revealed how truly isolating this notion is. Parents of a teenage girl may not prevent her abortion. A husband is not entitled to find out about his wife's pregnancy and the abortion of their child. And for a number of years, the abortionist was free not to tell his customer what he was going to do to her, the developmental stage of the fetus he would abort or the physical risks the mother faced.

Viability. *Roe* also relied on the legal point that the state has a compelling interest in protecting the fetus after *viability* and might even prohibit abortion at that stage. However, that state interest proved to be illusory. The Court added that states must permit abortions, even of a viable fetus, if necessary for the mother's health. In *Doe* v. *Bolton*, the Court defined *health* in the broadest possible terms.[3] Health includes anything "physical, emotional, psychological, familial, and the woman's age—relevant to the wellbeing [*sic*] of the patient."[4] Thus distress over her pregnancy is a constitutionally sufficient justification for a woman to terminate her pregnancy by abortion at any time. In effect states could not prohibit any abortion. As will be seen, although the state is hampered from protecting the child in utero, it may do so in other contexts.

Personhood. The third major legal doctrine bears particular significance for many of the challenges posed by new biotechnologies. This was the Court's conclusion that the unborn child is not a *person* for constitutional purposes. Justice Harry Blackmun, writing for the majority, observed that if the Fourteenth Amendment's use of the word *person* included the unborn child, Jane Roe would have no case, for the Fourteenth Amendment guarantees that no person may be deprived of life by the state without due process of law.[5] However, Justice Blackmun turned this limitation on government action into what Hadley Arkes called "a private right to kill."[6] By concluding that the fetus is not a constitutional person, the Court decided that he has no legal interest that could outweigh his mother's right to privacy, that is, her unfettered choice.

The devastating consequence of this legally imposed doctrine of abortion

---

[3]*Doe* v. *Bolton*, 410 U.S. 179 (1973).

[4]*Doe*, 410 U.S. at 192.

[5]The Fourteenth Amendment states, inter alia, "nor shall any State deprive any person of life, liberty, or property, without due process of law; nor deny to any person within its jurisdiction the equal protection of the laws."

[6]Hadley Arkes, "Prudent Warnings and Imprudent Reactions," in *The End of Democracy? II: A Crisis of Legitimacy*, ed. Mitchell S. Muncy (Dallas: Spence, 1999), pp. 44-85. "And my friend Russell Hittinger summed up our own situation in this way a few years ago: We have now created a private right to use lethal force, a private right to kill, for wholly private reasons. One person may now claim to kill a second person, a second being, for reasons that may not rise above convenience, and under those conditions a third person may not object" (pp. 64-65).

on demand throughout pregnancy was far beyond what anyone imagined. The number of legalized abortions soared as quickly as abortion mills could be built. In some cities the abortion rate nearly equaled the birth rate. Abortion was not safe or rare, just legal. Women continued to be maimed and killed by abortionists who moved from the back alley to Main Street. The kindly family physician envisioned by Justice Blackmun was replaced by anonymous out-of-state abortionists.

Reeling from *Roe*

The *Roe* and *Doe* legal doctrines presented a formidable challenge. In response Americans United for Life and others tested the extent of the newly created abortion license. The initial pro-life strategy focused on the legislatures. When the Supreme Court legalized abortion, it left the door open for state regulation. The strategy to change public policy focused on introducing bills in state legislatures, educating the public through committee hearings and defending the enacted laws when they were inevitably challenged in court.[7]

The pro-life movement also attempted to reverse the damage of *Roe* at the national level. One tactic was the Human Life Bill, introduced in 1981, which declared that the unborn child is a person from conception.[8] Another was the movement's multiple attempts to amend the Constitution, the only way to overcome the Supreme Court's decisions. One version that would have returned to the states their authority to regulate abortion attracted enormous attention during committee hearings. It failed in the Senate by 49-50, short of the two-thirds vote needed for passage.[9]

Meanwhile, changes in the makeup of the Supreme Court raised hopes for changes in its abortion doctrine. In 1983 the newest member of the Court, Justice Sandra Day O'Connor, dissented vigorously from a 6-3 decision striking down a municipal ordinance that required hospitalization, parental consent, detailed informed consent and a waiting period.[10] She fumed that "the *Roe*

---

[7]With few exceptions these regulations were struck down as unconstitutional by the Supreme Court. In the first decade after *Roe*, the Court rejected parental consent, spousal consent, a ban on saline abortions, a hospitalization requirement, detailed informed consent, a 24-hour waiting period, a requirement for "humane" disposal of fetal remains and medical care for a previable fetus. On the bright side, we won a significant victory in two cases which held that neither Congress nor the states are required to fund "medically necessary" abortions. *Harris v. McRae*, 448 U.S. 297 (1980), federal Medicaid funding of abortions limited by the Hyde amendment; *Williams v. Zbaraz*, 448 U.S. 358 (1980), state Medicaid funding.

[8] The summary and status of this bill (H.R. 900, 97th Cong., 1st sess.) can be found at <http://thomas.loc.gov/bss/d097query.html>. (The URLs cited in this chapter were accessed on January 16, 2004.)

[9]The Hatch-Eagleton amendment provided that "a right to abortion is not secured by this Constitution." <http://thomas.loc.gov/bss/d097query.html>.

[10]*Akron v. Akron Center for Reproductive Health*, 462 U.S. 416 (1983).

framework . . . is clearly on a collision course with itself" and that "there is no justification in law or logic for the trimester framework adopted in *Roe* and employed by the Court today."[11] Building on that implicit invitation, Americans United for Life ignited a strategy to reverse *Roe* through the courts by attacking *Roe*'s weakest pillars of legal and constitutional reasoning.

Life Without *Roe*?

By 1989 newly appointed Justices Antonin Scalia and Anthony Kennedy had shifted the balance to 5-4 in favor of upholding state abortion regulations. In *Webster* v. *Reproductive Health Services,* the Court upheld both Missouri's ban on using public facilities or public funds for abortion and its fetal-viability testing requirement.[12] Three years later the Court seemed poised to reverse *Roe* in *Planned Parenthood* v. *Casey.* It was a silver cloud that burst to reveal a dark lining. The Court upheld most of Pennsylvania's abortion regulations (informed consent, waiting period, reporting and parental consent) but reaffirmed *Roe* v. *Wade.*[13] Rather than demolish the shaky legal and constitutional pillars of *Roe,* the Court ignored them, substituting "new and improved" arguments. The Court sidestepped the ephemeral right of privacy and decided that abortion is a species of liberty protected by the Fourteenth Amendment. Where *Roe* pretended abortion was a medical decision made by the physician, *Casey* ignored the doctor and focused on the woman as the sole decision maker.[14]

This highly fractured decision ultimately rested, I believe, on one central reality: the Court could not imagine life without abortion. The three authors of the Joint Opinion wrote:

> For two decades of economic and social developments, people have organized intimate relationships and made choices that define their views of themselves and their places in society, *in reliance on the availability of abortion* in the event that contraception should fail. The *ability of women to participate equally in the economic and social life of the Nation* has been facilitated by their ability to control their reproductive lives.[15]

This "reliance interest" seems to have overcome any judicial doubts about the prudence or constitutionality of abortion. The impressive number of briefs

---

[11] *Akron,* 462 U.S. at 458 and 459.

[12] *Webster* v. *Reproductive Health Services,* 492 U.S. 490 (1989).

[13] *Planned Parenthood of Southeastern Pennsylvania* v. *Casey,* 505 U.S. 833 (1992).

[14] For an in-depth analysis of *Casey* and its contrast with *Roe,* see Paul Benjamin Linton, "*Planned Parenthood* v. *Casey:* The Flight from Reason in the Supreme Court," *St. Louis University Public Law Review* 13, no. 1 (1993): 15-136.

[15] *Planned Parenthood,* 505 U.S. at 856 (emphasis added). The three authors of the Joint Opinion were Justices O'Connor, Kennedy and Souter. Incidentally, all of them were appointed by Republican presidents.

marshaling evidence about fetal development (illustrating the biological facts of the humanity of the unborn child); the legal, logical and historical fallacies of *Roe* (revealing its shaky legal foundation); states' rights to regulate abortion (recalling the Court to its proper role); and legal protection for women's rights independent of the abortion doctrine (separating women's rights from abortion rights) failed to persuade the Court. Although abortion may be regulated to protect maternal health, it cannot be banned to protect fetal life. Abortion was further entrenched as a constitutional right. The Supreme Court has not retreated.[16]

The task for the pro-life movement, then, was to plead our case no longer with the courts, but with the American people. As long as judges believe that women need abortion and that society relies on abortion, it will remain a constitutional right. We had to face the reality that in twenty years, we had not succeeded in eliminating the scourge of legal abortion. It was time for a new strategy. The lesson was this: *don't put all your strategy eggs in one basket.*

Connecting with the Culture: Abortion's Impact on Women

Casey dispelled any doubts about reversing abortion policy solely through legal maneuvers. We would have to convince the Court that America would be better off without abortion. Meanwhile, I dreamed of the day when *Roe* and *Casey* would be irrelevant because women would stop having abortions. This would not happen because of a brilliant argument about the personhood or humanity of the unborn child. ("You're right, it *is* a baby! Why didn't I think of that?") We needed to appeal to the culture in a way that people could hear us. In today's postmodernist society, when rational argument fails, an appeal to self-interest, couched in emotive language, might connect. We needed to begin with the person whose decision was immediately relevant—the mother.

We developed a strategy of three arcs, which one day will connect in a com-

---

[16]The justices' commitment to unrestricted abortion (i.e., they allow some regulations but not a direct prohibition) was confirmed eight years later, in *Stenberg* v. *Carhart*, 530 U.S. 914 (2000). The Court could not bring itself to uphold a restriction on partial-birth abortion, a particularly gruesome abortion procedure. (The child is partially delivered, then the cranial contents are evacuated and her skull is crushed, and then the delivery of an otherwise intact infant is completed.) In order to do so, the Court rejected traditional standards of statutory interpretation, deference to a state's interpretation of its own statute and its own standard of constitutional review of a facial challenge (one made before the law goes into effect). In *Hill* v. *Colorado*, 530 U.S. 703 (2000), a case handed down the same day as *Stenberg*, the Court upheld Colorado's law prohibiting anyone within one hundred feet of an abortion clinic to get closer than eight feet to another person to persuade her not to get an abortion. The Court bent over backwards to ignore Colorado's infringement of free speech. In a blistering dissent, Justice Scalia retorted that "there is apparently no end to the distortion of our First Amendment law that the Court is willing to endure in order to sustain this restriction upon the free speech of abortion opponents." *Hill*, 530 U.S. at 753.

plete circle. The first arc of the strategy was based on a veiled truth about abortion: *abortion hurts women*. The second arc directly addressed the "reliance interest" so central to *Casey: we can live without abortion*. Abortion is not necessary for women's social and economic equality.[17] The final arc completes the circle: *the Constitution must protect unborn children and their mothers from abortion*. The unborn child must be shielded from legalized abortion.

The Abortion Lesson: From Caring About Babies to Caring About Women

This strategy did not immediately resonate with pro-life leaders. These men and women had fought for years to establish laws that would protect all unborn children from abortion in any circumstance. They were joined by thousands of everyday heroes. What drew so many people to an effort that would not directly benefit them? Why join the thankless fight to save other people's children? It was just that—the children. Abortion was about killing babies, about child murder. Whether they thought of bloody pictures of aborted fetuses tossed in garbage cans or soft-focus photos of cuddly newborns, their near-universal attraction was to "saving babies." The women who aborted were seen, at best, as weak-willed victims and, at worst, as heartless, casual murderers.[18] But the passion to protect children sustained many.

The early pro-life movement gradually migrated toward three general spheres of pro-life activity. Many of us, myself included, were called to fight the issue on the public policy level, in the courts and legislatures. Others chose direct action, including sidewalk counseling, picketing and praying in front of abortion clinics. The third sphere served and dissuaded abortion-minded women, primarily through the work of crisis pregnancy centers. While those operating in the latter two spheres could use explicitly religious language, for the most part those of us in public policy did not. Even moderate references to the morality of abortion drew accusations of trying to impose our religious viewpoint on America.

As a law student, I was comfortable with secular arguments against abortion. I moved from my thoughtless, conveniently pro-choice views toward a pro-life position first as a matter of civil and constitutional rights. Justice was denied to an entire class of people—the unborn—simply because they resided in a hostile womb. I was not ashamed of my faith, which was the source of my

---

[17]Clarke D. Forsythe and Paige C. Cunningham, "Is Abortion the 'First Right' for Women?" in *Abortion, Medicine and the Law*, J. Douglas Butler and David F. Walbert, eds., 4th ed. (New York: Facts on File, 1992).

[18]One attorney told me in all seriousness that he opposed our efforts to require abortion clinics to meet health and safety standards because he thought abortions should be just as lethal for the mother as for the unborn child.

strength, and shared it openly one-on-one and with sympathetic audiences. However, I tried to do what the apostle Paul did, speaking to the audience in a way that did not alienate them. In a talk I gave at Middlebury College on a post-*Roe* America (before the *Casey* decision in 1992), I was nearly finished before some of the students realized I wasn't a pro-choice feminist. By then, they had heard how abortion has hurt women, how *Roe* did nothing to advance women's legal rights and that reversing *Roe* would be true progress for women. Needless to say, this approach drew animosity—from other pro-lifers. But it did open doors that otherwise would have remained closed.[19]

Eventually, cultural and legal realities caused leaders and volunteers to consider new approaches. (In truth I believe it was the inspiration of the Holy Spirit.) Twenty years after *Roe,* the abortion issue seemed at a stalemate; opinion polls showed little change. As I discussed above, the Supreme Court and lower courts resisted measures that might curtail any abortions. Furthermore, an in-depth survey of moral beliefs and attitudes about abortion commissioned by Americans United for Life drew some troubling conclusions.[20] Although the majority of Americans believed abortion is killing or taking the life of a child, a significant number felt it should still be the woman's right to choose an abortion.[21] They were unwilling to make the connection between killing and a public policy prohibiting or discouraging that killing. It was time to reevaluate our public communications strategy.

We had to learn the lesson of *understanding the consequences of abortion.* We had to look beyond the nauseating reality that every abortion causes at least one death. Abortion is also evil because of its impact on women, their families, social institutions and culture.

We also had to learn *how to communicate in a secularized public square.* For years we had relied on phrases like "thou shalt not kill," "it's a baby," "abortion kills children" and "every life is sacred." Religious language and imagery appealed to the pro-life faithful but bypassed secular culture. After two dec-

---

[19]In July 1993 I testified before the Senate Judiciary Committee against the confirmation of Ruth Bader Ginsburg to the Supreme Court. As part of a panel of professional women, I spoke about the failures of legalized abortion and how, contrary to Justice Ginsburg's assertion, women do not need it to preserve our dignity. Women have been hurt by abortion, and it is not necessary for our full participation in economic, social and political life. A college classmate who had seen me on C-SPAN called Americans United for Life and said, "I saw Paige on television. I'm pro-choice, but I never thought about it that way. I work across the street from an abortion clinic, and now I wonder about the women going through the door."

[20]The oldest pro-life organization in our country, Americans United for Life (<http://www.AUL.org>) continues as the only law firm dedicated exclusively to nationwide efforts to reinstate respect for human life in American law and culture.

[21]Clarke D. Forsythe, "Abortion Is Not a 'Necessary Evil,' " *Christianity Today,* May 24, 1999 <http://www.christianitytoday.com/ct/9t6/9t6063.html >.

ades, as we searched for ways to connect with the unpersuaded, we probed how best to change a woman's abortion decision. Because we could not convince her on basic moral premises (e.g., killing a person is wrong and the unborn child is a person), then we must find some other point of contact. That point was self-interest, and the particular self-interest was abortion's impact on women.

In order to make a difference, we had to paint a picture of how abortion affects women directly. There was mounting evidence that abortion hurts women physically, emotionally, psychologically and spiritually. This evidence was confirmed by the experiences of thousands of women. Many have told the truth about their abortion "choice" and about how they were trapped into something they didn't want:[22] her boyfriend emotionally abandoned her, and she got the abortion in a desperate attempt to preserve a relationship that ultimately failed. Her husband insisted that "we just can't afford another baby now," only to admit later that it might have been possible to make it.[23] A college co-ed raised in an evangelical home secretly got an abortion to avoid shaming her parents.[24] Abortion clinic counselors treated women like customers and sold them an abortion, saying, "it's just a blob of tissue," "it won't hurt," "you'll feel so relieved" or "it's the safest choice." To overcome her natural aversion to the procedure, a young mother rationalizes that if abortion is a *constitutional* right, it must also be *morally* right. After her womb is empty, in her isolation she wonders why a "right" feels so wrong.

Once we were willing to communicate in secular language, we found surprising secular arguments against abortion. Some feminist supporters of abortion agree it is not a free choice for women, but a "grim option," chosen because the alternatives seem even worse.[25] The need for abortion could be eliminated if there were significant social changes to support women throughout pregnancy, childbirth and child rearing, so that women would not bear these burdens alone.[26] We also had to communicate *genuine respect for women*

---

[22]David C. Reardon, *Aborted Women: Silent No More* (Springfield, Ill.: Acorn, 2002); Frederica Mathewes-Green, *Real Choices* (Salem, Oreg.: Multnomah, 1994).

[23]Sue Nathanson, *Soul Crisis: One Woman's Journey Through Abortion to Renewal* (New York: New American Library, 1989).

[24]Several students related similar stories to me in the class on abortion and law that I taught at Wheaton College from 1999 to 2001.

[25]Caroline Whitbeck, a pro-choice feminist, makes this argument. She says that the grim option of abortion is "selected only because of a still greater aversion to the only available alternative." Caroline Whitbeck, "Taking Women Seriously as People," in *The Abortion Controversy: Twenty-five Years After Roe* v. *Wade*, ed. Louis P. Pojman and Francis C. Beckwith (Belmont, Calif.: Wadsworth), p. 434.

[26]Sally Markowitz, "A Feminist Defense of Abortion," in *The Abortion Controversy: Twenty-five Years After Roe* v. *Wade*, ed. Louis P. Pojman and Francis C. Beckwith (Belmont, Calif.: Wadsworth), pp. 389-98.

by including women who were ambivalent about abortion in our discussions. A woman considering an abortion is a moral agent, but her freedom to make a moral choice is often clouded by coercion, misinformation and deception. Thus, to "make a difference," we must give her accurate, noncoercive information, time to reflect on it, the truth about how abortion can hurt her and meaningful alternatives.

We didn't need to hammer women with the message that "abortion is wrong." But on what basis could we connect? One strategy was based on a study commissioned by the Caring Foundation. Their "right brain" research probed the psychology of pro-choice women. The analysis examined why traditional approaches have had so little effect. Surprisingly, the women in the study agreed that abortion is morally wrong, that it kills a baby and that God will forgive those who abort.[27] They also believed that when faced with a crisis pregnancy, abortion is the only choice that makes sense in a woman's life. Because it is so difficult and painful, it is also seen as courageous. Consequently, a message that targets women's real needs and emotions does not focus on a cuddly baby. The pregnant woman already knows it's a baby.[28] But she needs to know that abortion's seemingly quick resolution to her crisis is neither easy or problem free; it creates more pain than it relieves. What's more, choosing birth is the truly courageous choice, one that resonates with her inner values. This message touches the pregnant woman in a way that can influence her behavior.

This reassessment and realignment of strategies and messages is making a difference. Telling the truth about abortion's harmful impact on women resonates with what women intuitively know. Women contemplating an abortion are painfully aware that it is not an easy solution. In communities where television commercials targeted abortion-minded women and post-abortive women, the abortion rate has gone down, and opposition to abortion has gone up.[29] The Caring Foundation has expanded its outreach to Gen-

---

[27]Paul Swope, "Abortion: A Failure to Communicate," *First Things* 82 (April 1998): 31-35. The market research provided the material for a series of creative television ads targeting abortion-minded and post-abortive women.

[28]I have a political button that reads, "If it's not a baby, you're not pregnant."

[29]In his article ("Abortion," p. 34), Swopes cited pre- and post-market research for the television campaign featuring "pro-woman" ads. In every market there was a measurable, lasting shift to the pro-life position: "Have the ads been effective? Swope says that in Missouri, where his foundation originated and the ads have aired for years, the abortion rate has dropped 29 percent. In Michigan and Wisconsin where the ads have also been broadcast for a number of years, abortions have declined almost 40 percent." Bruce Sullivan, "Pro-Life Ads Counter Slick Abortion Rights Campaign," Conservative News Service, December 4, 1998 <http://www.conservativenews.org/InDepth/archive/199812/IND19981204b.html>. See also Paul Tuns, "Pro-life Stand an Asset in Recent U.S. Elections," *The Interim,* January 1999 <http://www.lifesite.net/interim/1999/jan/21unselections.html>, which notes that pro-life voters are more committed to electing pro-life candidates than are pro-choice voters.

eration Y, targeting them with a website in their own style.[30]

Meanwhile, Americans United for Life continues our strategy of reforming public policy to the extent permitted by the Supreme Court. We've learned the lesson of *cooperation with unlikely allies.* We work together with those outside the stereotypical right-wing conservative, religious fanatic, pro-life movement. Legislators who want to keep abortion as an option for women may still support parental involvement laws. Women who are pro-choice are also concerned about the link between abortion and an increased risk of breast cancer. Some feminists support Woman's Right-to-Know (informed consent) laws, health reporting requirements and clinic safety regulations.[31] These measures focus on the health of teenagers and women, rather than on fetal protection. They appeal to the "safe" part of President Bill Clinton's alleged desire that abortion remain "safe, legal and rare." Some measures, such as parental notice and parental consent, reduce the frequency of abortion, as well as teen birth and pregnancy rates. Other bipartisan legislation supports meaningful alternatives to abortion, such as Project WIN (Women In Need).[32] Feminists for Life has a college outreach program that works with pro-choice groups on campus to enable pregnant students to continue their education with practical support such as prenatal care and child care.

Ironically, radical proponents of "choice" are the most vigorous opponents of protecting unborn children whose mothers chose to carry to term. Abortion advocates resist fetal homicide laws and the federal Unborn Victims of Violence Act (laws that make it an additional crime to kill an unborn child during the commission of a crime).[33] They claim that fetal rights are best protected by

---

[30]See <http://www.gravityteen.com>. Development of this outreach is described by Sandra Choate Faucher, "The New Kids on the Block—Everybody Wants Them!" *Life Issues Connector,* January 2003 <http://www.lifeissues.org/connector/display.asp?page=03jan.htm>.

[31]Recent publications detail the damage to women's health caused by abortion. See, e.g., Elizabeth Ring-Cassidy and Ian Gentles, *Women's Health After Abortion: The Medical and Psychological Evidence* (Toronto, Ontario: The de Veber Institute for Bioethics and Social Research, 2002); John M. Thorp Jr., Katherine E. Hartmann and Elizabeth Shadigian, "Long-Term Physical and Psychological Health Consequences of Induced Abortion: Review of the Evidence," *Obstetrical and Gynecological Survey* 58 (January 2003): 67-79.

[32]Project WIN (Women In Need) was developed in Pennsylvania by pro-life Governor Robert Casey. Public funds are given to organizations that provide women with alternatives to abortion and that assist them through pregnancy and childbirth and that help them care for their children. In the first three years of its operation, Pennsylvania saw a measurable decline in abortions. Liz Townsend, "Bill to Fund Alternatives to Abortion Introduced in Congress," National College Students for Life website <http://www.nrlc.org/news/1999/NRL1199/billfund.html>.

[33]NARAL attacked the Unborn Victims of Violence Act as "misguided." "The "Unborn Victims of Violence Act": A Misguided Bill That Threatens Women's Rights," NARAL website, January 1, 2004 <http://www.naral.org/mediaresources/fact/prosecutors.html>. NOW

enhancing maternal rights, that fetal homicide pits the mother against the fetus and that these laws surreptitiously establish personhood for the fetus.[34] What an irony that those who trumpet support for "choice" also decry opportunities to expand women's choices. Although women who intend to give birth routinely get sonograms, the abortion industry actively opposes this option for abortion-minded clients. New York Attorney General Elliot Spitzer mounted a campaign against crisis pregnancy centers, apparently at the behest of NARAL.[35]

Even though some alliances bridge ideological divides, the abortion ethic is a tough one to challenge. It is deeply intertwined with the organized feminist movement, which sees it as the single most important achievement for women. The culture of abortion has redefined relationships between women and men. Despite feminist complaints about the imbalance of power that favors men, men have no legally recognized stake in abortion. Responsible fathers who want to parent their child have no legal rights. An irresponsible man can psychologically pressure his girlfriend or wife into an abortion, thereby avoiding financial and social responsibilities. Women are isolated and abandoned.

Ironically, abortion is not necessary for women's political, economic or social rights. Instead of helping women have an equal place in society, I believe it has harmed women. Because of women's exclusive legal power over their unborn children, they are often saddled with sole responsibility for their born children. Men feel free to shirk responsible fatherhood. Women in the workplace are pressured to abort in order to keep a job or to get ahead.[36] The intim-

---

called it a "direct threat to *Roe* v. *Wade*." "NOW Denounces House Passage of Unborn Victims of Violence Act; Urges Senate to Defeat This Direct Threat to *Roe* v. *Wade*," National Organization of Women website, April 26, 2001 <http://www.now.org/press/04-01/04-26-01.html>. The Religious Coalition for Reproductive Choice huffed that it imposes "one religious view about the beginning of life" <http://www.rcrc.org/get_involved/legislative_action/uvva.htm>.

[34]Kate Michelman, president of National Abortion and Reproductive Rights Action League (at the time), said in an NPR interview that "granting services to the unborn is just another step toward the end of establishing the fetus as a person, separate and distinct from the woman under the law so that abortions can be criminalized down the line." Kate Michelman, interview on NPR's *All Things Considered*, July 26, 2001.

[35]Marvin Olasky, "Fighting for Life and Informed Choice," Creators Syndicate, January 22, 2002 <http://www.townhall.com/columnists/marvinolasky/mo20020122.shtml>. For Planned Parenthood's perspective on the Spitzer investigation, see <http://www.ppnyc.org/new/releases/inthenews/crisispregnancy.html>.

[36]The University of California at Berkeley recently settled a case brought by a former assistant coach. Sharrona Alexander testified that she was told she would have to choose between getting an abortion and retaining her job. Jessica Hopp and Greg Sandoval, "Mystics Coach Was Cited in Pregnancy Suit," *Washington Post*, September 16, 2002 <http://www.washingtonpost.com>.

idation comes not just from supervisors, but from fellow employees who resent any accommodation for mothers.

In addition to facing discrimination and coercion, women also experience physical and psychological harm from abortion.[37] The truth of this message continues to be reinforced by medical and psychological research.[38]

This reorientation is not an abandonment of our pro-life concern about abortion's deeper horror—the death of an individual human being at the hands of another. But it is a realistic appraisal that in the current cultural and legal climate the most effective way to reduce abortion is by appealing to the one who holds the decision-making power: the pregnant woman. As Dr. Jack Wilke puts it, we are challenged to "love them both." By opening the mother's eyes to the potentially devastating effect of abortion on her, we may persuade her to avoid what the courts and abortion counselors tell her is her personal and legal right. Her rejection of abortion forestalls harm to two people. Her child's physical life is saved, and she is spared physical, emotional and spiritual suffering.

Abortion and the New Biotechnologies: Is There a Legal Connection?

One element common to both the abortion mentality and the biotech industry is the expendability of the embryo and fetus. In the former case, the mother may abort her fetus for any or no reason, virtually throughout pregnancy. In the latter case, particularly in the "making life" biotechnologies (embryonic stem cell research and cloning), embryos may be cloned for research or used as raw material to produce stem cells. This disdain for embryonic human life is directly traceable to the abortion legal doctrine and culture. The lesson to be learned is this: *changes in law and policy profoundly affect attitudes about who is a protected human being.*

The distorted view of "personhood" in *Roe* and *Casey* had several devastating consequences that are relevant to the challenges posed by biotechnology. First, the legal status of the unborn child has been diminished. Legal abortion (or reproductive) rights lurk behind the notion that the embryo may be created, used and discarded for medical research. Second, the practical treatment of an embryo as a "zero" when weighed against her mother's desire to abort has hardened attitudes toward pregnancy and childbearing in general. Children are treated more and more as a commodity to be acquired when the marriage is intact, the time is right and the quality of the child is acceptable. The fate of frozen embryos is indicative of this. If one parent does not want their embryos implanted, his or her choice prevails over the desires of the other

---

[37] Many of these harms are catalogued at <http://www.afterabortion.org>.
[38] See, e.g., Thorp, Hartmann and Shadigian, "Long-Term Physical."

spouse. Our understanding that children are a gift from God is under attack. Third, our culture has cheapened the value of life. When the child in the womb—the place where she should be most protected—is legally expendable, those already born are threatened. Maternal violence against children may be linked to the abortion mentality. Human life is treated instrumentally, as a means to an end (such as the pleasure of having children) rather than as intrinsically good (thus imposing on parents the duty to care for the children we have, regardless of the pleasure they give us).

Fortunately, abortion law does not control the outcome of biotech policy. Although abortion diminishes the legal status of the embryo and fetus during pregnancy, it does not follow that abortion legal doctrine protects destructive embryo research (DER). The right to abortion concerns women, pregnancy and the right to terminate that pregnancy by means other than childbirth. It fits within a larger framework of procreative rights, such as the right to use contraceptives or to contract for any variety of assisted reproduction technologies. DER, on the other hand, has no relationship to pregnancy. The law recognizes that pregnancy is "unique" and may cause "suffering too intimate and personal for the State to insist [that the mother remain pregnant]."[39] Even though many believe that abortion is "an act of violence against an innocent human life," the state may not prohibit it. Why? "[B]ecause the liberty of the woman is at stake in a sense unique to the human condition and so unique to the law."[40] The "unique" condition of pregnancy is not at issue in DER.

Biotech researchers may not rely on women's reproductive rights to claim freedom to do as they wish to the embryo in the laboratory. That is good news. Clarke Forsythe, president of Americans United for Life, stated that "legally, the path is completely open to protect the extracorporeal embryo from conception."[41] Unlike the case with abortion, the state's legal ability to protect the fetus does not depend on viability. There is no constitutional barrier to protecting the embryo and fetus from nontherapeutic experimentation and destruction. Forsythe argues that bans on human cloning are quite constitutional and that "scientists and doctors, as third parties, have no personal constitutional liberty to deprive an extracorporeal human being of life or dignity."[42]

The fetus is already legally protected in criminal as well as civil contexts. Many of these safeguards are the result of legislation, not judicial decree, and much has been done in the post-*Roe* era. Under fetal homicide laws, the fetus

---

[39]*Planned Parenthood*, 505 U.S. at 852.
[40]Ibid.
[41]Clarke Forsythe, telephone conversation with the author, February 28, 2003.
[42]Clarke Forsythe, "Human Cloning and the Constitution," *Valparaiso University Law Review* 32, no. 469 (Spring 1998): 542.

is considered the victim of a crime when her mother is assaulted, even if the mother did not know she was pregnant. A child may recover monetary damages in a civil action for injuries inflicted on her in the womb. The unborn child may inherit property, have a guardian *ad litem* appointed to represent his interests, be the subject of a custody dispute and be considered a child for purposes of terminating the parent-child relationship. The Department of Health and Human Services clarified its policy to include unborn children in the State Children's Health Insurance Program (S-CHIP); thus, prenatal care may be provided for fetuses whose mothers otherwise would not qualify for aid.[43] None of these protections is contingent on the recognition of the embryo or fetus as a constitutional "person." Thus, *Roe*'s denial of the personhood of the fetus does not have to be overturned in order to protect implanted embryos and those embryos outside the womb.

The federal government protects the fetus from nontherapeutic medical research. Any research must be for the benefit of the fetus, or it must pose no more than minimal risk to the fetus and be for the purpose of gaining knowledge that cannot be obtained through any other means.[44] This protection was established in 1974, after abortion was legalized.[45] Clearly, the government understood its responsibility to protect the fetus outside the abortion context.

But Is She a Person?

The rending of the whole human person into unrelated definitions of constitutional, philosophical, psychological and moral personhood has opened the door for all sorts of mischief. A living, pulsating human being (a fetus) is not a legal person, whereas a nonliving, inanimate organization (a corporation) is a constitutional person for certain purposes.[46] Although it is not necessary for the embryo to be a person for the state to protect him, the separation of legal personhood from biological species membership is disconcerting. The moral status of the fetus, and even of infants, is similarly under attack. Peter Singer,

---

[43]"HHS to Allow States to Provide SCHIP [*sic*] Coverage for Prenatal Care," U.S. Department of Health and Human Services, January 31, 2002 <http://www.hhs.gov/news/press/2002pres/20020131.html>.

[44]See 45 C.F.R. 45, part 46, subpart B <http://ohrp.osophs.dhhs.gov/humansubjects/guidance/45cfr46.htm#46.203>.

[45]See the overview article by Scott Rae, "Spare Parts from the Unborn: The Ethics of Fetal Tissue Transplantation," *Christian Research Journal* (Fall 1991) <http://www.iclnet.org/pub/resources/text/cri/cri-jrnl/crj0145a.txt>.

[46]"Something can be a person without being human, and can be human without being a person." John P. East and Steven R. Valentine, "Reconciling *Santa Clara* and *Roe* v. *Wade*: A Route to Supreme Court Recognition of Unborn Children as Constitutional Persons," in *Abortion and the Constitution: Reversing Roe v. Wade Through the Courts*, ed. Dennis J. Horan, Edward R. Grant and Paige C. Cunningham (Washington, D.C.: Georgetown University Press, 1984), p. 90.

on behalf of less-forthright utilitarians, claims that some animals hold a higher moral status than do handicapped newborns. In Singer's world, membership in the species *Homo sapiens* is neither necessary nor sufficient for one to be designated a person.[47]

The implications of this line of thinking for other biotechnologies are disturbing. If genetic membership does not admit one to the human family, how do we view genetically altered beings? What is the status of a mouse that has been inserted with human genes to test a cancer therapy? How much can we manipulate human genes and still have a person? Even if we have the power to permanently alter gene lines, do we have the moral or legal right to do so? *Roe* should not stop us from tackling the new bioethics.

Unlikely Allies: Pro-choice Does Not Equal Pro-cloning

Until recently few pro-life organizations opposed human cloning, perhaps because they believed it would not involve direct killing. Their only concern was to protect any born clone as a full human person. This is a shortsighted and naive position. Live-birth cloning, if successful, would result in children being born. However, hundreds of embryos likely will die in the attempt to produce one newborn. The mammalian cloning models support this conclusion. Further, the strongest impulse behind cloning is not to make carbon copies of ourselves but to make spare parts for ourselves. Cloned embryos could be mined for stem cells to produce tissue and organs for body repair and regeneration. Every therapy based on cloning would involve, at the very least, one embryo death.

Other pro-life organizations have been slow to sound the alarm because they are single-minded in their opposition to abortion. Many do not make an intellectual connection between a mother's right to abort her fetus and a biotech researcher's right to manufacture and manipulate embryos. Others, though moved by images of cuddly babies, are unmoved by images of biotechnology. Still others—most notably, politicians such as Senator Orrin Hatch— do not believe the unimplanted embryo is a human being deserving of legal protection.

In contrast to abortion opponents, there are abortion sympathizers who do see the threat of manipulative and destructive biotechnologies. They make a distinction between a woman's right to control her pregnancy (even if that includes abortion) and the wholesale creation and destruction of human life in remote laboratories. They are committed to protecting a "truly human future."

---

[47]Echoing Singer's philosophy, Lee Hall and Anthony Jon Waters have written a legal brief for personhood of the Great Ape. "From Property to Person: The Case of Evelyn Hart," *Seton Hall Constitutional Law Journal* 11 (Fall 2000): 1-67.

Pro-choice radical feminist Judy Norsigian testified before Congress against cloning, stating that "the embryo is not nothing."[48] Lori Andrews, a pro-choice law professor who pioneered many of the legal arguments in support of assisted reproduction, opposes human cloning. She argued that "the notion of replicating existing humans seems to fundamentally conflict with our legal system, which emphatically protects individuality and uniqueness."[49]

A group of these unlikely allies drew national attention in 2002 when conservatives joined forces with progressives to oppose research cloning. The alliance included "women's health advocates, the writer Norman Mailer, the sociologist Todd Gitlin and academics like Elizabeth Fox-Genovese, a scholar of women's history at Emory University, and Benjamin Barber, a noted political theorist at the University of Maryland."[50] When testifying before the Senate Judiciary Committee a few weeks later, liberal attorney and bioethicist Andrew Kimbrell (director of the International Center for Technology Assessment) stated,

> Over the last many months I have worked with a coalition of progressive environmental, consumer and women's health groups to attempt to ban reproductive human cloning and obtain at least a moratorium on human cloning for research. . . .
>
> A number of those in the progressive community have several major concerns about human cloning for research. Environmentalists, consumer groups, women's and children's health advocates all want to see unprecedented regulatory and ethical questions resolved before and [sic] human embryo cloning for research is allowed.[51]

Over one hundred progressive and conservative organizations and individuals signed a statement circulated by Norsigian, including Jeremy Rifkin, a leading critic of biotechnology; Francis Fukuyama, professor of international political economy at Johns Hopkins; William Kristol, editor of the *Weekly Standard;* and Stuart A. Newman, professor of cell biology and anatomy at New York Medical College. Norsigian clarified in a letter to the editor of the *Washington Post* that "this debate is not about abortion rights. The difference be-

---

[48]Judy Norsigian is a coauthor of *Our Bodies, Our Selves for the New Century: A Book by and for Women* (New York: Touchstone, 1998) and cofounder of the Boston Women's Health Book Collective.

[49]Lori Andrews, "Is There a Right to Clone? Constitutional Challenges to Bans on Human Cloning," *Harvard Journal of Law and Technology* 11 (Summer 1998): 656.

[50]Sheryl Gay Stolberg, "Some for Abortion Rights Lean Right in Cloning Fight," *The New York Times,* January 24, 2002, p. A25 <http://www.nytimes.com/2002/01/24/politics/24CLON.html>.

[51]Andrew Kimbrell (executive director, International Center for Technology Assessment), testifying on February 5, 2002, before the Senate Judiciary Committee (Feinberg hearing).

tween seeking to end an unwanted pregnancy and seeking to create genetic duplicate human embryos is immense."[52]

Both pro-life and pro-choice advocates agreed to disagree on an issue they feel passionately about in order to achieve a common goal. This type of alliance may be difficult for some "purist" pro-lifers to accept. Admittedly it is a challenge for us to cooperate on some matters of urgent concern while remaining deeply divided on other fundamental human life issues. We may be accused of fraternizing with the enemy. But to demand that we agree in all matters of strategy, tactics and motivations elevates these considerations to the level of moral principle. It also neglects the opportunity to penetrate the culture, which is still malleable on biotech issues.

Such alliances are costly—possibly more costly for the progressives. Their peers, colleagues and fellow activists are deeply and understandably suspicious of any linkage with pro-lifers, considering such collaboration as selling out; some are concerned that this will erode the pro-choice position. But the promising lesson is that *a common goal may be reached with cobelligerents,* even though we might not agree on some fundamental premises.

Destructive biotechnologies may be banned without first restricting abortion rights. In her testimony before the Senate, Norsigian made it clear that "we do not believe that cloning and genetically engineered children are extensions of 'reproductive choice.'"[53]

We can mobilize now to stop unethical biotechnologies. This may seem like we're throwing in the towel on abortion. I believe the distinction between abortion and other biotech issues is actually helpful in terms of the public policy strategy.[54] Why? We do not need to first reverse *Roe* before we stop cloning and DER.

The Cultural Challenge and the Biotech Moment

Many people do not understand the new biotechnologies. Nevertheless, they are uneasy about their arrival. Their unarticulated moral resistance is what Leon Kass calls the "wisdom of repugnance."[55] Just as the pro-life movement has tapped into public repugnance for abortion on demand to build support for its restriction, similar moral feelings may be mined to curtail harmful biotechnologies. Well-reasoned moral and religiously based arguments are essen-

---

[52]Judy Norsigian, letter to the editor ("Not About Abortion Rights"), *Washington Post,* June 15, 2002, p. A22 <http://www.washingtonpost.com/wp-dyn/articles/A54537-2002Jun14.html>.

[53]Judy Norsigian (executive director, Boston Women's Health Book Collective), testifying on March 5, 2002, before the Senate Health, Education, Labor and Pensions Committee.

[54]Let me hasten to add that the two issues share the ultimate principle of protecting the individual human being.

[55]Leon Kass, "The Wisdom of Repugnance," *The New Republic,* June 2, 1997, pp. 17-26.

tial for evaluating the ethics of each technology. Ultimately, the standard is whether the technology violates any of God's laws and principles. We must be able to articulate the immorality of these technologies as well as their threat to the human race. In addition to moral principles, we must also argue self-interest and cultural implications. We need to challenge policy influencers to think carefully about the repercussions of biotechnology. What will blind pursuit of biotech do to us? As Gilbert Meilaender put it, would a world designed by people willing to embrace such biotechnologies as genetic engineering be a place in which the genetically engineered want to live?[56]

Wise Arguments

Public policy restraints on biotechnology need not be based on the legal personhood of the embryo; there are many other compelling arguments. For example, progressive opposition to cloning rejects the personhood of the embryo. Instead, concerns revolve around both self-interest and social impact: the commodification of life, the threat to women's health from the hyperstimulation of ovaries to retrieve the millions of eggs that would be needed, the potential exploitation of vulnerable women for their eggs, the ethical concerns over intentionally creating "any human life form solely for its exploitation and destruction,"[57] the threat to many basic human rights and the unavoidable link to "germline genetic manipulations [that] would affect future generations in unpredictable and deleterious ways."[58] Furthermore, the clone herself may begin life with physical limitations. Dolly the sheep was euthanized because of a lung disease, living only half the normal life span of sheep. Cloned mouse fetuses have a higher rate of abnormality, and the adult mice have a higher incidence of tumors than do normal mice.[59] Are we willing to risk making babies with severe abnormalities and the corresponding mandate to abort or euthanize them?

Similarly, even an abortion advocate may be troubled by the consequences of *prenatal testing*. Prenatal tests are currently optional, yet many women feel pressured to undergo amniocentesis. How long will it be before all pregnant women are required by insurers to avoid the birth of a "defective" child? Also, couples who *want* a child opt for preimplantation genetic diagnosis (PGD or PIGD) performed on embryos fertilized in vitro. This is not just to ensure that their child doesn't have a genetic defect; parents can also reject implanting a

---

[56]Referred to by Marc D. Guerra in his review of *Our Posthuman Future: Consequences of the Biotechnological Revolution*, by Francis Fukuyama, *First Things* 126 (October 2002): 60.
[57]See Kimbrell's testimony.
[58]See Norsigian's testimony.
[59]Tom Spears, "Cloning Damages Genes, Harms Health, Warns Expert," *Ottawa Citizen*, September 11, 2002, p. A14.

healthy embryo of the "wrong" sex or one that will not be a suitable tissue donor for a sick sibling.[60]

A more challenging issue for the pro-life movement is *gene patenting*, since it does not directly involve "taking" or "making" life. There are currently hundreds of patent applications pending for human genes. Public policy objections can be based on issues of economics, scientific hoarding, freedom of medical research, fairness, commodification or ownership of human beings, and other violations of the purposes of patent laws. Although a purpose of patent law is to promote knowledge by protecting invention, the gold rush to patent human genes has had the opposite effect. A handful of commercial and academic entities seek to control all diagnostics, therapies and applications for human genes. This exclusivity drives up the cost of health care. For example, no woman may get a test for breast cancer without paying a royalty to Myriad Genetics, which holds the patent for BRCA1 and BRCA2, the specific breast cancer mutation genes.[61] Patenting inhibits medical research. No researcher may independently develop a better screening test or cancer therapy for breast cancer without first paying Myriad.[62] The exclusivity granted by a patent prevents other researchers from working on basic research on a particular gene, even if the patent holder refuses to conduct his own research.[63] Gene patenting also makes the taxpayer pay twice: first for the government-funded research and then for the diagnostics and therapies the scientists develop.

We must be alert to the corruption of language in the service of unethical ends. Call things what they truly are. *Abortion* has never gained a positive public response. Abortion activists and organizations go to great lengths to avoid the "A" word, even renaming their own organizations.[64] But still *abortion* has a negative connotation.

---

[60]The most notorious is the case of Adam Nash, who was selected to be a cord blood donor for his sister Molly, who has Fanconi's anemia. His story is briefly reported in Rhonda Rowland, "Genetic Testing of Embryos Raises Ethical Issues," Cable News Network, June 27, 2001.
<http://www.cnn.com/2001/HEALTH/06/27/embryo.testing/>.
[61]Screening costs range from $350 for one gene to over $2,500 for full gene sequencing.
[62]"European Parliament resolution on the patenting of BRCA1 and BRCA2 ('breast cancer') genes." John Sulston, "Heritage of Humanity," *Le Monde diplomatique*, December 2002 <http://mondediplo.com/2002/12/15genome>; and "Myriad," Consumer Project on Theology <http://www.cptech.org/ip/health/firm/myriad.html>.
[63]Anna Harrington, "Gene Patents Stifle Basic Research: An Economic Analysis," *Harvard Health Policy Review* 3 (Fall 2002) <http://hcs.harvard.edu/~epihc/currentissue/fall2002/harrington.php>.
[64]NARAL began as the National Association for the Repeal of Abortion Laws and redefined itself as the National Abortion Rights Action League. Later, it reinvented itself as NARRAL, the National Abortion and Reproductive Rights Action League. In 2003 it abandoned NARAL Pro-Choice Maerica, forcing media to use the contested "pro-choice rhetoric."

Language that describes and explains is powerful, and it can color the reality of a particular technology. The unthinkable is redefined to make it palatable and, eventually, permissible. For example, in a move calculated to overcome public abhorrence of cloning, pro-cloning advocates relabeled cloning as "somatic cell nuclear transfer"[65] and "nuclear transplantation to produce human pluripotent stem cells."[66] The new terms are merely definitions of cloning; they just sound less repugnant. Likewise, we must resist biotech's description of experimental cloning as "therapeutic" (for whom? certainly not for the soon-to-be-eviscerated cloned embryo) and live birth cloning as "reproductive" (cloning is inherently reproductive). A similar verbal sleight of hand created the "pre-embryo" to describe the embryo prior to implantation. It contradicts medical textbooks, but it is handy for persuading people that there is no harm in destroying the embryo if she resides in a Petri dish and that it is ethically acceptable to experiment on frozen "pre-embryos."

It is not too late for policy makers to correct the situation. In contrast with the abortion issue, it is not too late to preempt the "I'm personally opposed, but . . ." political cliché. We can build a public policy that safeguards against the destruction of embryonic human life, the manipulation of future generations, the genetic enhancement of the privileged few and the melding of humans with machines or animal species. The law is not settled. Unless Congress acts, the states have the power to prohibit destructive and unethical research within their borders. Several state legislatures are in the process of banning all human cloning. Congress is considering, again, a similar ban.[67] Federal funding (and the corresponding ability to regulate) for destructive embryo research was limited by President Bush to existing cell lines, ones in which the embryo had already been destroyed.

There are significant public policy reasons to limit these biotechnologies as well as others that, while they do not kill human beings, control future generations. Genetic germline engineering (where the genetic alteration is permanent), genetic information and diagnosis (which may be used to coerce women

---

[65]See, e.g., the petition submitted by medical school educators and scientists to the President's Council on Bioethics on July 12, 2002: "Therapeutic Cloning Research: There Should Be No Ban and No Moratorium; Medical School Educators' and Scientists' Petition," Seniors Allied for Biomedical Research website <http://www.sabr.us/body-general.htm>.

[66]See, e.g., Professor Irving Weissman's letter to Senator Hatch and to the President's Bioethics Panel <http://www.sabr.us/body-general.htm#weissman>.

[67]The House of Representatives had passed the Human Cloning Prohibition Act (the "Weldon bill") on July 31, 2001, by a vote of 265-162. The Senate did not move the bill. It would have banned all forms of human cloning. The House passed the Human Cloning Prohibition Act of 2003 (H.R. 534) on February 23, 2003, by a vote of 241-155. H.R. 534 banned all forms of human cloning; Rep. Dave Weldon was the lead sponsor. As of this writing, there have been no Senate hearings on the bill (S. 245).

to abort or may be used by employers, schools, insurers and the government to discriminate) and cybernetics and nanotechnology (which may meld humans with machines) can be regulated or prohibited. In addition to the above examples, biotechnologies raise the specter of redefining what it means to be human. The level of perfection a baby must reach to be "acceptable" is ratcheting up. The line between disease (e.g., dwarfism) and trait (e.g., shortness) is being blurred. Medical research is being exploited to enhance physical, mental and social prowess. Healing disease is not as rewarding as the possibility of creating *Übermensch*. The "digital divide" may soon be replaced by the "genetic divide." We have the responsibility to prevent these immoral exploitations.

Fraternal Twins?

Although they look different in many respects, abortion and biotechnologies and the ethical and cultural challenges that accompany them are undeniably related—not identical but perhaps fraternal twins. Abortion and the new technologies of making and manipulating human life grow in a common womb: power. It is the asserted power of one human being over the life or future of another. In asking, "who decides?" one makes an assumption that the decision is morally permissible. We must never lose sight of the truth that all choices are not equal. Taking the life of a young human, whether in the womb or the Petri dish, is immoral. Determining the future of as-yet-uncreated human beings is wrong. Redefining the meaning of being human in the pursuit of biotech advantage is unethical. All these improperly assume rights of ownership and have the effect of making human life a commodity.

The pro-life movement must see the connection between the devaluing of life in the womb and its devaluation by the new biotechnologies. It's not just about babies. It's not just about women's health and dignity. The issue is the worth of any human life, whether conceived in an experimental laboratory or discarded because of genetic profile. The issue is the power of one generation (or at least the elite group of scientific guardians) over all future generations. The issue is the future of the human family: who will be invited to the table, and who will be the disposable servant, the perfectly engineered accessory or the disinvited flawed outcast?

Our culture must see the connection between Supreme Court decisions that handed women a private license to kill and the instrumental view of nascent human life. We are quickly moving from a scenario where one woman can make a decision that affects the life of one unborn child, to a future where a handful of biotech scientists manipulate and discard thousands of embryos, permanently rearrange genetic identities and merge humans with machines and animals in the name of better health and the good life. When the embryo has an uncertain legal and moral status, "he" becomes an "it." Human genetic material becomes merely a means to an end, a part of the process of creating, shaping, modifying and perfecting other human beings.

Abortion and biotech, if considered twins, must never be said to look alike. Abortion is not widely welcomed, yet it is widely perceived as a necessary evil. Biotechnologies are viewed with a skepticism that is mixed with hope that they might benefit "me." We must ensure that unethical biotechnologies, unlike abortion, are never accepted as necessary.

Lessons Learned

Have we learned any lessons at all from our experience in resisting abortion? Because *our courts both dictate cultural change and respond to it,* we must secure a public policy without judicial interference. For example, Congress and the states can act now to bar unethical biomedical technologies, and Congress may prohibit the patenting of any form of human life. This multipronged strategy (which *avoids putting all your strategy eggs in one basket*) must extend beyond public policy to public education. People must *understand the consequences of biotechnology.* Christians seriously need to be retaught the doctrines of creation, imago Dei and the incarnation. While we respect animals and the rest of God's creation, we revere human life, in all its biological forms, because it alone bears the image of God.

This awareness is essential to ethical decision making, these profound truths may not initially persuade the larger culture. Therefore, we must learn *how to communicate in a secularized public square.* In addition to using the "yuk factor" (our natural repugnance to things such as human cloning), we must also inform the public of the harmful consequences of new biotechnologies. For example, gene patenting leads to hoarding of information, inhibition of medical research and higher costs for patients. We stand to gain great assistance in this endeavor through *cooperation with unlikely allies.* Some of the arguments most likely to carry the day in the halls of legislatures will probably be framed by people who do not rely on an explicitly Christian understanding, but who value the dignity and worth of human beings. They, too, grasp that *changes in law and policy profoundly affect attitudes about who is a protected human being.*

It is not too late in the day to hold back the biotech tide. By God's grace, may the dark skies be a temporary solar eclipse and not the inevitable advent of night.

8

AN UNNATURAL ASSAULT
ON NATURAL LAW

Regulating Biotechnology Using
A Just Research Theory

NATHAN A. ADAMS IV, Ph.D., J.D.
CHIEF LITIGATION COUNSEL, CHRISTIAN LEGAL SOCIETY

The most controversial aspects of biotechnology to date have focused on the experimental use of human subjects at the earliest point of human development. Until the development of in vitro fertilization, there had been some research on aborted human fetuses, but once the embryo could be cultivated in the lab, research interest grew. In many jurisdictions this was made illegal, but in the United States it was permitted in federal law, although funding was prohibited by the Dickey amendment. While such research was opposed strongly by the pro-life movement, liberal opinion was divided. There was much unease at the principle of creating embryos through in vitro specifically for the purpose of research and destruction, though pro-choice opinion was generally open to the use of "spare" embryos, those left over from in vitro processes, which would otherwise be discarded. There was, however, very little research of this kind.

The debate was dramatically rekindled by the announcement in 1997 of the cloning of Dolly the sheep, which raised the prospect of cloned human embryos in large numbers for research. Discoveries that followed led many scientists and corporate biotech interests to seek to safeguard their right to manufacture and use for experimentation large numbers of clonal human embryos. While opposing the birth of cloned babies, they advocated the creation and use of human embryos in large numbers to produce embryonic stem cells for potential medical treatments. As has been noted in chapter two by David Prentice, these claims are exaggerated: a plentiful and ethical supply of so-called adult stem cells is already available and has already begun to have clinical applications.

In this essay Nathan Adams explores the basic legal issues at stake in experiments on human beings. Behind any debate about particular statutes lies the idea of "natural law," according to which there exist fundamental moral truths that form the basis of all law. This is in contrast to what is generally called legal positivism, the idea that everything is relative and that law is simply what we choose to make it. Dr. Adams reviews these divergent ideas of law and their relationships with different views of the world as a basis for asserting a theory of when experiments are right, which he terms just research theory in parallel with just war theory, another fundamental application of natural law thinking. He shows how the Nuremberg Code develops principles that uphold and defend the dignity of the individual. He then assesses the approach of those who wish to create and destroy embryonic human beings in light of those principles.

NIGEL M. DE S. CAMERON

Natural law inspired by Judeo-Christian theology is perhaps the most distinctive contribution of Western civilization. The natural law tradition teaches that objective moral rights exist independent of those granted by government—rights that inhere in human beings by virtue of their humanity. Government may seek to detract from these rights through, for example, genocide, slavery or invidious racial discrimination, but the rights exist nevertheless as rationally discoverable, God-given, inalienable entitlements constitutive of humankind.

In the twenty-first century, the Western legal establishment's commitment to natural legal principles has markedly diminished, reaching such a nadir that the public and, worse yet, most Christians hardly bat an eye at crassly utilitarian policy recommendations. Just war theory continues to enjoy some vitality, but few discuss natural law's relevance to areas such as biotechnology including human cloning, embryonic stem cell research (ESCR) and genetic engineering. Instead, we have accepted jurisprudential premises at odds with the Christian faith and worldview about when to allow biotechnological experimentation.

This essay wrestles with the requirements of a natural legal approach to biotechnological research. Borrowing from just war theory, it propounds a just research theory for human subject experimentation. First, we discuss some basic facts about the human subject of biotechnology and law governing the living human embryo. Second, we distinguish the Christian worldview from naturalism and the natural legal perspective from its primary alternatives. Last, we explore the requirements of a just research theory for biotechnology and examine how closely proposed human cloning corresponds with it.

No less than any other subgroup in American culture, Christian families are afflicted with debilitating genetic diseases. We understand the appeal of technologies that may alleviate suffering, yet the natural legal tradition also obliges us to wrestle with the significance of humankind as created in God's image. Christians are not Luddites opposed to the advance of medical technology. To the contrary, modern medicine and science owe much to Christianity. Aware of humanity's ultimate depravity, however, Christians understand the need to guide innovation to ensure that its application and consequences are just and consistent with natural law.

The Human Subject of Biotechnology

Four banal yet critically important and scientifically verifiable facts about the subject of biotechnological research provide an important starting point for understanding the relevance of the natural legal perspective for biotechnology. Distinguishing these facts from the rhetoric fed and regurgitated by the media is difficult, but Scripture obliges Christians to shine light in the darkness to find our way toward a moral biotechnological policy.[1]

- The subject of biotechnological research is *living and genetically unique*.

- The embryo is *human* and *capable of developing into an adult*.

- Every adult passes through the embryonic stage of development.

- Derivation of an embryo's stem cells and various other components necessarily kills the embryo.

Considering these points in order, the human embryo that is the subject of biotechnological research is as living as any biological organism.[2] From the beginning it possesses every element necessary to grow into a genetically unique adult apart from the nurturing environment of the mother. The living human embryo is "totipotent," or capable of developing into every organ of the body; and, thus, it is more significant than a mere organ. Admittedly, the living human embryo does not look like or function in the same manner as an adult and apparently is not sentient, but this does not undermine the embryo's biologic living status:

> Embryos are in full possession of the very characteristic that distinguishes a living human being from a dead one: the ability of all cells in the body to function together as an organism, with all parts acting in an integrated manner for the continued life and health of the body as a whole.[3]

---

[1]See, e.g., Eph 5:8-14.

[2]See generally Maureen L. Condic, "Life: Defining the Beginning by the End," *First Things* 133 (2003): 50-54. "From the earliest stages of development, human embryos clearly function as organisms.... Human embryos are living human beings precisely because they possess the single defining feature of human life that is lost in the moment of death—the ability to function as a coordinated organism rather than merely as a group of living human cells" (pp. 50, 52).

[3]Ibid.

Some have referred to the embryo without scientific basis as a "pre-embryo," "activated cell," "cleaving cell," "egg" or, less impressively, "dot" or "goldfish."[4] Call the embryo what you will, the embryo is none other than human; it cannot develop into an adult of any other species any more than a tadpole can develop into a goldfish. Far from being merely a clump of human cells, "embryos are capable of growing, maturing, maintaining a physiologic balance between various organ systems, adapting to changing circumstances, and repairing injury."[5] Collections of human cells do nothing of the kind.[6] Furthermore, no adult human being can manage to avoid the embryonic stage of life. Nevertheless, just as dissecting any organism kills it, extracting the human embryo's stem cells and other constituent parts ends its ability to develop and function as a coordinated organism. This loss of integrated function, as opposed to a loss of comprehension, defines, as a matter of law, death for human beings.[7]

The law ordinarily ascribes to the person who has entered into a persistent vegetative state (characterized by loss of higher brain functions but not integrated bodily function), the deaf-mute and the drunkard languishing in the gutter the right to life.[8] Living human embryos do not yet enjoy this right, but no law precludes protecting them as long as the embryo is outside the womb, or *ex utero*. At present the law pertaining to these living human embryos is largely unchartered. The only constraint *stare decisis* may impose is treating living human embryos as "persons" within the court-interpreted meaning of the Fourteenth Amendment. *Stare decisis* does not compel treating living human embryos as mere expendable commodities as the research community recommends.

Roe v. *Wade* and its progeny acknowledge that the state possesses an important and legitimate interest in protecting potential life "separate and distinct" from the interest of the mother.[9] Cloning, ESCR and genetic engineering are all

---

[4]See Gina Kolata and Andrew Pollack, "A Breakthrough in Cloning? Perhaps or Perhaps Not Yet," *The New York Times*, November 27, 2001, p. A12 (in which ACT ethicist Ronald Green says he prefers to refer to embryos at this stage as "cleaving eggs"); Joannie Fischer, "Scientists Have Finally Cloned a Human Embryo," *U.S. News and World Report*, December 3, 2001 (referencing "pre-embryos"); testimony of Marlene Strege before the Government Reform Subcommittee on Criminal Justice, Drug Policy and Human Resources, for a hearing on "Opportunities and Advancements in Stem Cell Research" (referencing testimony of Senator Thomas Harkin, who referred to human embryos as "goldfish," and of Mary Tyler Moore, who referred to them as "dots").
[5]Condic, "Life," p. 52.
[6]Ibid.
[7]Ibid., pp. 50-51.
[8]See Hadley Arkes, *Natural Rights and the Right to Choose* (Cambridge: Cambridge University Press, 2002), p. 14.
[9]The interest *Roe* recognized commenced at viability, whereas the interest the *Casey* plurality recognized arose at conception. See *Roe* v. *Wade*, 410 U.S. 113, 163 (1973), and *Planned Parenthood of Southeastern Pennsylvania* v. *Casey*, 505 U.S. 833, 876 (1992).

procedures performed on an embryo outside of the womb. Accordingly, judging the constitutionality of thoughtful biotechnological regulation does not require courts to balance a woman's interest in aborting an embryo against the state's interest in protecting the living human embryo. Other precedent dealing with the First Amendment and other constitutional rights is also not a roadblock to thoughtful biotechnological regulation.[10]

Therefore, we have a unique opportunity for a short time to take dominion over the positive law and legislate substantive rights for living human embryos falling short of recognizing them as full juridical persons, but otherwise specially respecting them in accord with natural law. This strategy is complementary to the efforts of some to overturn *Roe* v. *Wade*, because recognizing incremental natural rights for living human embryos creates additional pressure and cognitive dissonance undermining the will to enforce abortion on demand. On the other hand, the strategies are independent, because it is not necessary to overturn *Roe* v. *Wade* to begin specially respecting living human embryos.

The Natural Legal Perspective and Its Alternatives

Whether law protects the living human subject of biotechnological research will depend on which worldview and philosophy of law (or jurisprudence) government adopts. Worldviews provide the foundation for jurisprudence, which determines the legal strategy for regulating biotechnology. Theology also matters insofar as it either mobilizes or immobilizes Christians to influence lawmaking.

Worldviews in conflict. Simply put, a worldview is a "conceptual scheme by which we consciously or unconsciously place or fit everything we believe and by which we interpret and judge reality."[11] Everyone has one whether or not they know it. It impacts our lives profoundly as a lens through which we see the world. A comprehensive worldview incorporates consistent beliefs about God, reality (or metaphysics), knowledge (or epistemology), morality and humankind.[12]

Concerning these, the classic Christian worldview affirms that a supremely powerful and personal God created the world ex nihilo (from nothing) and

---

[10]See generally Nathan A. Adams IV, "Creating Clones, Kids and Chimera: Liberal Democratic Compromise at the Crossroads," *Notre Dame Journal of Law, Ethics and Public Policy* 17 (March 2003).

[11]Ronald H. Nash, *Worldviews in Conflict: Choosing Christianity in a World of Ideas* (Grand Rapids, Mich.: Zondervan, 1992), p. 16.

[12]Ibid., p. 26. See also Charles Colson and Nancy Pearcey, *How Now Shall We Live?* (Carol Stream, Ill.: Tyndale House, 1999), p. 14: "Every worldview can be analyzed by the way it answers three basic questions: Where did we come from, and who are we (creation)? What has gone wrong with the world (fall)? And what can we do to fix it (redemption)?"

maintains it; humans may attain knowledge of God through Scripture, sensory perception and introspection; human beings are moral agents subject to God-given immutable moral laws that are as fixed and universal as are physical ones; and human beings are sinful, fallen and in rebellion against God, but they reflect a distorted image of God and are divine right-bearers.[13]

In contrast, the secular worldview (also called *naturalism*) denies the existence of God or his personal character; considers creation the result of random events and a battle of the fittest persevering out of biologic selfishness; believes knowledge is limited to sensory perception; believes human beings create their moral order for convenience and enforce it solely through public coercion; and consider human beings different from, but not necessarily more important than, creation except to the extent that our sentience or affinity for the arts distinguishes us.[14]

Jurisprudences in conflict. Juxtaposed worldviews lead to widely differing jurisprudences. The battle royal pits the natural legal tradition against legal positivism or legal realism. Natural law presumes the existence of deontological or absolute and objective moral truth, whereas legal positivism and legal realism deny it and affirm an atheistic vision of morality premised upon a relativistic or hedonistic ethic.[15]

Natural law. Natural law is a "higher law" because it provides a reference point for judging the justness or unjustness of human-made or so-called positive laws.[16] Although of divine origin, natural law is accessible to human reason, rather than knowable only through special revelation.[17] The apostle Paul wrote about this when he discussed the requirements of the law "written on [the] hearts" and consciences of Gentiles, so that their thoughts both accuse and defend them (Rom 2:14-15). Thomas Aquinas famously elaborated on this principle in *Summa Theologica* by emphasizing that "the light of natural reason, whereby we discern what is good and what is evil, which is the function of the natural law, is nothing else than an imprint on us of the Divine light."[18]

---

[13]Nash, *Worldviews in Conflict*, p. 34-53; Colson and Pearcey, *How Now*, p. 20.
[14]See Colson and Pearcey, *How Now*, pp. 20-21.
[15]See also Phillip E. Johnson, *Reason in the Balance: The Case Against Naturalism in Science, Law and Education* (Downers Grove, Ill.: Intervarsity Press, 1995), pp. 141-42.
[16]Robert P. George, *The Clash of Orthodoxies: Law, Religion and Morality in Crisis* (Wilmington, Del.: Intercollegiate Studies Institute Books, 2001), p. 169.
[17]Ibid.; Russell Hittinger, *The First Grace: Rediscovering the Natural Law in a Post-Christian World* (Wilmington, Del.: Intercollegiate Studies Institute Books, 2003), pp. xxiii, 42-44, 46, 50, 54, 61.
[18]Thomas Aquinas *Summa Theologica* 1.Q91.A2, in Peter Kreeft, ed., *A Summa of the Summa: The Essential Philosophical Passages of St. Thomas Aquinas'* Summa Theologica *Edited and Explained for Beginners* (San Francisco: Ignatius, 1990).

The divine light is the image of God, or imago Dei, that all humankind, and only humankind, shares.[19] It is "the source of the inestimable dignity of the human creature."[20] No other species shares it, and no member of our species is without it—no matter how deficient, disabled, deaf, mute, sick, young or old.[21] The Alzheimer's patient shares it as much as the brilliant physicist does. The effort to sever the relationship between the imago Dei and membership in the human species by imposing additional criteria such as comprehension, limbs or birth is unsupported by reason or Scripture.[22] It relies on an unbiblical dualism between mind and body regarding the latter as less important than the former.[23]

According to Aquinas, either positive law accords with natural reason premised on the imago Dei and is, thus, just; or it fails to accord with it and is, thus, unjust and, indeed, a perversion of positive law.[24] Unjust positive laws violate God's law and the human character. In this respect, William Blackstone argued that natural law constitutes a check on humankind's free will and is so interwoven with the happiness of individuals "that the latter cannot be attained but by observing the former; and, if the former be punctually obeyed, it cannot but induce the latter."[25]

Legal positivism and legal realism. In contrast to natural law, legal positivism and legal realism have become associated with a view of law deeply skeptical of moral truth.[26] According to these philosophies, law is a simple act of public will subject to amendment whenever it suits lawmakers.[27] Within this tradition, law is exclusively an emanation from government. There is no law besides positive law. Once more, law need not reflect any morality or immutable principles; rather, it is simply the result of a contest of interests following an agreed upon procedure that ultimately derives its authority from the state.[28] Goodness has nothing to do with it.

Justice Oliver Wendell Holmes argued that law is ultimately merely the

---

[19]See Gen 1:27, "So God created man in his own image, in the image of God he created him; male and female he created them."

[20]Nigel M. de S. Cameron, *The New Medicine: Life and Death After Hippocrates* (Wheaton, Ill.: Crossway, 1991), p. 172.

[21]Ibid., p. 173.

[22]See ibid.; Arkes, *Natural Rights*, pp. 83-84; Condic, "Life," pp. 52-54.

[23]Colson and Pearcey, *How Now*, pp. 119, 122-23.

[24]Aquinas *Summa Theologica* Q.93.A.3, Q.95.A.2.

[25]William Blackstone, *Commentaries on the Laws of England* (Chicago: Chicago University Press, 1979), 1:38-46.

[26]See Arkes, *Natural Rights*, p. 14.

[27]Ibid., p. 31.

[28]See ibid.; Hans Kelsen, "The Pure Theory of Law," pt. 1 and 2, *Law Quarterly Review* 50 (1934): 474; 51 (1935): 1, 8-10, 28-31, 47-50; Karl Llewellyn, "Some Realism About Realism," *Harvard Law Review* 47 (1931): 1222-23, 1233-42.

force that a government brings to bear to enforce its commands.[29] People obey it purportedly not because they feel morally obliged to do so, but because they fear the consequences if they do not. Moral rights exist in positive law only to the extent that those in control legislate them into existence. According to this view, moral rights have no independent objective significance; thus there is no "injustice" except to the extent that behavior fails to conform to positive law.[30] Not tethered to any divine commandment, strict legal positivists and realists are free to vindicate any principles or none at all.

Utilitarianism. One of the most common alternative ethics that legal positivists and realists favor in the biotechnology debate is utilitarianism. The principle of utility has changed little since the early 1800s, when Jeremy Bentham explained it as achieving the greatest happiness for the greatest number.[31] Method is immaterial to the utilitarian if the consequence of an action satisfies this maxim. In this respect, utilitarianism is sometimes referred to as *consequentialism* and criticized for not taking into account the rightness of the rules or method leading to the consequences.[32] Utilitarianism may also be viewed as a form of "welfarism," because the relevant consequences are only those that increase or decrease the welfare of those affected; third parties who may be indirectly affected are irrelevant.[33]

Hedonism. Hedonism is an entirely unprincipled approach to law also evident in the modern medical research establishment. Hedonism is strictly an apology for self-interested experimentation. Richard Dawkins explained why this makes sense: "We are survival machines—robot vehicles blindly programmed to preserve the selfish molecules known as genes."[34] In *The Hedonistic Imperative*, one author writes that the "post-Darwinian agenda" that biotechnology will facilitate enables us "to discard the legacy-wetware of our evolutionary past" including "pathways of pain and malaise evolved only because they served the inclusive fitness of our genes in the ancestral environment."[35] Post-Darwinian hedonists care little about the subjects of biotechnological experimentation and only about their vision of an improved human race.

---

[29]Oliver Wendell Holmes, "The Path of the Law After One Hundred Years," *Harvard Law Review* 110 (1997): 991.

[30]George, *Clash of Orthodoxies*, p. 153; Hittinger, *First Grace*, pp. 115-16.

[31]Jeremy Bentham, "Principles of Morals and Legislation," in *Great Political Thinkers: Plato to the Present*, ed. William Ebenstein (New York: Holt, Rinehart & Winston, 1969), p. 516.

[32]R. M. Hare, "A Utilitarian Approach," in *A Companion to Bioethics*, ed. Helga Kuhse and Peter Singer (Oxford: Blackwell, 1998), p. 80.

[33]Ibid., pp. 80-81.

[34]Richard Dawkins, *The Selfish Gene*, 2nd ed. (Oxford: Oxford University Press, 1989).

[35]David Pearce, *The Hedonistic Imperative*, BLTC Research website <http://www.paradise-engineering.com/hedab.htm >. (The URLs cited in this chapter were accessed on January 16, 2004.)

Theologies in conflict. Although the Christian and secular approaches to the law of biotechnology could not be further juxtaposed nor the stakes greater, some Christians are paralyzed by theological questions. For example, some ask, when does the imago Dei vest? The nascent biotechnological debate in this country has revealed a hidden rift between those who believe it vests at conception (coital or noncoital) and those who believe it vests only upon implantation or later. In truth the question itself may miss the mark because the notion of the imago Dei first and foremost requires us to ask, what does it require of me? Whether or not another is vested with the image of God, your investiture with the divine imperative, besides divine revelation (the Bible), renders basic moral truths accessible to you—truths about, for example, the morality of creating human life outside of the context of marriage.

We should also recognize that those who conclude the imago Dei vests at some point after one becomes a member of the human species necessarily credit the rationale of those who favor abortion until a certain trimester. These contend that what matters for purposes of defining one's moral and legal culpability for killing a human being is his or her age, not the human being's life. Frequently, this view is accompanied by a spatial or geographic defense of abortion, that is, that moral and legal responsibility for aborting an infant should not attach until the last toe of the infant emerges from the uterus. For these persons, the imago Dei vests on a specific month, day, hour and minute other than conception at a peculiar location, but not the minute earlier or centimeter shorter.

A second confusing theological issue relates to the divine imperative to take dominion over and redeem creation. Christians have long recognized that the revealed Word requires us to pray and care for the infirm. Christians pioneered medical services for this purpose but have never agreed, as some theologians now contend, that this end justifies immoral means, such as killing one human being to aid another or, even worse, creating human beings with the premeditated purpose of killing them to aid another (which is literally the purpose of so-called research cloning). Some will object that the church, medicine and law have not previously weighed a human embryo's life against an adult's. Although true as far as it goes, we have rejected experimentation on vulnerable human populations, including the mentally infirm, the imprisoned, children and fetuses, and we have deemed it unethical and generally unlawful even though others stand to benefit.[36]

It would be a perverse twist of Christian compassion to vindicate a utilitarian weighting of what is in the best interest of the greatest number over a deontological one that teaches all human beings are divine right-bearers and that

---

[36]See section *"Jus ad experimentum:* just cause," below.

taking human life is wrong. Favoring this view or even doing nothing is not a neutral decision. It ensures the vindication of the secular worldview over the Christian worldview, legal positivism, utilitarianism and hedonism over natural legal principles, abortion rights over human life, a contract and property rights model for governing living human embryos over a special respect paradigm; and it portends additional human rights abuses against other living human beings, the vulnerable and incompetent ones first.

A Just Research Theory for Human Subject Experimentation

It is a generally knowable and natural legal proposition that living human embryos deserve better treatment than commodities, organs or cells deserve. Powerful evidence for this proposition and the vitality of natural law and the divine imprint on the human conscience comes from an unlikely source: a few secular courts and even abortion rights-oriented law professors have agreed that the state should accord living human embryos "special respect," albeit not the full complement of rights enjoyed by juridical persons.[37]

Short of recognizing the embryo as a juridical person, the law can enforce a wide variety of familiar legal protections to grant living human embryos special respect. An important first step would be to accord living human embryos the protection of the code of conduct for human experimentation that Western medicine and law have developed over the past half-century.[38] This code of conduct can be conceptualized within the natural legal tradition as a just research theory for human subject medical experimentation. To exempt an entire class of living human beings from it would contradict the natural law and accomplish nothing short of a revolution in the positive law of medicine just as the biotechnological revolution is posed to change medicine permanently.

Just Research Theory

For a framework to discuss the requirements of a just research theory within the natural legal tradition, I turn by way of analogy to a more familiar legal theory premised on natural law, just war theory. Just war theory teaches that war, the most extreme form of violence, can begin for just or unjust reasons and be fought at least in its conventional form in a just or unjust manner. Thus,

---

[37]See, e.g., *Davis v. Davis*, 842 S.W. 2d 588, 597 (Tenn. 1992); John A. Robertson, "In the Beginning: The Legal Status of Early Embryos," *Virginia Law Review* 76 (1990): 437, 446-47. See also Francis Fukuyama, *Our Posthuman Future: Consequences of the Biotechnology Revolution* (New York: Picador, 2002), pp. 174-77.

[38]For other recommendations on how to specially respect living human embryos, see Adams, "Creating Clones," pp. 141-49; and Samuel B. Casey and Nathan A. Adams IV, "Specially Respecting the Living Human Embryo by Adhering to Standard Human Subject Experimentation Rules," *Yale Journal of Health Policy, Law and Ethics* 2 (Autumn 2001): 111, 124-26.

the morality of war can be judged twice, first with respect to the reasons states commence wars and, second, with respect to how they fight them.[39] *Jus ad bellum* (literally, the right to war) denotes the former, whereas *jus in bello* (literally, the law in war) denotes the latter. An unjust war may be fought justly, or a just war may be fought unjustly.

Questions about *jus ad bellum* precede questions about *jus in bello* and hinge on an inquiry into six conditions (the first of which is the most important): the justice of the cause, right intention of the government, competence of the authority, chance of success, limited nature of the objectives, and last resort.[40] Nonaggression is a key condition of most just war making.[41] This reflects our commitment to a pluralist world of independent nation-states, which when attacked may defend themselves. Indeed, the preeminent purpose of the nation-state is to defend the right of a people to live corporately within certain boundaries.[42]

Reflecting this purpose, classic just war theory does not render armed force inherently suspect or presumably immoral.[43] Instead, "the classic tradition views armed force as something that can be used for good or evil, depending on who is using it, why, to what ends, and how."[44] It is used for good to the extent government defends the security of the governed against attack. Human subject experimentation is perhaps even less presumably suspect morally than is the use of armed force. In a fallen world subject to sickness and death, this experimentation is vital to mitigate the effects of the Fall where the prerequisites of just research theory are met.

With respect to the other *jus ad bellum* requirements, the primary legitimate goal of war is the restoration of peace.[45] "Vengeance, subjugation, and conquest are unjustifiable purposes."[46] The requirement of competent authority or "lawful declaration" limits the right to initiate war and use force to the state and its legally authorized agents, not other crusading parties.[47] Before under-

---

[39]Michael Walzer, *Just and Unjust Wars: A Moral Argument with Historical Illustrations* (New York: BasicBooks, 1977), p. 21.

[40]A. Holmes, ed., *War and Christian Ethics* (Grand Rapids: Baker, 1975), pp. 4-5; George Weigel, "Moral Clarity in a Time of War," *First Things* 129 (January 2003): 22-23.

[41]Walzer, *Just and Unjust Wars*, pp. 51-53. This excludes legitimate preemption and just cause to recover something wrongfully taken or to punish evil (pp. 80ff.; Weigel, "Moral Clarity," p. 24).

[42]Walzer, *Just and Unjust Wars*, p. 55.

[43]Weigel, "Moral Clarity," p. 22.

[44]Ibid. The foundational presumption of the just war tradition is that "rightly constituted public authority is under a strict moral obligation to defend the security of those for whom it has assumed responsibility" (ibid.).

[45]Holmes, *War and Christian Ethics*, p. 5 (terming this the only morally legitimate reason for war) and p. 29 (Cicero same).

[46]Ibid.

[47]Ibid., p. 5.

taking war, *jus ad bellum* requires that there be a reasonable chance of success. The aims of war must also be limited and proportional to its objectives. Finally, last resort requires exhaustion of alternatives where it is reasonable to believe they exist.[48]

Once at war, *jus in bello* hinges on discrimination and proportionality.[49] According to the discrimination principle, warfighters must make every effort to avoid deaths of noncombatants by observing noncombatant immunity (e.g., not raping women and children, not attacking or murdering civilians) and prisoner-of-war rights. The proportionality principle requires that the means used to achieve victory be proportionate to the limited military objectives. Military necessity prohibits other than essential armed force to achieve military objectives. Thus, unlimited war and destruction is rarely justified.

Just war theory and the war convention emerged over a period of centuries from the crucible of war itself as an imperfect attempt to render war less hellish, particularly for those least consulted and least responsible.[50] Likewise, just research theory is a response to atrocities involving nontherapeutic (violent) human subject experimentation, which is a relatively new feature of Western medicine as it becomes more commonplace with advances in biotechnology.[51] Similar to just war theory, just research theory governs both *jus ad experimentum* or the right to experiment (literally, the law to experiment) and *jus in experimento* or rights in experimentation (literally, the law in experimentation).

Jus ad experimentum: just cause. Whereas the key condition for just war making is nonaggression, the key condition for just human experimentation is autonomy. In other words, the right to experiment on humans pursuant to natural legal principles hinges on the subject's autonomously deciding after full disclosure of the risks of experimentation whether to submit to it. Medical autonomy protects the status of human subjects as human beings worthy of respect; affirms self-determination, liberty and equality; minimizes fraud and duress; encourages self-scrutiny on the part of the researcher; and compensates for the imbalance in power between the researcher and subject and for their divergent interests nurtured by the research enterprise. Medical autonomy protects all human subjects but especially vulnerable or incompetent

---

[48]Some believe last resort requires serial exhaustion of alternatives to war making (see ibid., p. 5), whereas others argue differently. Weigel, "Moral Clarity," p. 26-27.

[49]Holmes, *War and Christian Ethics*, p. 5, 29; Walzer, *Just and Unjust Wars*, chaps. 8-9. Of these limitations, only proportionality is utilitarian in character.

[50]Walzer, *Just and Unjust Wars*, pp. 45-46.

[51]The first case in the United States addressing a mildly nontherapeutic procedure arose in 1941, when a court approved the consent a guardian gave for her fifteen-year-old nephew to provide a skin graft to a badly burned cousin. See *Bonner* v. *Moran*, 126 F.2d 121 (App. D.C. 1941).

ones, including the mentally impaired, prisoners, the elderly and nonadults.

The strongest endorsement of the medical autonomy principle is set forth in the Nuremberg Code, which emerged from World War II and, more particularly, from the crimes Nazis committed against humanity as chronicled at the Doctor's Trials.[52] The Nuremberg Code effectively precluded research on human subjects, unless they provided voluntary informed consent. Some view the code as a secular restatement of the Hippocratic oath adopted centuries earlier as a pagan oath in response not to experimentation, but to widespread participation by physicians in abortion, suicide and euthanasia.[53] The Nuremberg Code states in pertinent part:

> The voluntary consent of the human subject is absolutely essential. This means that the person involved should have legal capacity to give consent; should be so situated as to be able to exercise free power of choice, without the intervention of any element of force, fraud, deceit, duress, overreaching, or other ulterior form of constraint or coercion; and should have sufficient knowledge and comprehension of the elements of the subject matter involved as to enable him to make an understanding and enlightened decision.[54]

Unfortunately, Western medicine's commitment to *jus ad experimentum* has diminished over time, as the theory's grounding in obligation to God has disappeared from declarative texts and the pressure to routinize human subject research has increased. Protections are buttressed every so often when scandalous abuses are published, such as the Willowbrook hepatitis study and the Tuskegee trials, where researchers studying syphilis failed to inform African-Americans of the availability of penicillin.[55] However, the prevailing international code of experimentation—the World Medical Association's Declaration of Helsinki—and U.S. law now permit in certain circumstances persons responsible for human subjects to consent to experiments on them.[56] U.S. law

---

[52]See *United States* v. *Karl Brandt*, in *Trials of War Criminals Before the Nuremberg Military Tribunals Under Control Council Law No. 10* (Washington D.C.: U.S. Government Printing Office, 1949-1953), 2:181-82. See also Cameron, *New Medicine*, pp. 69-89.

[53]Cameron, *New Medicine*, pp. 26-28. The Hippocratic oath states in relevant part, "I will use treatment to help the sick according to my ability and judgment, but I will never use it to injure or wrong them. I will not give poison to anyone though asked to do so, nor will I suggest such a plan. Similarly I will not give a pessary to a woman to cause abortion. But in purity and in holiness I will guard my life and my art." Ibid., p. 25.

[54]The Nuremberg Code is available in a variety of texts including *British Medical Journal* 313 (December 7, 1996): 1448 <http://www.cirp.org/library/ethics/nuremberg/>.

[55]See W. J. Curran, "The Tuskegee Syphilis Study," *New England Journal of Medicine* 289 (October 4, 1973): 730-31.

[56]The World Medical Association's Declaration of Helsinki is available in a variety of texts and online at <http://www.cirp.org/library/ethics/helsinki>. See also 45 C.F.R. sec. 46 <http://www.access.gpo.gov/nara/cfr/waisidx_00/45cfr46_00.html>.

memorializes this so-called proxy consent standard by permitting experimentation on a subject when the researcher has the "legally effective" informed consent of the subject's "legally authorized representative."[57]

Case law suggests that a proxy can never validly consent to some types of hazardous research. Most recently, a state supreme court held that parents could not validly consent to expose their children to lead paint poisoning as part of medical experimentation.[58] In contrast, it is well established that guardians may consent to mildly nontherapeutic medical procedures with known risks like a skin graft for the benefit of a family member.[59] U.S. law requires that researchers solicit children's assent to research when, in the researchers' judgment, the children are capable of providing informed assent.[60] On the other hand, U.S. law explicitly forbids proxy consent to nontherapeutic research on even *ex utero* human fetuses,[61] as well as federally funded nontherapeutic research on prisoners.[62] Accordingly, although we have tolerated some substantial departures from the just cause principle by permitting proxy consent, U.S. and international law still substantially vindicate the autonomy principle in human subject experimentation law.

Other requirements. The prevailing medical code of conduct also vindicates the remaining requirements of *jus ad experimentum*. With respect to right intention, the Declaration of Helsinki provides that the exclusive morally legitimate objective for human subject experimentation must be "to improve prophylactic, diagnostic, and therapeutic procedures and the under-

---

[57]45 C.F.R. sec. 46.101(a).

[58]*Grimes* v. *Kennedy Krieger Institute*, 782 A.2d 807 (Md. 2001): "In our view, parents whether improperly enticed by trinkets, food stamps, money or other items, have no more right to intentionally and unnecessarily place children in potentially hazardous non-therapeutic research surroundings, than do researchers. In such cases, parental consent, no matter how informed, is insufficient."

[59]See, e.g., *Bonner* v. *Moran* (noted above); *Hart* v. *Brown*, 289 A.2d 386 (1972), approving the transplant of a kidney from one seven-year-old twin to another, where the donor was expected to live a normal and productive life afterwards and the recipient twin had only a 50 percent chance of surviving for five years without the kidney.

[60]45 C.F.R. sec. 46.408(a).

[61]42 U.S.C.A. sec. 289(g): "The Secretary may not conduct or support any research or experimentation . . . on a nonviable living human fetus ex utero or a living human fetus ex utero for whom viability has not been ascertained unless the research . . . may enhance the well-being . . . of the fetus or . . . will pose no added risk of suffering, injury, or death to the fetus and the purpose of the research or experimentation is the development of important biomedical knowledge which cannot be obtained by other means"; <http://www.access.gpo .gov/uscode/title42/title42.html>. See also 45 C.F.R. sec. 46.209.

[62]45 C.F.R. sec. 46.302: "Inasmuch as prisoners may be under constraints because of their incarceration which could affect their ability to make a truly voluntary and uncoerced decision whether or not to participate as subjects in research, it is the purpose of this subpart to provide additional safeguards for the protection of prisoners."

standing of the aetiology and pathogenesis of disease."[63] Human subject experimentation is only justified "if there is a reasonable likelihood that the populations in which the research is carried out stand to benefit from the results of the research."[64] U.S. law allows research not directly benefiting the subject only when the study will "yield generalizable knowledge about the subjects' disorder or condition that is of vital importance for the understanding or amelioration of the subjects' disorder or condition" and other restrictive conditions are met.[65]

U.S. and international law likewise require that human subject experimentation be conducted "only by scientifically qualified persons and under the supervision of a clinically competent medical person."[66] Conflicts of interest between the researcher and human subject should be eliminated and conflicts of value mitigated.[67] Furthermore, "The responsibility for the human subject must always rest with a medically qualified person and never rest on the subject of the research, even though the subject has given consent."[68] The results of studies, positive and negative, must be published accurately.[69]

Human subject experimentation must also be premised on a reasonable chance of success as demonstrated by adequate laboratory and, where appropriate, animal experimentation (also called "modeling"), and thorough knowledge of the "natural history of the disease" and the scientific literature.[70] "Physicians should abstain from engaging in research projects involving human subjects unless they are confident that the risks involved have been adequately assessed and can be satisfactorily managed."[71]

Research projects involving human subjects "should be preceded by careful assessment of predictable risks and burdens in comparison with foreseeable benefits to the subject or to others."[72] The clearly formulated scope of the study and nature of the invasion should not exceed its limited objectives and thereby

---

[63]Declaration of Helsinki, par. 6.

[64]Ibid., par. 19. See also 45 C.F.R. sec. 46.406(c): "Research on children posing more than minimal risk may be federally funded if the procedure is likely to yield generalizable knowledge about the subjects' disorder or condition which is of vital importance for the understanding or amelioration of the subjects' disorder or condition." A similar regulation is found in 21 C.F.R. sec. 50.52 <http://www.access.gpo.gov/nara/cfr/waisidx_03/21cfrv1_03.html>.

[65]21 C.F.R. sec. 50.53.

[66]Declaration of Helsinki, par. 15. See also Nuremberg Code, par. 8; 21 U.S.C.A. sec. 355; 21 C.F.R. sec. 50.

[67]See also Declaration of Helsinki, par. 13, 22, 27.

[68]Ibid., par. 15; see also Nuremberg Code, par. 1.

[69] Declaration of Helsinki, par. 27.

[70]Ibid., par. 11; Nuremberg Code, par. 3.

[71]Declaration of Helsinki, par. 17.

[72]Ibid., par. 16.

cause unnecessary suffering or injury.[73] U.S. law requires "risks reasonable in relation to anticipated benefits, if any, to subjects, and the importance of the knowledge that may reasonably be expected to result."[74]

Finally, human subject experimentation requires exhaustion of alternatives where it is reasonable to believe they exist. In the words of the Nuremberg Code, the results of human subject experimentation must be "unprocurable by other methods or means of study."[75] Where laboratory or animal modeling is an adequate alternative or where research can be conducted on cadavers or legally competent persons, rather than incompetent ones,[76] it must be exhausted.[77]

Jus in experimento. Western law and medicine have also been committed to *jus in experimento* since the 1940s. The principle of consent ensures immunity from involuntary experimentation similar to noncombatant immunity. Even proxy consent protects incompetent human subjects from more than minimally nontherapeutic experimentation. The discrimination principle and just cause principle would appear to merge at this point, whereas the nonaggression principle applies to the nation-state and discrimination principle to the combatant; however, the just cause *ad experimentum* principle may be conceptualized as protecting the status of human beings generally, whereas the discrimination principle protects specific subjects against abuse. As with military discrimination, every effort must be made to protect the lives and autonomy of nonconsenting and especially incompetent living human beings.

Exposing human subjects only to proportionate risks out of medical necessity provides the parallel to proportionality and military necessity. The Nuremberg Code forbade any human experimentation that could lead to "death or disabling injury."[78] Likewise, U.S. law requires minimization of risks to human subjects,[79] where "minimal risk" means "the probability and magnitude of harm or discomfort anticipated in the research" may not be "greater in and of themselves than those ordinarily encountered in daily life or during the performance of routine physical or psychological examinations or tests."[80] Subjects "likely to be vul-

---

[73]Ibid., par. 13; Nuremberg Code, par. 4.
[74]45 C.F.R. sec. 46.111(a). See also Declaration of Helsinki, par. 18; Nuremberg Code par. 3, 6.
[75]Nuremberg Code, par. 2.
[76]Declaration of Helsinki, par. 11, 24.
[77]See also 45 C.F.R. sec. 46.209 (until determined nonviable, fetuses may not be subject to research if its purposes can be obtained by other means).
[78]Nuremberg Code, par. 5.
[79]45 C.F.R. sec. 46.111(a).
[80]Ibid., sec. 46.102(i). The Department of Health and Human Services (HHS) funds research on children posing more than minimal risk only if the increase in risk over minimal risk is minor; see ibid., sec. 46.406(a). The Federal Drug Administration (FDA) funds research not directly benefiting human subjects only under the same condition; see 21 C.F.R. sec. 50.53.

nerable to coercion or undue influence, such as children, prisoners, pregnant women, mentally disabled persons, or economically or educationally disadvantaged persons" are entitled to additional safeguards.[81] No subject is to be exposed to risks unreasonable in relation to the projected benefits.[82]

Like classic just war doctrine, just research theory has been largely self-policing. Physicians and soldiers are primarily responsible for following their respective codes of conduct. Beyond tort liability, U.S. law provides no remedy for a violation of just research theory, aside from terminating a federal research grant or not qualifying for another.[83] This has left the institutional review boards of research institutions with tremendous discretion that is subject to abuse if conflicts of interest or value arise between subjects and researchers. Reported abuses manifest a critical need to tighten rules as the military has with its code of warfare, but the extent to which *jus in experimento* has worked is remarkable—once again, testimony to our divine conscience.

Just Biotechnological Experimentation

Biotechnology poses a unique challenge to just research theory because the living human embryo looks the least like us and because the incestuous relationship between the scientific and industrial community multiplies the potential conflicts of interest and value inherent in the research.[84] Media has assaulted our consciences for over three decades seeking to convince us that the in vitro baby is something other than a living human being who merits legal protection. Our consciences dulled, we are now prone to accept the lie that the living human embryo is merely a goldfish and, thus, should also be excluded from any protection beyond that offered by the Uniform Commercial Code (contract law). We are also conditioned to believe the oxymoronic assurance that the experimentation will be performed "ethically."

The ethics the biotechnological community has in mind represent an assault on natural law, because researchers would permit an entire class of living human beings to literally be produced and experimented on at will (so-called research cloning) in a manner certain to lead to their death—without any significant preceding animal experimentation demonstrating the research's benefits for others, without any demonstrated necessity for the research, and without the valid consent of any person legally authorized to give it. This research would fail even the weak ethical standard of utilitarianism, because researchers cannot demonstrate that the harm to living human embryos will benefit

---

[81]45 C.F.R. sec. 46.111(b).
[82]Ibid., sec. 46.111(a). See also Declaration of Helsinki, par. 18; Nuremberg Code, par. 3, 6.
[83]See Adams, "Creating Clones," p. 119.
[84]See ibid., pp. 119-23.

even one other human being. This is the worst form of utilitarianism or hedonism because no proven remedies—only speculation—is juxtaposed against the cost in human lives the research demands.

Jus ad experimentum violated: no just cause. The biotechnology community's formula for biotechnological research fails the most important prong of *jus ad experimentum,* just cause, because, first, living human embryos obviously cannot consent to the experimentation on them and, second, generally, there is neither a valid proxy to give consent to the experimentation nor a legally valid consent to be had. Media generally are oblivious to both concerns, and they report uncritically that researchers obtained a valid consent to experiment from (in the case of research cloning) egg or DNA donors or (in the case of other biotechnological research) the embryo's parents.

Many times, these donors are not valid proxies because they lack a fiduciary relationship to the living human embryo or, in other words, a relationship requiring the donor to look out for the embryo's best interest. Donors commonly disclaim any responsibility for an embryo when they transfer the embryo or egg and DNA to a research institution, so that they are not obliged to care for any person born after the transfer. Research institutions that receive the embryos obviously do not have the embryos' best interest at heart. Therefore, there is usually no legally recognized proxy even to give consent to biotechnological experimentation.

In the unusual case where a valid proxy can be found, the next legal question is whether the proxy can validly consent to deadly experimentation on their progeny. As set forth above, the common law has never recognized the right of a parent to permit hazardous experimentation on a ward and, indeed, U.S. law explicitly precludes consenting to nontherapeutic research on *ex utero* human fetuses and more than minimally risky experimentation on human beings.[85] To permit a parent or guardian to authorize deadly experimentation on their progeny would represent a radical departure from this precedent and the autonomy principle undergirding *jus ad experimentum.*

No reasonable chance of success or proportionality. Certain types of biotechnological research such as human cloning and ESCR also are not yet premised on a demonstrated reasonable chance of success and, thus, the harm caused by the research is disproportionate to its ends. Few, if any, successful animal models of human cloning or ESCR exist;[86] thus, the rationale for research cloning and killing human embryos (i.e., that we must do it to benefit the infirm) is entirely speculative. Without adequate preceding laboratory and

---

[85]See *infra* pt. II(A)(1).
[86]See the testimony (and the supplemental statement) of David Prentice (professor of life sciences, Indiana State University) before the Government Reform Subcommittee on Criminal Justice, Drug Policy and Human Resources, for a hearing on "Opportunities and Advancements in Stem Cell Research."

animal experimentation, researchers cannot know the risks associated with ESCR, so it is impossible to show its proportionality to its speculative ends. Worse, to the extent cloning has occurred, it has invariably proven to lead to genetic abnormalities in animals, meaning that the likely harm to human beings the research could cause is unjustified.

No last resort. Human cloning and ESCR also fail the last resort test of *jus ad experimentum* for two reasons: first, proven alternatives to ESCR exist and, second, ESCR can be performed on stem cell lines already extracted from deceased human embryos. The pharmaceutical industry is investing heavily in proven adult stem cell research models that do not lead to the loss of human life and are achieving the objectives of ESCR. Unfortunately, media generally confuse this successful adult stem cell research with ESCR and lead many to the wrong conclusion that ESCR is a proven medical therapy when it is only an unproven experimental strategy. ESCR is nevertheless also proceeding, though it is federally funded only if performed on cell lines previously extracted from deceased human embryos, so that there are no federal incentives to kill more.[87]

Jus in experimento violated. The biotechnological establishment's formula for research also violates *jus in experimento*. Biotechnological research is the most hazardous kind of research for the human subject. Research cloning necessarily kills the living human embryo. This is far afield of the permissible "minimally risky" human subject experimentation that U.S. law countenances. Media confuse this issue by focusing not on the subject of the research dissected for its stem cells, but on the speculative benefits the stem cells may have for recipients. Nazi physicians likewise hinged their defense of their practices at Nuremberg on the potential benefit their experimentation would have for German soldiers and citizens. Western civilization justly rejected their defense in the 1940s, but the same argument has persuaded many now that we ought to experiment on living human embryos.

In general, our inability and the media's unwillingness to distinguish therapy from experimentation and patients from human subjects in the biotechnological field are dangerous. Patients undergo *therapy*, whereas human subjects undergo *experimentation*. Therapy leads to benefits for patients, whereas experimentation "contributes to generalizable knowledge" without necessarily or even ordinarily benefiting human subjects.[88] Research cloning will always re-

---

[87]See Casey and Adams, "Specially Respecting," pp. 123-24, citing Omnibus Consolidated Appropriations Act of 2001, Public Law 106-554, sec. 510 (December 21, 2000).

[88]See U.S. Dept. of Health, Education and Welfare, Office for Protection from Research Risks, *The Belmont Report* (Washington, D.C.: OPRR Reports, 1979), p. 3. *Therapy* denotes "interventions that are designed solely to enhance the well-being of an individual patient . . . and have a reasonable expectation of success," whereas *research* is "an activity designed to test a hypothesis . . . and contribute to generalizable knowledge."

main, at best, experimental (at worst, it is murder) because by definition it will never benefit its human subject, the living human embryo, or the subgroup of living human beings to which the embryo belongs and the research is directed. To the contrary, research cloning extracts stem cells from healthy living human embryos not affected by a disease or condition for use in persons affected by them.[89]

The Natural Legal Alternative

The alternative formula that natural legal principles require to specially respect living human embryos does not require doing nothing. To the contrary, it calls for, among other things, redoubled public and private adult stem cell research to achieve all of the objectives of ESCR. Should we discover objectives of ESCR that adult stem cell research cannot achieve, then it requires adequate animal modeling proving, contrary to the best existing evidence, that ESCR would be more successful. If this is demonstrated, it requires that we exhaust research on cell lines already extracted from deceased living human embryos and other suitable alternatives to research on living human embryos. In all likelihood, we will never reach a crossroads requiring us to choose between proceeding with ESCR on living human embryos and not healing human beings; but should we arrive there years from now after taking these steps, we will have shown that ESCR has a reasonable chance of success, established the risks relative to the benefits of proceeding with it on living human embryos and satisfied last resort in keeping with *jus ad experimentum*.

We would be left to consider violating just cause—and to evaluate decision makers' intentions and authorities' competence—before permitting the biotechnological research. If the research intends to benefit the subgroup of human beings with which the living human embryo is associated—and if we assume scientifically qualified persons who have eliminated their conflicts of interests and mitigated their conflicts of value are prepared to proceed—then we shall have to decide whether excusing the violation of just cause in this limited circumstance is warranted.

We might decide that this scenario represents a legitimate exception to the autonomy principle just as, say, preemption is a legitimate exception to the nonaggression principle. The principles of *jus in experimento* could still be employed to minimize the number of living human embryos killed. Whatever decision we made after taking these steps would be far more consistent with the

---

[89]In contrast, genetic engineering at least has the potential someday to prove therapeutic. Genetic engineering also raises troubling questions outside the scope of this chapter, such as how we should react to modifying an embryo's genetic imprint either for the purpose of eliminating inheritable diseases or for merely increasing the height, intelligence and other traits of adults. See Adams, "Creating Clones."

requirements of natural law than would be disregarding and thereby weakening just research theory and rushing headlong now into unjustified nontherapeutic human subject experimentation.

Conclusion

In many respects Western history is all about redeeming humankind from a persistent tendency to accord living human beings less than the fundamental rights with which God endowed us. At each historical milestone, for example, the German Lutheran Reformation of 1517, the English Puritan revolution of 1640, the American Revolution of 1776 and the abolition movement of the 1840s, Christian activism has been crucial to ensure that law affirmed the imago Dei. Tragedy resulted when Christians retreated, failed to act or supported other historical upheavals such as the Russian revolution of 1917 or putsch of the National Socialist Party in 1933.

A medical revolution is dawning on Western civilization that requires Christian activism now as much as at any prior historical crossroads. It presents unique challenges including how we shall treat living human embryos, as well as human clones and quasihuman chimera, if they are born. One vision is to render living human embryos mere property so that they can be produced, patented, priced, packaged and offered for purchase pursuant to contract and property law principles. Another vision, that of natural law, requires that we specially respect living human embryos. The visions could not be more different. Choosing the positivistic one now or simply doing nothing as biotechnology takes over medicine will inevitably overwhelm the prevailing natural legal influence on medicine with serious consequences for all human and quasihuman beings, especially the most vulnerable populations.

The strategic time to confront this unnatural assault on natural law is now. Christians know better than most that the proposition that scientific inquiry will naturally pursue our best interest is fundamentally flawed. Better than most we can also confront the fallacy and sensational rhetoric that well-being and, indeed, eternal life hinge on medicine. Medicine practiced rightly is certainly a way to redeem creation, but true redemption can be found only in Jesus Christ. Unfortunately, many have not come to this realization yet and put their faith in science instead. Due to their efforts and the sheer speed of biotechnological innovation, waiting just a few years to set regulations in place to respect human life could result in centuries of inhumanity. To avoid this outcome, consider what the imago Dei compels you to do.

9

LESSONS FROM
THE CLONING DEBATE

The Need for a Secular Approach

WESLEY J. SMITH, J.D.

Wesley Smith is a prolific writer who has long served the pro-life cause as counsel for a national movement opposed to euthanasia, and he has more recently turned his energies to making the case against cloning. In places such as the Weekly Standard and National Review Online he has proved an indefatigable critic of the egregious claims of the biotech industry as they have sought to advance their cause and block legislation that would bring a comprehensive ban on human cloning. He is a Senior Fellow at the Discovery Institute.

In this essay he reflects on the cloning debate and its lessons for the pro-life cause as we look ahead to the generation of debate that awaits us. After summarizing in lay terms the major issues at stake, he distills his many articles into a series of arguments: the case made by those who favor cloning answered point by point, not simply to convince readers of this book that cloning should be prohibited, but to give us arguments to use with others. He makes a strong case that while Christians will have special Christian reasons for the view they take on biotechnology issues, the public square needs arguments that are not rooted overtly in theology. So that is his focus: how to make the case against cloning, and for human biotech, in the public arena of the twenty-first-century United States.

It is important to understand that the cloning debate offers us a unique opportunity to prepare for what comes next. It is the first round of many, since it represents a discussion of how we handle in public policy one of the first major breakthroughs in biotechnology. It will be followed by some of ambiguous character and some, like cloning, that are overtly and immediately dangerous. One key task facing the church and the pro-life movement is to use the current debate, and what it is teaching us, to prepare for what lies ahead. Smith draws attention to the fact that cloning has brought together conservatives and liberals, Christians and secularists. While from the start astute Christians have sought to argue the abortion issue in public terms, our now being yoked together with others of such diverse commitments means that the nature of the discussion has changed. Whatever the outcome of the current debate on cloning in federal law, it needs to prepare us for a generation-long debate on what Smith calls "whether human life will remain truly human." In the words with which he closes, "What could be more important than that?"

NIGEL M. DE S. CAMERON

The public and the government used to care very much about what positions "the churches" held on important issues of public policy. Indeed, church advocacy was once so important and powerful that even totalitarian governments were sensitive to positions advocated by Christian leaders. For example, in 1933, the new Nazi government backed down from its attempt to legalize euthanasia after an outcry against the proposal led by church leaders.[1] It was not until 1939 that Adolf Hitler signed a secret decree permitting the killing of disabled babies; later adult disabled German citizens were added to the list of killables with the notorious "Operation T4." But even Hitler felt forced to suspend the T4 program—although not the eugenic infanticide euthanasia—after Catholic Archbishop Clemens August Graf von Galen courageously preached a sermon against the German euthanasia program.[2] (German doctors continued to murder disabled adults despite the "official" suspension of T4.)

That was then. This is now. Today the opinions of the churches hold far less sway with the government, in general society and even among parishioners. There are several reasons for this. First, our emphasis on the importance of the individual has reduced the influence exerted by churches and other organized groups over personal conduct and beliefs. Second, the accelerated pace of the secularization of society has resulted in less sway for religious outlooks. This has resulted—perhaps most significantly among young people—in a refusal to listen to or abide by any arguments considered to be "religious," regardless of the cogency or validity of the points made or the depth of their empirical content. Third, many religionists whose faith determines how they will live their individual lives worry that by bringing these perspectives to the public square, they would be "imposing" their religious beliefs on society.

It is also increasingly difficult to determine just what a "church" position is on any controversial public issue. Where once most churches differed on doctrinal issues but generally agreed on moral issues, today churches rarely speak

---

[1]Wesley J. Smith, *Forced Exit: The Slippery Slope from Assisted Suicide to Legalized Murder* (New York: Times Books, 1997), p. 76.
[2]Michael Burleigh, *Death and Deliverance: Euthanasia in Germany, 1900-1945* (New York: Cambridge University Press, 1994), p. 178.

uniformly on any moral issue. On any given public controversy you will find vast differences of opinion among church organizations. For example, the United Church of Christ supports legalizing assisted suicide, whereas the Roman Catholic Church opposes it. Just consider the vast differences between positions taken generally by the World Council of Churches and those of conservative, pro-life Christian religious organizations as a further illustration of the point. This being so, how can society follow the lead of churches when religious people and groups are deeply divided among themselves?

With this state of disagreement, should faith-oriented people withdraw from the crucial moral and public policy debates of the day? Absolutely not. Religious values have just as much place and importance in the marketplace of ideas as those based in philosophy, ideology or just plain personal preferences. Moreover, large numbers of people continue to respond positively to arguments based on religious principles and precepts. Thus, speaking from a religious value system may profoundly influence people who accept those values. Indeed, appealing to religious values remains an important aspect of public policy advocacy on many important public policy issues such as cloning.

This being said, I do believe that religious people who desire to engage the public issues of the day in the public square need to develop a multifaceted approach to their advocacy. Yes, they should equip themselves to make religious-based arguments to fellow believers. But preaching to the choir will generally not succeed in influencing the wider society; more is required. You must be able to effectively argue your points of view from distinctly secular bases.

This is not as daunting as it may sound. Often the secular cases against the proliferating antihuman agendas, such as cloning, are as powerful and evocative as the religious arguments are. Moreover, in a diverse and religiously polyglot society, standing up for right public policies requires that believers learn how to address these crucial issues from various religious bases as well as being able to engage in well-reasoned secular analysis.

Good communication considers where the hearer and reader are coming from, not just the point of view of the speaker or writer. Otherwise, even the best ideas, expertly and cogently expressed, are likely to bounce off the audience's consciousness like a tennis ball hitting a brick wall. For example, if you tell your coworker that you oppose human cloning because it is "playing God," and he or she responds, "So what? I don't believe in God," you have reached a dead end to the conversation unless you can argue forcefully against cloning from a non-God-oriented perspective.

Understanding Basic Terms

In order to communicate effectively, you must understand basic terms. This is especially true when dealing with seemingly complex issues of science, politics and morality. I say "seemingly" because the issues being addressed in this book are not as complicated as many cloning advocates want you to think. (After all, if you believe you can't understand the issue, it is easy to accept the premise that you are not entitled to an opinion on it.) Indeed, while performing the actual physical act of cloning is difficult and intricate, understanding how the process is accomplished and what it means morally is easily within anybody's grasp.

Let's start with a few definitions that you will need to know:

Somatic cell nuclear transfer (SCNT). This is the primary form of human cloning. (There are other potential types of cloning, but for purposes of clarity and brevity, we will concern ourselves only with SCNT.) Most readers will have heard of Dolly, the cloned sheep. Dolly was created through the SCNT process. In theory, we too could be brought into being this same way because humans—like animals such as sheep, mice and cows, which have been cloned successfully—are mammals.

Human SCNT would be accomplished by taking a human egg (oocyte) and removing its nucleus. (The nucleus contains the chromosomes, where the genes reside.) The clone donor (the person being cloned) then provides a "somatic cell," such as a skin cell. (All of our cells are somatic cells, except those from ovaries in women and testes in men, which are called "germ cells.") The nucleus is removed from the skin cell and placed into the empty space in the egg left from the prior removal of its nucleus.

A brief electrical charge is then administered to the genetically modified egg. If the cloning "works," the egg will be transformed into an embryo and begin to divide in the same manner as if it had been fertilized. (I call this the point of "inception" and deem it morally equivalent to the point of conception.) The new embryo would be the near-identical twin—albeit at the embryo stage—of the clone donor since the two would share the identical genetic makeup contained in their forty-six chromosomes. (The egg provides approximately 3 percent of genetic makeup, and thus the cloned embryo is not 100 percent identical to the clone donor.)[3]

After the SCNT process is complete, there are no further acts of cloning. At this point, the future fate of the cloned embryo depends on what its makers decide to do with it. It can be used in medical and scientific research. It can be implanted in a womb toward the end of gestation to a targeted point of fetal development. It can be brought all the way to bringing the cloned baby into the world. But to whatever use it is put, the only act of cloning is SCNT. In other words, contrary to the arguments of some cloning proponents, there is

---

[3]For a good, easy-to-understand description of SCNT, see David A. Prentice, *Stem Cells and Cloning* (San Francisco: Benjamin Cummings, 2003).

no distinction to be made between "reproductive" cloning or "therapeutic" or "research" cloning. These refer to the fate or use of the cloned embryo, not to the act of cloning itself.

Cloning for biomedical research. There are many and varied terms used for human cloning that is undertaken for the purpose of engaging in medical or scientific research (e.g., *therapeutic cloning, SCNT for stem cells,* etc.). The fluidity of the lexicon has caused much confusion in the public debate. For this reason, the President's Council on Bioethics recommended that the term *cloning for biomedical research* (CBR) be used to indicate cloned embryos made via SCNT that are to be used for research rather than for reproductive purposes. Unless indicated otherwise, I will follow the council's advice and use this term.[4]

Cloning to produce children. Cloning undertaken for the purpose of bringing a baby into the world is often called *reproductive cloning.* However, the President's Council on Bioethics recommended the use of the term *cloning to produce children* (CPC) to identify SCNT undertaken for the purpose of implanting in a woman's womb, gestation and birth. Again, this is the terminology I will use.[5]

Stem cell. This is the popular name for a cell that is "undifferentiated." Another term that is sometimes used is *immature cell.* If a cell is undifferentiated, it means that it has not yet become "differentiated": the cell has not yet become one of the more than two hundred types of tissue cells found in the human body (e.g., blood, bone, fat, brain, etc.). To put it more scientifically, a differentiated cell is a "specialized cell type that carries out a specific function in the body, such as heart muscle cell, a neuron in the brain, or a red blood cell carrying oxygen to other cells in the body."[6] Thus, a cell that is undifferentiated—a stem cell—has yet to be transformed into one of these many specific tissue types.

Stem cells are found, most famously, in blastocysts, embryos that have developed and divided for approximately one week. Some researchers believe that by extracting embryonic stem cells—a process that destroys the embryo— they may be able to cause the cells to differentiate into specific tissue types. The hope is to use these stem cells as medical cures for degenerative diseases such as Parkinson's disease, multiple sclerosis and heart disease. (This is called "regenerative medicine" because it would heal by rebuilding damaged organs or tissues.) Advocates of embryonic stem cell research (ESCR) propose using embryos created by in vitro fertilization (IVF) treatments, which are in excess of need as the primary source of embryonic stem cells. But as we shall

---

[4]The President's Council on Bioethics, *Human Cloning and Human Dignity: The Report of the President's Council on Bioethics* (New York, Public Affairs, 2002).
[5]Ibid.
[6]Prentice, *Stem Cells*, p. 3.

see below, some believe the embryos used would have to come from clones.

Stem cells are also found in other tissues, and thus regenerative medical treatments might well be developed without using embryonic stem cells. Umbilical cord blood and placentas contain stem cells; they are found also in bone marrow, blood, the brain, the heart, fat, hair, skin and even the pulp of baby teeth, among other places. Many believe that these "adult" or "nonembryonic" stem cells could offer the benefits of embryonic stem cells without the moral problems associated with destroying embryos. This potential will be discussed in a little more detail later in this chapter.

Therapeutic cloning. Scientists fear that injecting a patient with embryonic stem cells extracted from embryos leftover from IVF procedures, or those that have been created for IVF, might trigger an autoimmune rejection response to the new tissues similar to what occurs when an organ is transplanted. In other words, the body's immune system could seek out the injected tissues and attempt to destroy them. This could mean that patients receiving embryonic stem cell therapy might have to spend the rest of their lives taking strong immune-system-suppressing drugs to prevent tissue rejection.

One way some researchers hope to get around this difficulty is through "therapeutic cloning." This would involve using SCNT to create a cloned embryo of a patient who is to be treated with embryonic stem cells. When the cloned embryo reached the blastocyst stage, it would be destroyed and its stem cells extracted. These would then be cultured into the millions and injected into the patient. In theory the body would not reject these embryonic stem cells (as it might stem cells taken from an IVF embryo) because, having come from a cloned embryo of the patient, they would be an almost exact genetic match. The prospect of developing therapeutic cloning as a viable medical treatment is the primary reason many cloning supporters claim to oppose outlawing banning SCNT to make human life.

Secular Responses to Arguments in Favor of Human Cloning

Now that we understand the most important terms used in the ongoing cloning debate, let's look at the primary secular arguments made in favor of human cloning and some potential secular responses to them.

Argument: Only abortion opponents oppose human cloning; thus, if you are not pro-life, you should support human cloning. Polls demonstrate that the majority of Americans support the right to abortion, at least in some cases.[7] On

---

[7]For example, a January 22, 2003, *CBS News* poll revealed that 22 percent of respondents believed that abortion should not "be permitted." Another 38 percent believed abortion should be permitted with "stricter limits than now," and a further 39 percent opined that abortion should be "generally available."

the other hand, polls also show that most Americans oppose human cloning.[8] Thus, claiming that cloning is a "choice issue" seeks to change the subject and transform the cloning debate into the mirror image of the abortion controversy in the belief that cloning supporters will thus be able to gain the upper hand.

Response. Abortion is factually irrelevant to the issue of human cloning. This may seem counterintuitive since both abortion and many facets of the human cloning debate concern life or death for unborn human life. But that is where the similarity ends.

Why is abortion legal in the United States? Whether one agrees or not, as a matter of protecting the privacy and personal autonomy of women, the courts have decided that the law will not force women who experience an unwanted pregnancy to use their bodies in ways they do not wish to, that is, to gestate and give birth. The political expression of this idea is "right to choose."

But "choice" has nothing whatsoever to do with human cloning. Why? Because in human cloning, no woman is being forced to do anything with her body. Indeed, the act of human cloning (SCNT) takes place outside the woman's body. Hence, the personal autonomy of women—the principle foundation of legalized abortion—is not an issue. This means that the decision whether to support or oppose human cloning should have nothing whatsoever to do with whether one is pro-choice on abortion. Indeed, there are many pro-choice cloning opponents, such as the members of the Center for Genetics and Society.[9] In other words, the abortion argument is nothing more than a red herring designed to distract people from the actual issues of the cloning debate.

Argument: A cloned embryo isn't really human life. Some cloning proponents attempt to justify their support of cloning for biomedical research on the basis that cloned embryos are not really human life. There are many versions of this argument, several of which will be discussed below.

Argument: The product of SCNT is really only an unfertilized egg. The idea behind this assertion is this: since a cloned embryo is not the consequence of the merging of sperm and egg, it is not really an embryo at all, but remains an "unfertilized egg."

One of the primary proponents of this argument is Senator Dianne Feinstein (D-CA). She is the coauthor of legislation that would permit CBR but outlaw implantation of the cloned embryo and require that it be destroyed after fourteen days to prevent a cloned baby from ever being born in the United States.

---

[8]For example, a Gallup poll from May 6, 2002, found that 61 percent of Americans oppose the "cloning of human embryos for use in medical research," with 34 percent in favor. Gallup News Service, August 16, 2002.

[9]See Center for Genetics and Society website at <http://www.genetics-and-society.org>. (The URLs cited in this chapter were accessed on January 16, 2004.)

The beauty of our legislation is that it would allow this most promising form of stem cell research, somatic cell nuclear transplantation, to be conducted on a human egg for up to 14 days only, under strict standards of Federal regulation. . . . The reason for this 14 days is to limit any research before the so-called primitive streak can take over that egg. This stem cell research can only take place on an unfertilized egg. . . . An unfertilized egg is not capable of becoming a human being. Therefore we limit stem cell research to unfertilized eggs.[10]

Response: This argument is utterly self-defeating. If you implant an "unfertilized egg" into a woman's womb, it can never result in a baby being born. Indeed, fertile women of childbearing age release unfertilized eggs from their ovaries every month, and these never result in a baby—unless the egg becomes fertilized by sperm. And while it is true that an unfertilized egg is incapable of becoming a human being, this is not the case with an embryo: introduce an embryo in a woman's womb, and if it implants and all goes well, a baby will be born about nine months later. Thus, the only reason to outlaw the implantation of the products of human SCNT in order to prevent their coming to birth is because they are embryos. Indeed, this was the unanimous conclusion of President's Council for Bioethics even though the members were divided over whether the law should permit CBR.[11]

Argument: Cloned embryos are really only "pre-embryos." One of the most pervasive arguments made by promoters of human cloning is that embryos younger than two weeks' development are really "pre-embryos," meaning that these early embryos have not achieved the moral status of being a human embryo, which is a nascent form of human life.

Response. There is just one problem with that assertion: biologically there is no such thing as a pre-embryo. Indeed, the term was created not for purposes of science but politics and public policy advocacy. Indeed, Princeton University biology professor and cloning enthusiast Lee M. Silver admits in his book *Remaking Eden: Cloning and Beyond in a Brave New World* that the term *pre-embryo* has "been embraced wholeheartedly . . . for reasons that are political, not scientific." He further writes that the term "is useful in the political arena—where decisions are made about whether to allow early embryo (now pre-embryo) experimentation."[12]

Or turn to basic embryology. The authors of the textbook *Human Embryology and Teratology* have refused to recognize the existence of a "pre-embryo" because

---

[10]Remarks by Senator Dianne Feinstein on the floor of the U.S. Senate. *Congressional Record*, June 14, 2002, p. S5580.
[11]President's Council, *Human Cloning and Human Dignity*, p. 56.
[12]Lee M. Silver, *Remaking Eden: Cloning and Beyond in a Brave New World* (New York: Avon, 1997), p. 39.

(1) It is ill-defined; (2) it is inaccurate . . . ; (3) it is unjustified because the accepted meaning of the word embryo includes all of the first 8 weeks; (4) it is equivocal because it may convey the erroneous idea that a new human organism is formed at only some considerable time after fertilization; and (5) it was introduced in 1986 largely for public policy reasons.[13]

We thus see that *pre-embryo* is merely an advocacy term employed by cloners and supporters of other forms of destructive embryonic research to obfuscate the truth: research on early embryos—whether the embryo is formed by fertilization or through cloning—destroys human life.

Argument: An embryo is really just a cell. A more recent attempt to strip the humanity from the cloned embryo claims that that embryos are the moral equivalent of mere cells, such as those you destroy everyday when you brush your teeth. A classic example of this argument was propounded by Alan Russell, executive director of the Pittsburgh Tissue Engineering Initiative, in an opinion column in the *Pittsburgh Post-Gazette:*

> All cells contain DNA, which gives them the ability to reproduce. But cloners have discovered that if one removes the DNA from mom's egg cell (producing an empty cell) and replaces it with her daughter's DNA, the newly produced cell can survive. . . .
>
> We then have in our hands a fresh cell, which from now on will look like her daughter's cell. . . . In a dish, technology will exist to take that cell and simply convince it to multiply—clone itself. . . . The process is called cloning because the new cell created in the laboratory has the ability to copy itself again and again before turning itself into the liver cell that your loved one so desperately needs.[14]

Response. This argument is disingenuous. First, as we have seen, the product of SCNT is not called a clone because its cells divide. If that were true, all of our cells would be clones since all cells replace themselves through cellular division.

Second, while it is true that replacing the egg nucleus with the DNA of the cloned person is the primary technique used to clone in the laboratory, this genetic transfer is not all that happens. As stated earlier, the cloner must next stimulate the genetically modified egg to grow in the same fashion as if it had been fertilized. Thus, just as Dolly the cloned sheep was not the same sheep as the ewe who provided the DNA used in Dolly's cloning, a human cloned embryo would not merely be a somatic cell line; he or she would be a separate and distinct living human entity.

---

[13]Ronan O'Rahilly and Fabiola Muller, *Human Embryology and Teratology,* 3rd ed. (New York: Wiley-Liss, 2001), p. 88.

[14]Alan Russell, "Human Therapeutic Cloning: Life-Saving Medicine, not Scary Monsters," *Pittsburgh Post-Gazette,* December 2, 2001.

Finally, the "new cell" does not "copy itself again and again" until, as if by magic, it suddenly becomes various body tissues. Rather, if the cloned embryo survives long enough, he or she would go through exactly the same stages of gestational development as any other baby would: from an embryo, to a fetus, to a baby at birth. Indeed, the cloned embryo's makeup would be identical to a "natural" embryo's at the same stages of development.

Argument: If it has the ability to twin, it isn't human. Some cloning supporters claim that an embryo isn't really human life until it can no longer become an identical twin. The idea seems to be that until the time in embryonic development when identical twinning cannot occur, the embryo isn't really a human individual. Since human research clones would be destroyed prior to that time, according to this argument, destroying the clone would not actually take a human life. (However, note that in early 2004, New Jersey enacted a law that legalized SCNT, implantation and gestation through the ninth month.[15])

Response. The argument is mere sophistry. Naturally occurring identical twins originate from the same fertilized egg. (Fraternal twins develop from different fertilized eggs.) Twinning occurs early in gestation when the single embryo splits into two identical embryos—a natural form of cloning. These identical embryos are now siblings.

Before twinning, an embryo, whether naturally conceived or cloned, is an individual, self-contained embryonic human life with a gender and an individual genetic makeup. After identical twinning, there are now two, individual, self-contained human lives, each having an identical gender and genetic makeup. In other words, there are now two distinct human lives instead of one. But just because there is a time in the embryo's existence when it has the potential to "twin" (a relatively rare event), that does not mean it is not a unique and fully human form of life prior to the time in which twinning can no longer occur. Besides, even identical twins are not really identical. Yes, they have identical chromosomes, but that is not all there is to human life. For example, identical twins emerge from the womb with different fingerprints.

Summary. Would a cloned embryo be a nascent form of human life? Clearly, the *biological* answer is an unequivocal yes. (It wouldn't be Martian, after all.) That does not necessarily settle the issue since, as we shall see, many people believe that it takes more than simple biological membership in the human species for an entity or being to have meaningful moral value. But at the very least, public policy debates on these issues should be founded on the biological facts. Otherwise, the quality of public discourse sinks into the realm of political spin, wishful thinking, emotionalism or myth.

---

[15]S-1909/A 2840, signed into law January 6, 2004.

Argument: Embryos are not "persons," and so it is not immoral to use them for research purposes. This argument raises the question, is being a human life meaningful in and of itself? Or to put it another way, does human life have ultimate value simply and merely because it is human?

Many in bioethics and biotechnology argue that what is morally important is not being biologically human but having certain cognitive abilities, such as being self-aware over time and being able to think rationally. Since embryos are clearly without consciousness, proponents of this view assert that no wrong is done in destroying them for their tissues, particularly if the tissues could help born human persons.[16]

Response. If the value of life is based on consciousness rather than on humanhood, then other members of the human family can also be used as a natural resource. For example, many in bioethics extend the "nonperson" category to newborn infants, people with Alzheimer's, people diagnosed to be in a permanent coma and the like.[17] If we deem it acceptable to use embryos because they are not persons in this way, then why not use fetuses? And if fetuses, why not newborns or people in comas? And, in reviewing the professional literature, we find that these arguments *are already being made.* For example, some bioethicists and members of the transplant medical community urge that the definition of death be redefined to include a diagnosis of permanent unconsciousness for the purpose of making the comatose eligible as organ donors.[18] Basing these decisions on "personhood" is a slippery slope leading to the exploitation and oppression of the most weak and vulnerable human lives.

Argument: Cloning is essential if we are to develop new medical treatments. Regenerative medicine, if it can be developed, would use stem cells to rebuild damaged tissues and organs as a treatment for degenerative conditions such as Parkinson's disease, heart damage and spinal cord injury. The "best" stem cells for this, proponents claim, are embryonic stem cells, since theoretically, they can be transformed into every kind of tissue in the body. But since these tissues (taken from embryos leftover from IVF procedures) could cause the patient's immune system to reject the tissues, researchers must learn how to clone patients so that the resulting embryos can be used in therapeutic cloning procedures. Thus, according to this claim, if

---

[16]For a more detailed critique of "personhood theory," see Wesley J. Smith, *Culture of Death: The Assault on Medical Ethics in America* (San Francisco: Encounter, 2000).

[17]See, e.g., Peter Singer, *Rethinking Life and Death: The Collapse of Our Traditional Ethics* (New York: St. Martin's, 1994).

[18]See, e.g., R. Hoffenberg et. al. (for the International Forum for Transplant Ethics), "Should Organs from Patients in Permanent Vegetative State Be Used In Transplantation?" *Lancet* 350 (November 1, 1997).

we are to develop a thriving regenerative medical sector, CBR must be not only allowed but encouraged.

Response. Permitting CBR is one of history's most radical ideas. Consider this: for the first time in human history human life would be created not to be brought to birth, *but rather for the purpose of being used as a natural resource:* it would be destroyed for the purpose of extracting tissues. Not only that, but under many proposals, the destruction of human embryos created via SCNT would be required by law. This may be a first in human history. One doesn't have to be religious to get a queasy stomach over the prospect of sowing and harvesting human life as if it were a mere corn crop. This moral concern is a core issue in the debate.

But morality aside—and let me be clear, it should *never* be set aside—therapeutic cloning is not practicable. Indeed, the chances that therapeutic cloning will ever become a widely available and viable medical procedure are extremely slim. First, the animal studies demonstrate that embryonic stem cells, when injected into adult bodies, tend to form tumors.[19] *This is a different problem than tissue rejection and would not be solved by using cloned embryos* instead of those arising from natural fertilization. Second, even if the tumor problem could be overcome (which is certainly no given), the impracticalities of therapeutic cloning make its use as a viable medical treatment highly unlikely. Think about what would be required.

First, cloned embryos would have to be made from patients and would have to be sustained to the point where embryonic stem cells developed. To date, this has not been successfully accomplished.

Then a viable stem cell line would have to be created. This is far more difficult than it sounds. Indeed, in animal models there is a low rate of success at developing stem cell lines. This means that many clones of each patient to be treated with therapeutic cloning would have to be created in order to derive just one stem cell line.

Next, the stem cell line would have to be induced to produce the specific tissue type required—again, no easy task.

Finally, if all of this were successful, the patient could be treated with the cells.

Clearly, this process would be so complicated, time-consuming, intricate and impractical that therapeutic cloning, if it could ever be perfected, would be available only to very few, meaning to the very rich. The more likely scenario is that therapeutic cloning is unlikely to ever become a widespread med-

---

[19]See, e.g., J. Fallon et al., "In Vivo Induction of Massive Proliferation Directed Migration, and Differentiation of Neural Cells in the Adult Mammalian Brain," *Proceedings of the National Academy of Sciences USA,* December 19, 2000.

ical therapy. Indeed, even some embryonic stem cell researchers are beginning to acknowledge that the promise of therapeutic cloning is more hype than realistic expectation.[20]

Happily, there are alternatives to therapeutic cloning that do look very promising. Some human trials have already undertaken using adult stem cells as treatment. Human studies have demonstrated that adult stem cells extracted from the blood and bone marrow appear to rebuild damaged hearts. One patient has been treated for Parkinson's disease with his own brain stem cells, with apparent success. (Of course, one patient does not a cure make.) Treatments for other conditions, such as type 1 diabetes and multiple sclerosis, are currently in or nearing adult stem cell human trials.

The good news is that with adult stem cells, no moral problem is presented because the patient's own tissues become medicine. This also means that there is no problem with tissue rejection. And, so far at least, adult tissues do not seem to cause tumors, although certainly far more studies are needed with regard to this issue. In summary, not only is it highly unlikely that therapeutic cloning will ever become a significant form of medical treatment, but even if it could be developed, it may very well be unnecessary. In contrast, adult stem cells might well provide most or all of the benefits promised by therapeutic cloning proponents—with none of the moral problems associated with destroying and harvesting human life.

Clearly, the arguments that favor human cloning are unpersuasive, both from the moral and practical standpoints. But there is still more to the story. Let's turn now to some of the secular arguments against human cloning that may help convince your secular friends that this is a biotechnology that should not be allowed.

Secular Arguments Against Human Cloning

Some of the most potent arguments against permitting human cloning have nothing to do with religion or the charge that cloning is "playing God." Unfortunately, these are not often widely covered in the mainstream media. However, this factor can work to your advantage since it may induce a "Gee, I never thought of that!" kind of reaction that could be the first step in changing minds and hearts.

Argument: Cloning for biomedical research will lead to cloning to produce children. There seems to be near universal agreement that CPC should be out-

---

[20]See, e.g., "Stem Cells Won't Be Used as Therapies but Will Spawn Them, Pioneer Gearhart Predicts," *Washington Fax*, November 19, 2002. Gearhart stated, however, that he believes that ESCR—which is different than therapeutic cloning—could provide researchers a chance to learn how to harness adult stem cells for use in regenerative medicine.

lawed; but division persists as to whether to permit CBR, based on its supposed potential to help treat degenerative illnesses and injuries. Thus, some have advocated a federal law that would legally prohibit implanting a cloned embryo but permit such embryos to be created for research purposes so long as they were destroyed after fourteen days.[21] There is only one problem with this approach: *legalizing CBR would result in attempts to bring cloned babies into the world.*

Why would this be the result? First, typically such legislation would authorize the manufacture of cloned human embryos to the blastocyst stage, a necessary step toward successfully creating a cloned human baby. (New Jersey even permits implantation and gestation!) Not coincidentally, the blastocyst stage is when an embryo's stem cells can be extracted and also when it becomes implantable in a womb, because it then has the capacity to begin forming a placenta. Once researchers succeeded in creating blastocysts, there would be no realistic way to use them exclusively for stem cell extraction. Some day, some researcher would implant them in a womb, leading eventually to the first born cloned baby.

Second, such legislation would also open the door to various other cloning experiments designed to maximize the chances for human reproductive cloning to become a reality. Such experiments would include the creation of part-human, part-animal embryos (chimeras) for study. Nothing in any legislation introduced in the United States would prevent such bizarre experiments.

Third, if enacted, such a law would give research into human cloning the invaluable imprimatur of the government of the United States. The law doesn't merely reflect our values—it tells many people right from wrong. Passing a law explicitly sanctioning the creation of cloned embryos would send a loud message to society that this is a proper and moral act. As a consequence, the pace of cloning research would likely increase substantially, heightening the chances that a cloned baby would someday be born.

If we want to prevent the birth of cloned babies, the only way is to outlaw human cloning for any purpose.

Argument: Cloning will lead to the exploitation of women. There are two absolutely essential ingredients for successful SCNT cloning. One is a somatic cell from the clone donor. No problems there: each human being has trillions. The other is the human egg. And here is where both CPC and CBR hit a brick wall, for we can create only as many patient clones as there are eggs available for use in SCNT. Thus the entire argument over cloning may boil down to the answer to one crucial and unavoidable question: where are researchers going to get the millions of eggs that would be needed to treat the tens of millions of

---

[21]See, e.g., the S-303, 108th Congress.

patients who could theoretically benefit from therapeutic cloning or who would want to give birth to a cloned baby?

The simple answer is, they won't get them. Let's focus only on the number of eggs needed to treat patients with therapeutic cloning. Assuming that cloning researchers could overcome the rejection problem and tumor problems—even assuming perfect clinical conditions—there is no way past the fact that at least one human egg would be required for each patient receiving embryonic stem cell therapy. Now, consider the number of people with medical conditions that embryonic stem cell therapies are supposed to treat—people with Parkinson's disease, Lou Gehrig's disease, multiple sclerosis and Huntington's disease, as well as those who have suffered strokes or spinal cord injuries. According to an estimate by National Academies of Science, there are more than one hundred million such patients in the United States alone, meaning that even in a perfect cloning world, where the success ratio was one clone per genetically modified egg, we would need at least one hundred million human ova for use in embryonic stem cell cloning. There is simply no way that many eggs will be harvested.

But that is only the beginning of the numbers crunch. As daunting and insurmountable as number one hundred million may seem, it is more likely that for the foreseeable future it would undoubtedly take many eggs to successfully create just one human clone embryo. This means that the actual number of eggs that would be necessary for clinical application of therapeutic cloning would be utterly staggering.

Dr. David Prentice, professor of life sciences at Indiana State University and an expert in stem cell research and an opponent of human cloning, has done the math for only one patient group: diabetics. The results are devastating to the prospect of ever seeing therapeutic cloning enter medicine's armamentarium.

There are approximately sixteen million diabetics in the United States.

Prentice assumed that 20 percent of cloning attempts would succeed in reaching the blastocyst stage of development. (This number is based on published reports of cases where researchers have successfully obtained blastocysts from animal cloning. The number is more than fair since cloning a genetically sound human embryo would be far more difficult than cloning an embryonic mouse, sheep or cat.)

He next assumed that stem cells would be successfully derived from 10 percent of these clone embryos. (This figure is also fair. It took thirty-six embryos for James Thomson of the University of Wisconsin to create five human embryonic stem cell lines, a 13.8 percent success rate. The Jones Institute used 110 embryos to get only three stem cell lines, a 2.7 percent success rate.)

Using these figures, Prentice computed that it would take *800 million eggs* just to treat the sixteen million American diabetics with clone embryonic stem cells.

There simply aren't enough women of childbearing age to supply all these eggs.

Now let's look at what it takes to obtain human eggs. Harvesting human eggs requires that a woman be given strong hormones to stimulate her ovaries to release seven to ten eggs in her monthly cycle rather than the usual single egg. (This process is called *hyperovulation*.) Assuming (generously) that ten eggs are harvested from each procedure, we would still need *80 million egg donations* from women of childbearing age. Considering the number of people in the United States with other diseases who have been promised they will benefit from clone ES cell therapy, the actual number of women that would be required to donate eggs just to treat patients in this country can hardly be imagined.

Now, consider the difficulties involved with hyperovulation. The procedure is not exactly a walk in the park. After the ovaries are stimulated to release multiple eggs, the ova are surgically extracted. A partial list of potential side effects from the procedure includes rupture of the ovaries, severe pelvic pain, accumulation of fluid in the abdomen as well as around the heart and lungs, bleeding into abdominal cavity, acute respiratory distress and pulmonary embolism. That being so, how many American women are going to be willing to provide eggs for use in cloning?

Of course there are hundreds of millions of women in the developing world who could provide eggs. But that would require a disgusting market in human ova in which poor women would submit to hyperovulation for pay without any personal therapeutic benefit. Moreover, these women would probably not have access to quality medical care if they experienced side effects. So, once again, cloning has the potential to reduce some humans to mere natural resources—in this case, poor women of childbearing age. In short, such a market in human eggs would result in the exploitation of women.

Argument: Cloning will lead to a new eugenics. Leon Kass, chairman of the President's Council on Bioethics, has written, "It is our difficult task to find ways to preserve [society] from the soft dehumanizations of well-meaning but hubristic biotechnical 'recreationism'—and to do it without undermining biomedical science or rejecting its genuine contributions to human welfare."[22]

What did Kass mean? There are a dedicated cadre of bioethicists, philosophers and ethicists who literally want to use genetic engineering to seize control of human evolution. This movement to create a "posthuman" world is known as *transhumanism*.

Transhumanism is a nascent and explicitly eugenic philosophy that advocates seizing control of human evolution through bioengineering. Transhumanists come from the highest levels of academia. For example, the founder

---

[22]Leon R. Kass, "Preventing a Brave New World," *New Republic*, May 21, 2001.

of the movement, Nick Bostrom, is a professor of philosophy at Yale University who recently received a three-year fellowship at Oxford University.

Transhumanists are biotech absolutists. They assert that humans should not merely be allowed to metamorphose themselves through plastic surgery, cybertechnology and the like, but should have the right to control the destiny of their genes via progeny design and fabrication. This could include replacing natural chromosomes with artificial chromosomes, increasing or decreasing the number of chromosomes in offspring or clones and even "mixing species boundaries."

Cloning is the one essential technology that must succeed if transhumanists are to be empowered to pursue their misguided quest. As Princeton biologist (and enthusiastic proponent of genetic engineering) Lee Silver has admitted in his book *Remaking Eden: Cloning and Beyond in a Brave New World*, "without cloning, genetic engineering is simply science fiction. But with cloning, genetic engineering moves into the realm of reality."[23]

It is folly to attempt to reengineer human life into a "better version." But the only way to truly prevent it may be to outlaw all human cloning. Otherwise, we may find ourselves faced with a future in which even "normal" babies are deemed inadequate, forcing prospective parents to engage in a never-ending genetic arms race in which "designer babies"—enhanced for greater beauty, intelligence, strength, sports ability, musical talent or other attributes—move us toward a new super race. Indeed, Silver predicts a day when

> all aspects of the economy, the media, the entertainment industry, and the knowledge industry are controlled by members of the GenRich class. [This is the name he gives to the genetically enhanced.] GenRich parents can afford to send their children to private schools rich in the resources required for them to take advantage of their enhanced genetic potential. In contrast, Naturals [i.e., genetically normal humans] work as low-paid service providers or as laborers, and their children go to public schools.

Eventually, Silver predicts, "The GenRich class and the Natural class will become the GenRich humans and the Natural humans—entirely separate species with no ability to cross-breed, and with as much romantic interest in each other as a current human would have with a chimpanzee."[24]

Of course there would be a lot of bumps in the road between here and there. We are, after all, the species that created the unsinkable ship *Titanic*. Only with genetic engineering, it wouldn't be a luxury ship that could sink, but perhaps the genetic future of the entire human race.

---

[23]Silver, *Remaking Eden*, p. 129.
[24]Ibid., pp. 6-7.

Here's another point to ponder: As the new eugenics accelerates, fewer and fewer "genetically inferior" humans would make it through gestation. Embryos are already eugenically selected for implantation or discard at IVF clinics, and expectant parents are often pressured to terminate pregnancies when prenatal testing discloses the presence of Down syndrome or other genetic anomalies. The same fate would likely await embryos or fetuses found to have genetic predispositions to diseases such as breast cancer or Alzheimer's and to mental illness. Moreover, as our knowledge about the interaction of genes increased, unborn life found to possess non-health-related "undesirable" traits might also be rejected. These unfortunates might include those diagnosed as having a propensity toward obesity, homely features, alcoholism or other addictive behaviors, homosexuality, undesirable stature, poor athletic ability, low intelligence, criminal or other antisocial behavior, and so on—the list could go on for pages.

Had such a world existed in years past, Ludwig van Beethoven might never have been allowed to be born, considering his genetically destined deafness. If Abraham Lincoln suffered from bipolar disorder (also known as manic-depressive illness), as some have speculated, he might well have been "selected out" in favor of an embryo likely to have a less troubled nature. For that matter, we might have lost Winston Churchill when his genetic screeners warned his parents that he would have a predisposition for alcoholism. And what about Eleanor Roosevelt? Had her homeliness been able to be predicted in utero, her parents might have decided to spare her the woe of ever being born.

And think about the people we encounter every day who have traits that others might want to genetically weed out but who enrich our lives: the wisecracking waitress with the club foot who makes Saturday morning breakfasts such a joy; the teacher whose students laugh at her speech impairment behind her back only to discover later that she changed their lives; the developmentally disabled man whose loving nature makes him the community favorite; the wise grandparent who nurtured and mentored his grandchildren and then died too young of genetically caused colon cancer.

Aldous Huxley wrote of his prophetic novel, "The theme of *Brave New World* is not the advancement of science as such; it is the advancement of science as it affects human individuals."[25] Eugenics is evil because holds that all people are not created equal. Such thinking objectifies the lives of disfavored individuals, leading with the force of gravity to a fundamentally unjust society. Should the new eugenics ever take hold, the dysfunction described in *Brave New World* would seem mild by comparison.

---

[25]Aldous Huxley, foreword to *Brave New World* (New York: Harper Perennial, 1998), p. xi.

The Stakes in the Debate

I hope that the arguments I have presented in this chapter present a compelling case against permitting human cloning that will resonate with people of all political stripes and religious sensibilities. The cloning debate is not one between secularists and religionists, or between left and right on the political spectrum. Rather, it is, quite starkly, a debate of right versus wrong. How this plays out in a democratic society will tell the tale of twenty-first-century morality and whether human life will remain truly human. Could there be anything more important than that?

10

BIOTECH AND PUBLIC POLICY

The European Debate

HENK JOCHEMSEN, Ph.D.

This book sets out to address a chiefly American audience about what has been an American debate. Yet it is also a global debate. Indeed, one of the most intriguing aspects to current discussion is the manner in which debates on Capitol Hill are mirrored by discussion in such multilateral bodies as UNESCO and the United Nations General Assembly. As it happens, the most advanced discussion of these policy questions has taken place in Europe, principally through the Council of Europe (not to be confused with the smaller European Union), which includes all the democracies in Europe, including Russia—more than forty states in total. Historically, social issues of this kind were the province of the council, while the EU focused on economic questions, although recent developments in the EU have broadened its agenda.

The Council of Europe has developed the only international treaty on bioethics: the Convention on Human Rights and Biomedicine, which was opened for signature in 1997. Broadly speaking, the European approach has been conservative in nature. This reflects in part the unique situation in Germany, where for reasons of history a deep caution in respect to medicine and biotechnology is found across much of the political spectrum. It also reflects the influence of the Catholic church in many European countries, as well as the influence of environmentalists (through the Green Party). European debate has also focused heavily on agricultural biotech, and there has been deep opposition to "genetically modified" foods right across the continent. To some degree this has distracted from the issues of human biotech, although these issues are coming into clearer focus.

Henk Jochemsen has long been a leading Christian voice in the European bioethics debate, serving as director of one of the handful of evangelical Christian bioethics centers in Europe. His background in molecular biology and bioethics and his current appointment to the chair of medical ethics at the Free University of Amsterdam prepare him well for the task of reviewing the European debate.

NIGEL M. DE S. CAMERON

A substantial number of independent states in Europe have their own policy in matters of life sciences and bioethics, unless they have signed some form of (international) agreement or are bound otherwise to regulations pertaining to those fields.

Two major European institutions have generated a context of regulations and agreements also in matters of bioethics, the Council of Europe (see fig. 2) and the European Union (see fig. 3). In this chapter I will not so much give an overview of the way in which the various states have or have not regulated issues in bioethics, but rather present and discuss the major documents that have been produced in these two organizations and that influence the member states to at least some extent.[1] We will limit ourselves to documents that pertain to human life and health, foregoing the fierce and interesting discussions on bioethics in agriculture and food. This will give a fair impression of the way those issues are being dealt with in the context of the (self-named) First World.

I will begin by briefly presenting the two organizations, and then I will deal with the main documents of each of them.

Two Circles of European States

The Council of Europe. The Council of Europe (CoE) is an intergovernmental organization that was established in 1949 by ten states. It now has forty-five member states. The aims of the CoE are

- to protect human rights, pluralist democracy and the rule of law

- to promote awareness and encourage the development of Europe's cultural identity and diversity

- to seek solutions to problems facing European society (e.g., discrimination against minorities, xenophobia, intolerance, environmental protection, human cloning, AIDS, drugs, organized crime, etc.)

- to help consolidate democratic stability in Europe by backing political, legislative and constitutional reform[2]

---

[1] A helpful overview of bioethical discussions in European contexts and main European states until 1994 is given by A. Rogers and Denis Durand de Bousingen, *Bioethics in Europe* (Strasbourg: Council of Europe Press, 1995).

[2] Excerpted from <http://www.coe.int/ DefaultEN.asp>. (The URLs cited in this chapter were accessed on January 16, 2004.)

Forty-Five Member States
Albania (13.07.1995)
Andorra (10.11.1994)
Armenia (25.01.2001)
Austria (16.04.1956)
Azerbaijan (25.01.2001)
Belgium (05.05.1949)
Bosnia & Herzegovina
 (24.04.2002)
Bulgaria (07.05.1992)
Croatia (06.11.1996)
Cyprus (24.05.1961)
Czech Republic
 (30.06.1993)
Denmark (05.05.1949)
Estonia (14.05.1993)
Finland (05.05.1989)
France (05.05.1949)
Georgia (27.04.1999)
Germany (13.07.1950)
Greece (09.08.1949)
Hungary (06.11.1990)
Iceland (07.03.1950)
Ireland (05.05.1949)
Italy (05.05.1949)

Latvia (10.02.1995)
Liechtenstein (23.11.1978)
Lithuania (14.05.1993)
Luxembourg (05.05.1949)
Malta (29.04.1965)
Moldova (13.07.1995)
Netherlands (05.05.1949)
Norway (05.05.1949)
Poland (26.11.1991)
Portugal (22.09.1976)
Romania (07.10.1993)
Russian Federation
 (28.02.1996)
San Marino (16.11.1988)
Serbia and Montenegro
 (03.04.2003)
Slovakia (30.06.1993)
Slovenia (14.05.1993)
Spain (24.11.1977)
Sweden (05.05.1949)
Switzerland (06.05.1963)
Former Yugoslav Republic
 of Macedonia (09.11.1995)
Turkey (09.08.1949)
Ukraine (09.11.1995)

United Kingdom
 (05.05.1949)

**States Candidate for
Membership**
Belarus (12.03.1993)
Monaco (21.10.1998)

**The Observers to the
Committee of Ministers**
Canada (29.05.1996)
Holy See (07.03.1970)
Japan (20.11.1996)
Mexico (01.12.1999)
United States of America
 (10.01.1996)

**The National Parliaments
Observers to the
Parliamentary Assembly**
Canada (28.05.1997)
Israel (02.12.1957)
Mexico (04.11.1999)

Figure 2. The Council of Europe[3]

The major institutions of the CoE are the Committee of Ministers, which is the CoE's decision-making body, comprising the foreign affairs ministers of all the member states (or their permanent representatives); and the Parliamentary Assembly, which is the CoE's deliberative body, the members of which are appointed by national parliaments. In the context of this chapter the CoE's Steering Committee on Bioethics deserves being mentioned too. It is the expert committee, set up in 1985, that has its mandate from the Committee of Ministers and is responsible for preparing texts on bioethics, which are then debated in the Parliamentary assembly. Its members are elected by the member states.

The European Union. According to the official website of the European Union (EU),

> The European Union (EU) was set up after the 2nd World War. The process of European integration was launched on 9 May 1950 when France officially proposed to create "the first concrete foundation of a European federation." Six countries (Belgium, Germany, France, Italy, Luxembourg and the Netherlands) joined from the very beginning. Today, after four waves of accessions (1973: Denmark, Ire-

---

[3]See <http://www.coe.in/T/E/Com/About_Coe/Member_states/default.asp>.

land and the United Kingdom; 1981: Greece; 1986: Spain and Portugal; 1995: Austria, Finland and Sweden) the EU has 15 Member States and is preparing for the accession of 13 eastern and southern European countries.

The European Union is based on the rule of law and democracy. It is neither a new State replacing existing ones nor is it comparable to other international organisations. Its Member States delegate sovereignty to common institutions representing the interests of the Union as a whole on questions of joint interest. All decisions and procedures are derived from the basic treaties ratified by the Member States.

Principal objectives of the Union are:
Establish European citizenship (Fundamental rights; Freedom of movement; Civil and political rights);
Ensure freedom, security and justice (Cooperation in the field of Justice and Home Affairs);
Promote economic and social progress (Single market; Euro, the common currency; Job creation; Regional development; Environmental protection);
Assert Europe's role in the world (Common foreign and security; The European Union in the world).

The EU is run by five institutions, each playing a specific role:
European Parliament (elected by the peoples of the Member States);
Council of the Union (composed of the governments of the Member States);
European Commission (driving force and executive body);
Court of Justice (compliance with the law);
Court of Auditors (sound and lawful management of the EU budget).[4]

A special group that needs to be mentioned here is the European Group on Ethics in Science and Technologies to the European Commission (EGE): "The Group is an independant, [sic] pluralist and multidisciplinary body which advises the European Commission on ethical aspects of science and new technologies in connection with the preparation and implementation of Community legislation or policies."[5] Though in a somewhat different form, the EGE was set up in 1991; it got its present name and terms of reference in 1998. It produces opinions on ethical aspects of new technological developments, among others, in the field of biotechnology and medicine, which are made available to the public.

In the limited space of this chapter only a selection of topics that concern the protection of human life and human rights in the context of new biomedical and biotechnological advances can be discussed.

---

[4]Excerpted from <http://www.projecteu.com/eu.htm>.
[5]Excerpted from <http://europa.eu.int/comm/european_group_ethics/index_en.htm>.

Member States	Portugal	Slovakia
Austria	Spain	Slovenia
Belgium	Sweden	
Denmark	United Kingdom	**Candidate Countries**
Finland	Cyprus	Bulgaria
France	Czech Republic	Romania
Germany	Estonia	Turkey
Greece	Hungary	
Ireland	Latvia	**Applications Pending**
Italy	Lithuania	Croatia
Luxembourg	Malta	Former Yugoslav Republic
The Netherlands	Poland	of Macedonia

Figure 3. The European Union as of May 2004[6]

Bioethics in the Council of Europe

Recommendations. The Parliamentary Assembly has over the years adopted a number of "recommendations" on bioethical issues. Those recommendations have no binding force for the member states, but they give a political sign and have a certain influence on policy and public opinion. I will mention a few of those recommendations.

"Recommendation 934 on Genetic Engineering" focuses on genetic modification of organisms and gene therapy in humans. Important principles in this R, in addition to the right to the health and safety of humans, are

- freedom of scientific inquiry, though that is linked immediately with duties and responsibilities in regard to health and safety to the public in general and scientists

- informed consent of patients involved in gene therapy

- the right to inherit a genetic pattern that has not been artificially changed, which is based on the rights to life and to human dignity protected by articles 2 and 3 of the Council of Europe's Convention for the Protection of Human Rights and Dignity of the Human Being with regard to the Application of Biology and Medicine: Convention on Human Rights and Biomedicine (known widely as the Convention on Human Rights and Biomedicine). This latter, newly phrased right is widely debated and criticized. In fact Recommendation 934 itself already states that this right should not impede developments of the therapeutic applications of gene therapy: the right is conditioned by the phrase, "except in accordance with certain principles which are recognised as being fully compatible with respect for human rights."[7]

---

[6]See <http://www.eurunion.org/states/home.htm>.
[7]Council of Europe, Parliamentary Assembly, Recommendation 934, sec. 7.b.

Interestingly Recommendation 934 asks the Council of Ministers to examine the patentability of microorganisms genetically altered by recombinant DNA techniques. There was no regulation or *communis opinio* on this issue, although two years before, the Supreme Court in the United States had decided in favor of a patent on a (supposedly) genetically modified bacterium.

Some recommendations deal with the use of human gametes, embryos and fetuses for various purposes. These are "Recommendation 1046 on the Use of Human Embryos and Foetuses for Diagnostic, Therapeutic Scientific Industrial and Commercial Purposes" (adopted September 24, 1986) and "Recommendation 1100 on the Use of Human Embryos and Foetuses in Scientific Research" (adopted February 2, 1989).

Recommendations 1046 and 1100 point out the biological and genetic continuity of the human embryo after fertilization throughout its whole developmental process and the impossibility of making clear-cut distinctions between embryos in different developmental stages, and they require that embryos be treated with the respect due to human dignity. At the same time they recognize that opinions vary on the use of the embryo or fetal tissue and ask for initiatives that should lead to a common legal instrument in the issues at stake.

In Recommendation 1046, the Parliamentary Assembly calls on the governments of the member states to forbid (among other things),

- creation of human embryos by IVF for research

- research on viable human embryos and experimentation on living human embryos whether viable or not

- "the creation of identical human embryos by cloning or any other method"

- "the fusion of [human] embryos or any other operation which might produce chimeras"[8]

Among the rules given in the appendix to Recommendation 1046, it is stated that "no intervention . . . on the living [human] embryo *in vitro* or *in utero* or on the foetus whether inside or outside the uterus shall be permitted, unless its object is the well-being of the child to be born."[9] The use of tissue from (aborted) dead fetuses is accepted under certain conditions.[10]

In sum, the mood in the CoE on the question of the status of the human embryo—though certainly not unequivocally pro-life—is pretty much inclined to grant the human embryo a considerable degree of protection. This is most

---

[8]Council of Europe, Parliamentary Assembly, Recommendation 1046 sec. 14.A.ii, iv.
[9]Appendix to Council of Europe, Parliamentary Assembly, Recommendation 1046, sec. B.i.
[10]Ibid., sec. B.1.vi; appendix to Council of Europe, Parliamentary Assembly, Recommendation 1100, sec. D and E.

likely due to a still quite broadly present (in those years) vacillation with respect to biotechnological interventions in humans and to the influence of
strongly Roman Catholic states (like Malta), of the Vatican, which has an ob-
server status in the deliberations of the CDBI ("Council of Europe's Steering
Committee on Bioethics" in English), and of the Greens, who (especially in
Germany) took a strong antigenetic intervention position.

Convention on Human Rights and Biomedicine. The most important document from the CoE on matters of bioethics is the Convention of Human Rights
and Biomedicine. Its roots go back to Recommendation 1100 (passed in 1989),
which asks for the framing of a common legal instrument with respect to human reproduction and biomedicine, and more explicitly to Recommendation
1160 (passed in 1991), in which the assembly recommends that the Committee
of Ministers "envisage a framework convention comprising a main text with
general principles and additional protocols on specific aspects."[11]

After many deliberations, the text of Recommendation 1160 was adopted
by the Committee of Ministers on November 19, 1996, and the Convention on
Human Rights and Biomedicine was opened for signature by the member
states in the conference in Oviedo, Spain, on April 4, 1997. By January 28, 2004,
the thirty-one states had signed the convention, although only seventeen of
these had also ratified it. Among these seventeen are only four of the fifteen
EU countries. It is noteworthy that so far the UK and Germany have not signed
it, probably because the UK has a more permissive regulation of embryo research than the convention accepts and because in Germany the acceptance of
nontherapeutic medical research with incompetent persons, even under very
strict conditions, is a politically sensitive issue.

The convention (which consists of a preamble and thirty-eight articles and
is divided into fourteen chapters) intends to address three concerns related to
recent developments in genetics and biomedicine:

- protection of individuals against improper use of the new possibilities

- the interests science and society have in progress in these fields and their
  possible contrast to the interests of the individual

- the protection of the human species against unwanted tinkering with its genetic heritage

The first concern finds expression in several articles. The most notable of
these is article 2, "Primacy of the Human Being," which reads, "The interests
and welfare of the human being shall prevail over the sole interest of society

---

[11]Roger and Durant de Bousingen, 1994, see note 1, p. 321. <http://assembly.coe.int/
Mainf.asp?link=http%3A%2F%2Fassembly.coe.int%2FDocuments%2FadoptedText%2Fta9
1%2FEREC1160.htm>.

and science." Other articles in this context are article 10, addressing the right of the respect for private life and to information on one's health; article 11, prohibiting discrimination on grounds of genetic heritage; article 14, prohibiting the choice of a future child's sex, except where serious hereditary sex-related disease is to be avoided; article 21, prohibiting financial gain by the human body or its parts as such; and article 22, allowing the use of body parts for purposes other than that for which they were removed only with the appropriate information and consent.

Article 18 can also be seen in this context. This article deserves special attention because it deals with an important issue in an ambiguous way, which is typical for a lot of European regulations in bioethics: "Where the law allows research on embryos in vitro, it shall ensure adequate protection of the embryo. The creation of human embryos for research purposes is prohibited."[12]

The ambiguity of article 18.1 is in the words *adequate protection*. Those who want to protect the embryo against destruction read this article as saying that research is allowed only if it is in the interest of the embryo itself (cf. discussion of Recommendations 1046 and 1100, above). But those who want to use the embryo in research that leads to the death of the embryo take this provision to mean that destructive use of embryos in research is allowed only for good medical scientific reasons, not just for any research.[13] It is interesting that the explanatory report, which contains extensive clarifications to other articles, does not give any explanation of this article. Apparently the plurality of opinions did not allow any further stipulation.

Article 18.2 is clear in itself and is valuable to those who want to grant full protection to the human embryo. But here the legal weakness of the convention becomes apparent. Those states who do not want to fulfill this provision will not ratify the convention or may make a reservation in respect of this (or any other) provision of the convention. In fact the convention itself provides (in art. 36) for the possibility of making such a reservation, to the extent that any law then in force in its territory is not in conformity with the provision. This is probably the reason why countries in which the government wants to leave open the possibility of this kind of biomedical research have not signed or at least have not ratified the convention.

The second concern finds expression in articles 17.2, 20.2 and 26. Articles

---

[12] Convention on Human Rights and Biomedicine, art. 18. Oviedo (Spain) 1997. <htto://conventions.coe.int/treaty/EN/cadreprincipal.htm>.

[13] For example, the EGE interprets this condition as follows: "to adopt a legislation fixing the conditions and limits of such research," as if any legislation independent of its content fulfills the condition of the convention. (European Group on Ethics in Science and New Technologies, "Opinion 15: Ethical Aspects of Human Stem Cell Research and Use," November 14, 2000, sec. 1.14.)

17.2 and 20.2 provide for an exception to the general rule of informed consent and of the unacceptability of involving incompetent patients in procedures that are not for their own benefit. Article 17.2 allows for the exceptional involvement of incompetent persons in nontherapeutic medical research under strict conditions, and article 20.2 permits, under strict conditions, the removal of regenerative tissue from incompetent persons for transplantation.

In these cases the interests of other persons belonging to a certain group are given priority over a regulated infringement of the protection of the individual. These stipulations were already quite broadly accepted but received further support from this convention.[14]

The third concern finds its expression most clearly in articles 12 and 13. Article 12 stipulates that a predictive genetic test "may be performed only for health purposes or for scientific research linked to health purposes." This article is related to the second concern outlined above: that the protection of the social position of individuals has priority over the (financial) interests of social actors like employers and insurance companies (and their clients). But it is also pertinent for the third concern because results of genetic tests may also be used in policy measures that aim to control the "genetic quality" of a population.

Article 13 allows genetic modifications only for preventive, diagnostic and therapeutic purposes and only if the aim is not to introduce any modification in the genome of any descendent. So enhancement and germline genetic modification are prohibited, thus seeking to protect the human species against unwanted and "wanted" modifications.

The overall impression of this convention is that in spite of its ambiguities, in general it exerts a moderating influence on the general acceptance of new biomedical possibilities that could imply a threat to certain groups of human beings.

Additional protocols. The CDBI is working on special protocols to the convention.

In 1998 an additional protocol to the convention—on the prohibition of cloning human beings—was signed. This protocol essentially contains one article prohibiting any intervention aimed at creating a human being genetically identical to another living or dead human being, where being genetically identical is defined as having the same nuclear gene set.

In January 2002 an additional protocol on organ and tissue transplantation was adopted. Work is proceeding on protocols on medical research, on the protection of the human embryo and fetus and on genetics.

---

[14]For example, art. 24 of the latest version of the Declaration of Helsinki on ethical principles for medical research involving human subjects (Edinburgh, 2000) essentially allows for the same as art. 17 of the convention.

Bioethics in the European Union

In the context of the EU bioethical issues are debated frequently and at different levels, and it is impossible to give a complete overview of all the debates and their results. Important players in this field are the European Commission (EC) and the European Parliament (EP).[15] Since the EC is advised by the EGE, this group also is quite influential.[16] In this section I will present opinions and resolutions of the relevant players on some sensitive topics in bioethics.

I will begin by discussing a few resolutions of the European Parliament and then will briefly refer to the Charter of Fundamental Rights of the European Union. I will also discuss opinions of the EGE on the issues at stake here.

Artificial reproduction techniques. The subject of bioethics has concerned the EP for many years already. In the course of the last few decades the EP has accepted various resolutions on topics in this field. One of these topics is artificial reproduction.

In 1989 the EP accepted two resolutions on biomedicine, both prepared by the EP Committee on Legal Affairs and Citizens' Rights. One resolution deals with the ethical and juridical problems related to genetic manipulation, and the other deals with the artificial insemination in vivo and in vitro.[17]

The resolution on artificial insemination essentially states that

- the number of embryos created in the course of an IVF treatment should be restricted to the number that can be transferred to the woman in one treatment cycle (i.e., embryos should only be frozen if for special reasons immediate transfer to the womb is not possible)

- experiments on human embryos in vitro should be forbidden

- embryos should not be frozen (cryopreservation) for more that three years

It is clear that this resolution would not allow scientists to use embryos to cultivate embryonic stem cells, let alone to create (clone) embryos for research. If (national) legislations had followed these resolutions, artificial procreation medicine would be much more restricted than it now in fact is, and the ethical problems related to frozen supernumerary embryos would have been avoided. Apparently the pressure on infertile couples to do everything possible to have a child, together with researchers' desire to perform research with

---

[15]The EC's website is found at <http://europa.eu.int/comm/index_en.htm>; the EP's website is found at <http://www.europarl.eu.int/home/default_en.htm>.

[16]The EGE (<http://europa.eu.int/comm/european_group_ethics/index_en.htm>) was set up by the EC and consists of twelve members named by the EC for periods of three years on the basis of expertise, taking into account a variety of perspectives. The EGE is independent and examines issues at the request of the EC, the EP or on its own initiative.

[17]Official Journal C096, April 17, 1989, p. 171.

human embryos, has led to a much more permissive policy with respect to artificial procreation and the creation of embryos in vitro, even though in Europe this practice has generally been more explicitly regulated than in the United States.

No further resolutions on human artificial reproduction techniques as such have been accepted by the EP. However, the much related issue of research using human embryos has been the subject of several other official documents, of which the Fiori resolution (discussed below) is probably the most significant—and controversial.

Genetic manipulation. In 1989 the EP also adopted an extensive resolution on medical genetics. This contained the following main points:

- The transfer of genes to human gametes should be forbidden.

- The zygote should be protected and should not be subjected to experiments other than those that may lead to results that directly favor the well-being of the embryo and the mother, and that respect the physical and psychological integrity of the woman involved.

- It should be an offense to keep an embryo alive in order to use it as a source of tissue or organs; and the cloning of human beings should be prosecuted.[18]

On June 29, 1990, the EP decided to approve a research program funded by the EU for analysis of the human genome. This program entails an integrated approach to the medical, ethical, social and juridical aspects of the use of the research's results, and it holds that the research should be in agreement with certain generally accepted ethical principles (e.g., informed consent of human subjects involved in the research, protection of privacy, etc.). Germline genetic modification is excluded from funding. The observation of ethical principles as a requirement for funding research has been maintained in the subsequent EU research programs (as I will discuss below).

Issues related to developments in human genetics were intensely debated in 2000 and 2001 in a series of hearings organized by the EP's broad Temporary Committee on Human Genetics and Other New Technologies in Modern Medicine, which was chaired by the Italian MEP (Member of the European Parliament), Francesco Fiori. This committee drafted a concept resolution that was debated in the EP in November 2001.[19] Though it was rejected after a long and

---

[18]Ibid., p. 165. <http://europa.eu.int/servlet/portail/RenderServlet?search=RefPub&lg=en &nb_docs=25&domain=&in_force=NO&year=1989&month=4&day=17&coll=JOC&nu_jo =96&page=165>.

[19]The unofficial version of the Fiori resolution (A5-0391/01) as amended before it was rejected in the final vote on November 29, 2001 can be found at <http://www.europarl.eu .int/committees/genetics_home.htm>.

confusing debate (in which scores of amendments were discussed), it contains several statements that were broadly supported in the EP. With respect to embryo research, it is more permissive than were former resolutions, which essentially only approved of therapeutic embryo research. The Fiori resolution accepts the use of surplus embryos for uses such as the cultivation of human embryonic stem cells.

Other broadly supported recommendations in this (rejected) resolution plead for the following:

- cooperation between the countries in this field of genetic testing and therapy

- synergy between public and private research

- harmonization of quality regulations on genetic testing

- adequate regulation of the principle of informed consent in the context of genetics testing

- adequate regulations of the protection of privacy in the use of genetic data (e.g., by seeing to it that data can only be used for the purpose for which they were obtained)

- further compliance with essential values in the field of genetics and in society at large (e.g., by furthering the social acceptance of people with congenital disorders)

On some points it positively refers to the Convention on Human Rights and Biomedicine.

On medical genetics the EGE produced two opinions, one on gene therapy[20] and one on prenatal diagnosis.[21] The Opinion on Gene Therapy essentially entails the following bioethical position:

- Somatic cell therapy is promising but still experimental and should be restricted to serious diseases and the protocols should be carefully reviewed by a local and a national ethical body.

- Equal access to gene therapy should be assured; a special status should be attributed to orphan diseases.

- Because of scientific uncertainties and its ethical controversial nature, germline therapy is not at the present time ethically acceptable.

---

[20]The Group of Advisers on the Ethical Implication of Biotechnology, "Opinion 6: Ethical Implications of Gene Therapy," December 13, 1994. (This group was the predecessor of the current EGE).

[21]European Group on Ethics in Science and New Technologies, "Opinion 6: Ethical Implications of Prenatal Diagnosis," February 20, 1996.

Recent health problems with patients who received somatic gene therapy for a fatal immunological disorder demonstrate the wisdom of the first statement, which was written just over eight years ago.

Meanwhile the public discussion on germline gene therapy continues. In December 2002 an international meeting of experts in Europe, convened by the International Forum for Biophilosophy, concluded that there are no reasons for stopping research on inheritable genetic modification (i.e., germline genetic therapy) in humans, for it "may sooner or later lead to a safe and effective application." The so-called right to be born with a human genome that has not been artificially modified was not recognized as being a clear and compelling right. Such a right was postulated in the EP resolution on genetic manipulation of 1989.[22]

The EGE Opinion on Prenatal Diagnosis recommends the following:

- Pregnant women should in no way be coerced to undergo prenatal testing.

- Prenatal testing should only be performed after informed consent has been given in the context of (nondirective) genetic counseling.

- Testing should not be separated from counseling.

- The choice to continue or terminate pregnancy is the prerogative of the woman or the couple alone; no discrimination should be made as a consequence of this decision.

- Prenatal diagnosis should be offered only on the basis of medical indications; the choice of sex or other characteristics for nonmedical reasons should be prohibited.

This opinion is quite liberal. The only restriction to prenatal testing and the possibility of selective abortion is that it should concern a medical problem, not just a social problem (e.g., the child has the unwanted sex).

Embryo research, cloning and stem cell research. The status of the human embryo and (related to this) the permissibility of therapeutic or destructive embryo research have been among the most debated topics in the European scene.[23] The EP resolutions of 1989 mentioned above already dealt with it and took the view that only therapeutic research should be allowed, although they did accept cryopreservation under urgent circumstances and, at least implicitly, prenatal testing and selective abortion. At the same time it should be real-

---

[22]Official Journal C096, 17 April 1989, p. 169.

[23]For an extensive survey of the regulations and legislation of embryo research in European Union countries (including the new candidate member states), see B. Gratton, "Survey on the National Regulations in the European Union Regarding Research on Human Embryos," July 2002 <http://europa.eu.int/comm/european_group_ethics/ docs/nat_reg.pdf>.

ized that these procedures were widely in practice in many countries.

In its opinion on human embryo research the EGE takes a more permissive position.[24] This opinion advises the EC on the question whether destructive embryo research should in principle be considered for funding by the EC also (in the context of the so-called Fifth Framework Programme). The EGE notices a diversity of opinions and regulations on this point in European countries. It considers the distinction between therapeutic research and destructive research to be artificial since "it would be an unacceptable risk to implant into a woman's uterus an embryo which previously has been subjected to research and hence may have been damaged" (art. 2.7). So it concludes that funding should not a priori exclude human embryo research—meaning destructive embryo research—though such funding should be only granted under strict conditions. This opinion does not explicitly deal with the creation of embryos for research.

On January 1998 the EP accepted a resolution on cloning.[25] In it the EP invites the member states of the EU to ratify the Council of Europe's Convention of Human Rights and Biomedicine and its additional protocol that forbids human cloning. This resolution further invites the EU member states and the United Nations to see to it that the prohibition of human cloning will be legally binding.

This position was confirmed in a resolution on human cloning adopted on September 9, 2000.[26] In it the European Parliament

> considers that "therapeutic cloning," which involves the creation of human embryos solely for research purposes, poses a profound ethical dilemma, irreversibly crosses a boundary in research norms and is contrary to public policy as adopted by the European Union. . . . [It] calls on the UK government to review its position on human embryo cloning. [And it] repeats its insistence that there should be a universal and specific ban at the level of the United Nations on the cloning of human beings at all stages of formation and development.[27]

It is noteworthy, however, that the earlier mentioned Fiori resolution, which recommended a ban on all human cloning, was rejected. The main reason for its rejection was probably that the members of parliament could not reach a consensus on the issue of human therapeutic cloning. Some parties wanted to leave open the possibility that "therapeutic cloning" would be al-

---

[24]European Group on Ethics in Science and New Technologies, "Opinion 12: Ethical Aspects of Research Involving the Use of Human Embryos in the Context of the Fifth Framework Programme," November 23, 1998.
[25]PB C 034, February 2, 1998, p. 164.
[26]European Parliament Resolution on Human Cloning (B5-0710, 0751, 0753, 0764/2000), September 7, 2000.
[27]Ibid., sec. 2, 3.

lowed under strict conditions. The amended resolution had become ambivalent, even contradictory with respect to human cloning just before it was integrally rejected. It asked for a ban on the use of embryos created in vitro for any purpose other than bringing about a pregnancy. This would rule out cloning for research (so-called therapeutic cloning). On the other hand, it "considers that research on therapeutic cloning for the purpose of treating serious diseases should be supported," while at the same time it "calls on Member States which have not yet done so to pass laws banning the production of genetically identical human embryos by means of cloning."[28] This latter statement is confusing in itself. Strictly speaking it could mean that only the creation of genetically identical embryos is rejected, leaving open the production of an embryo genetically identical to an already born person and allowing for therapeutic cloning. If it intends to say that all cloning, even until the embryonic stage, should be banned, then clearly therapeutic cloning would not be approved. More recently the European Parliament's Committee for the Environment and Public Health has backed calls from fellow MEPs (Members of the European Parliament) for a comprehensive ban on human cloning.[29] This demonstrates the sharp division among the members of parliament and reflects society's dissension with respect to embryonic stem cell research that uses "spare" embryos or embryos created explicitly for research purposes. The division is underlined by the fact that a year earlier the European Parliament, the Council of the Union and the European Commission endorsed the Charter of Fundamental Rights of the European Union (which will be discussed further below).[30] Chapter 1, article 3.2 of this charter pleads for a prohibition of reproductive cloning. Since in a draft it asked for the prohibition of the cloning of human beings, it should be understood that there was no consensus to also ask for a prohibition of research cloning.

That division also surfaced in the context of attempts by the United Nations to come up with a worldwide regulation of human cloning. Whereas the United States, together with Spain and the Philippines, argued for a total ban on all human cloning, other countries, notably France and Germany, put forward a proposal that would outlaw baby cloning (so-called reproductive cloning) but would accept—or at least not prohibit—research cloning. This position is supported by the United Kingdom, the only Western country that legally accepted and regulated therapeutic cloning; it did so in the Human Fer-

---

[28]Ibid., sec. C, resp. 4.
[29]Cordis RTD News, "MEPs Back Calls for Ban on Human Cloning and Stem Cell Research," March 26, 2003.
[30]The Charter of Fundamental Rights of the European Union (2000/C 364/01) was signed on December 7, 2000, in Nice by the member states of the EU, and is available at <http://www.europarl.eu.int/charter/default_en.htm>.

tilisation and Embryology Act (1990) amended for this purpose in January 2001. This position was upheld in a recent decision of the House of Lords that rejected a challenge of that amendment by the Pro-life Alliance.[31]

More recently the German government seems to have changed its position: it now also supports a total ban on human cloning.[32] However, French President Jacques Chirac recently asked UNESCO to come up with a convention to prevent abuses of human cloning. What he means is not fully clear. Presently in France only therapeutic research with human embryos is allowed. But the proposed revision of the 1994 law on transplantation, medically assisted procreation and antenatal diagnosis seems to also allow destructive research on human embryos and embryonic stem cells under certain conditions. This same proposal does explicitly prohibit reproductive cloning, but it does not mention therapeutic cloning. Since it does rule out the creation of embryos for research, it is deemed to also prohibit research cloning, although this is not absolutely clear.[33] However, by mentioning "abuses," Chirac seemed to be referring to reproductive cloning, implying that he might not want to completely ban research on embryonic cells even though he wants to encourage research on adult cells first and foremost.[34]

Meanwhile the EGE presented its opinion on the ethical aspects of human stem cell research.[35] In this informative document the EGE takes a relatively cautious position. It defends the use of "surplus" embryos for the cultivation of embryonic stem cells. However, it considers the creation of embryos for embryonic stem cell research ethically unacceptable when spare embryos represent an alternative source. The EGE considers that on the basis of the proportionality principle and the precautionary approach at present, the creation of embryos by cloning (somatic cell nuclear transfer, SCNT) for research on stem cell therapy would be premature. Alternatively, the EGE recommends funding research on the possibilities of adult stem cell therapy. Furthermore the group stresses the necessity of ensuring that the demand for spare embryos and oocyte donation does not increase the burden on women.

The European Commission, supported by the EP following the EGE opin-

---

[31]BBC News, "Lords Uphold Cloning Law," March 13, 2003.

[32]Deutsche Welle news, "Germany to Host International Cloning Ban Conference," January 10, 2003 <http:// www.dw-world.de>.

[33]See Gratton, "Survey on the National Regulations," pp. 23-26.

[34]BBC News, "France Warns of Cloning Abuses," February 23, 2003. The prestigious Comité Consultatif National D'éthique (CCNE) came up with a report in which a small majority was in favor of allowing research cloning.

[35]European Group on Ethics in Science and New Technologies, "Opinion 15: Ethical Aspects of Human Stem Cell Research and Use," November 14, 2000.

ion, has decided that its research funding program (the Sixth Framework Programme) will not fund research that involves the creation of embryos for research purposes, including research on SCNT.[36] Those applying for funding are asked to confirm that their proposed research does not involve

- research activity aimed at human cloning for reproductive purposes

- research activity intended to modify the genetic heritage of human beings, which could make such changes heritable

- research activity intended to create human embryos solely for the purpose of research or for the purpose of stem cell procurement, including by means of somatic cell nuclear transfer

- research involving the use of human embryos or embryonic stem cells, with the exception of banked or isolated human embryonic stem cells in culture

So the European scene on human embryonic stem cell research continues to demonstrate dissension and confusion. Leading bodies are taking, for the moment, a relatively cautious position—not rejecting all forms of cloning, but not funding research in this field either. At the same time scientists and industries try to keep open all research possibilities. But a majority of countries seems to be inclined to ban all cloning if only to keep the public quiet and to prevent further resistance against biomedical and technologic research.

A survey of the regulations of embryo research in the countries of the European Union indicates that thirteen of the fifteen countries allow for some form of embryo research with "spare" embryos and that only two of the fifteen countries (viz. Belgium and the UK) permit the creation of embryos for research purposes, including research cloning.[37]

---

[36]Crucial information for the Sixth Framework Programme applicants <http://www.europa.eu.int/comm/research/fp6/index_en.html>.

[37]See Gratton, "Survey on the National Regulations." To these rough statistics the following remarks should be added: (1) Of the two countries that do not allow embryo research, at least one country permits IVF, which in practice can easily involve a kind of therapeutic research. (2) In practice the distinction between using spare embryos for research and creating embryos for research is not as clear as the formulation may suggest, since in the course of an infertility treatment so many embryos can be created that almost certainly a number will not be used for procreation; it depends on other regulations—e.g., whether cryopreservation is allowed or not, or whether in practice those embryos can be used in nontherapeutic research. (3) "Therapeutic cloning" is not so far explicitly regulated in most countries; in general it is deemed to fall under a prohibition to create embryos for research, but this is debated in several countries (e.g., in Austria). Furthermore, in a number of countries, influential advisory committees of the government have published reports that sometimes arguein favor of allowing research cloning (e.g., in Sweden and Spain).

A 1998 survey on the regulation of medically assisted procreation and embryo research among the members of the CoE gives a lot of additional information, but it has become obsolete, esp. with respect to embryo research and cloning. See <http://www.coe.int/T/E/

Charter on Fundamental Rights. On December 7, 2000, the EU member states signed a new document to strengthen the protection of fundamental rights in the light of changes in society, social progress and scientific and technological developments—the Charter on Fundamental Rights of the European Union related to technological innovations. This document is endorsed by the three main institutions of the EU: the EP, the Council of the Union and the European Commission. The charter consists of seven chapters, titled "Dignity," "Freedoms," "Equality," "Solidarity," "Citizens' Rights," "Justice" and "General Provisions." A number of those fundamental principles and rights pertain to medicine and biotechnology. I will mention here some important articles relating to biotechnology (medical genetics) and medicine, and I will add comments to some of them in brackets.

ARTICLE 1

Human dignity

Human dignity is inviolable. It must be respected and protected.

ARTICLE 2

Right to life

1. Everyone has the right to life.

2. No one shall be condemned to the death penalty, or executed.

ARTICLE 3

Right to the integrity of the person

1. Everyone has the right to respect for his or her physical and mental integrity.

2. In the fields of medicine and biology, the following must be respected in particular:

— *the free and informed consent of the person concerned, according to the procedures laid down by law,*

— *the prohibition of eugenic practices, in particular those aiming at the selection of persons [Are eugenic practices only practices that involve coercion by the state? Otherwise one could also call prenatal selection of fetuses or embryos eugenic practices, unless one would deny that those unborn human beings are persons.],*

— *the prohibition on making the human body and its parts as such a source of financial gain,*

Legal_Affairs/Legal_co-operation/Bioethics/Texts_and_documents/CDBI-INF(98)8PMA
-1.pdf>.

— *the prohibition of the reproductive cloning of human beings [see also above].*

ARTICLE 8

Protection of personal data

1. Everyone has the right to the protection of personal data concerning him or her. [This is important for medical, including genetic, data.]

ARTICLE 21

Non-discrimination

1. Any discrimination based on any ground such as sex, race, colour, ethnic or social origin, genetic features, language, religion or belief, political or any other opinion, membership of a national minority, property, birth, disability, age or sexual orientation shall be prohibited. [This article can be an important argument against discrimination in social contexts (e.g. jobs, health insurance) on the basis of a genetic predisposition to a disease.]

ARTICLE 24

The rights of the child

3. Every child shall have the right to maintain on a regular basis a personal relationship and direct contact with both his or her parents, unless that is contrary to his or her interests. [What does this article mean for children born through reproductive techniques involving donor gametes or surrogacy? Does "parent" mean only social parent or (also) genetic parent?]

ARTICLE 35

Health care

Everyone has the right of access to preventive health care and the right to benefit from medical treatment under the conditions established by national laws and practices. A high level of human health protection shall be ensured in the definition and implementation of all Union policies and activities.

In general it can be concluded that this charter contains an interesting compilation of important rights. At the same time many of those rights are laid down already in other treaties, declarations and conventions as well as in national legislation, or they are limited by such. Furthermore, some of the key concepts are interpreted differently, implying that some articles do not pro-

vide the protection one would want. This pertains especially to the failing protection of nascent human life.

Conclusion

Bioethics in Europe is a very dynamic field, not only because of the continuing
scientific and technological developments in the field of biomedicine and biotechnology, but also because of the variety of voices and changing coalitions.
My goal here has been to inform, so consequently this essay has a descriptive
character, interjected with a few interpreting observations and questions. In
this final section I will make some more general evaluative remarks. These are
not the result of extensive research, but they represent my personal impres-
sions after having followed the main trends in European ethics of biomedicine
for about fifteen years.

A characteristic of today's Europe is its plurality of ethical approaches. In
the first place, there is the traditional Judeo-Christian understanding of the human being, with its emphasis on respect for life, including the unborn human
being, and the high value it attributes to the marriage relationship. This tradition manifests itself politically most clearly in the Christian and Christian-
Democratic parties of several European countries (like Austria, Italy, Germany,
the Netherlands, Belgium, and some central European and Scandinavian
countries) and to a lesser extent in politically central and conservative parties
(in, e.g., Spain, the UK and some central European countries). The religious
background is mainly Roman Catholicism, sometimes expressed in a way of
doing ethics called *personalism*. (This does not mean that those parties and personalism are not informed also by other religious and philosophical traditions
like Protestantism and humanism.) This tradition defends the protection of the
human being from its conception and the marriage relationship as the context
for procreation.

A second tradition emphasizes human rights, laid down in international
declarations, as a basis for bioethics. This is a rather legal approach, but in contrast to the situation in the United States, where court decisions dominate the
field of medical ethics, it takes accepted rights as its starting point. The Charter
of Fundamental Rights in its form is a good recent example of this approach,
even though different traditions are reflected in its content. This approach
sometimes uses the language of the principlist approach, of which Tom L.
Beauchamp and James F. Childress's *Principles of Biomedical Ethics* is the main
representative.[38] In this approach the right to life sometimes finds itself in conflict to the right to self-determination. The outcome of this tension is decisive

---

[38]Tom L. Beauchamp and James F. Childress, *Principles of Biomedical Ethics* (New York: Oxford
University Press, 2001).

for the position one takes with respect to the protection of nascent human life in the context of medically assisted procreation and prenatal diagnosis.

A third influential ethical approach is the already mentioned principlist approach embedded in a utilitarian ethical outlook. Characteristics are a strong emphasis on individual patient autonomy and utilitarian reasoning, defending new technologies with reference to the desired effects for the patient. In this approach the human embryo is granted only a relative protection, and the value of relations is the value the individuals themselves attribute to it at a certain moment. In many European countries this approach is moderated not only by the earlier mentioned traditions, but also by a stronger concept of the medical profession as a profession whose mission is both to provide a medical service at the request of a patient and to serve the health interests of the patient as professionally understood. However, it seems to me that both the traditional concept of profession and the position of the medical profession are waning.

11

CONFRONTING TECHNOLOGY AT THE BEGINNING OF LIFE

A Morally Grounded Policy Agenda for the United States

RICHARD M. DOERFLINGER, M.A.

The chapters of this book have ranged over issues of science, ethics, law and strategy. In this final essay we turn to the practical situation in which we find ourselves in the early twenty-first century—confronted with rising developments in biotechnology and the pressing need for our democratic process to respond with policy decisions that are equal to the moment.

Richard Doerflinger has long served as the key liaison between Catholic moral thinking on the pro-life and broader biotech agenda, and the policy process on Capitol Hill. In this summary statement he reviews recent debate in such bodies as the President's Council on Bioethics and its predecessor, the National Bioethics Advisory Commission, and sets out recommendations for policy. In this process he draws on the common Christian moral tradition, natural law, the Nuremberg Code and other sources of public moral reflection. He notes the inherent utilitarianism of so much apologetic for untrammeled biotech. He pleads that ethical norms should never be traded for putative medical benefits. And he writes in the confidence that even at this late stage in the history of the West, and in the face of pluriformity of opinion on many basic questions, it remains possible for the United States to set its policy course in a direction that is well-disposed to biotechnology but also firmly committed to the protection and dignity of human life.

NIGEL M. DE S. CAMERON

Issues surrounding human embryo research, cloning and reproductive technologies may appear to be poor candidates for forging a public policy consensus in our very diverse society.[1] To an even greater extent than older issues

---

[1]Doerflinger is deputy director of the secretariat for pro-life activities at the U.S. Conference

such as abortion, they present a challenge to Christians seeking to present a reasoned case for legislation based on sound moral values.

In fact, however, a substantial (though not unanimous) consensus has long existed in American society in support of certain key values and principles relevant to these issues. Tragically, these values and principles—and even key facts—have sometimes been acknowledged by secular bodies, only to be obscured or neglected when the time came to use them as a basis for public policy. The result has been an inconsistent patchwork of laws and regulations through which these values can sometimes be perceived only with difficulty.

What follows, then, will focus on general values that are compatible with the Christian tradition and are offered from within the Roman Catholic branch of that tradition, but that have also found expression in secular documents and reports as well as longstanding legal enactments. A constructive agenda on these issues can proceed by seeking to elicit these core values from enactments that have gone before, and then working to ensure that they are more consciously and consistently put into practice in the future.

Ethical Norms Should Not Be Traded for Medical Benefits

The first and most important ethical value at stake is simply the inescapable need for ethical limits themselves. A research enterprise driven simply by a utilitarian calculus, dedicated to the principle that "the end justifies the means," is best seen not as an exercise in one approach to ethics but as a threat to any ethic worthy of the name.

The temptation to engage in unethical exploitation of humans for medical research is as old as modern medicine. As soon as Western thinkers began to see medicine as a science that could advance and acquire new knowledge, the temptation arose of using human beings as mere means to this end.

When Dr. Claude Bernard sounded an alarm against this temptation in the nineteenth century, the preferred victims were prisoners convicted of serious crimes. He insisted that the physician must not deliberately do harm to any of his neighbors simply to acquire knowledge that may help others:

> The principle of medical and surgical morality, therefore, consists in never performing on man an experiment that might be harmful to him to any extent, even though the result might be highly advantageous to science, i.e., to the health of others. But performing experiments and operations exclusively from the point of

---

of Catholic Bishops. Major portions of this chapter are adapted from his testimony on June 12, 2003, on behalf of the U.S. Conference of Catholic Bishops, before the President's Council on Bioethics.

view of the patient's own advantage does not prevent their turning out profitably to science.[2]

Here in 1865 Dr. Bernard was already making the important distinction between therapeutic and nontherapeutic experimentation. The fact that an experiment may benefit the research subject is only one moral requirement among others; but it is one thing to provide a human being with an experimental treatment whose outcome may also help in treating others in the future, and quite another thing simply to use the human subject as a means, imposing significant risks on him or her solely to benefit others.

In the Nuremberg Code (1947) the United States and its allies responded to the horrors of the Nazi war crimes by restating this principle, to ensure that human dignity would not again be trampled on in the pursuit of medical knowledge. The code's key norms could be summed up as follows:

First, there should be no *unnecessary* risk to human subjects. The knowledge gained must be important for the good of society and "unprocurable by other methods or means of study," and the study must be preceded by animal studies and other precautions to minimize any risk to humans.

Second, "the voluntary consent of the human subject is absolutely essential." This must be an informed consent: the research subject must understand the nature and purpose of the experiment and its possible risks before consenting to participate.

Third, one must never cause serious injury or death in the name of medical knowledge. "No experiment should be conducted where there is an a priori reason to believe that death or disabling injury will occur."[3]

This code was the inspiration for many later declarations, including the Declaration of Helsinki first approved by the World Medical Association in 1964. Its key principle is that in medical research on human subjects, considerations related to the well-being of the human subject should take precedence over the interests of science and society.

The Helsinki declaration noted that this principle must apply to *all* human beings and that "some research populations," including those who cannot give consent for themselves, "need special protection."[4] It seems this principle

---

[2]Claude Bernard, *An Introduction to the Study of Experimental Medicine* (1865), quoted in Stephen Post, *Inquiries in Bioethics* (Washington, D.C.: Georgetown University Press 1993), p. 145.

[3]See the Nuremberg Code at <http://www.cirp.org/library/ethics/nuremberg/>. The code acknowledges one possible exception to this last norm, which if taken absolutely would itself be problematic: "those experiments where the experimental physicians also serve as subjects." Researchers have a moral responsibility to take due care of their own lives as well. (The URLs cited in this chapter were accessed on January 16, 2004.)

[4]World Medical Association, Declaration of Helsinki, available at <http://www.wma.net/e/policy/b3.htm>

was intended to extend to the unborn. The World Medical Association's parallel statement on the ethics of the practicing physician, the Declaration of Geneva, provided an oath by which the physician swears: "I will maintain the utmost respect for *human life, from the time of conception.*"[5]

Despite these solemn declarations, the utilitarian approach to research ethics has become popular among scientists and others who want to justify harmful experiments on human embryos today. When asked in 1994 whether the National Institutes of Health's Human Embryo Research Panel should base its conclusions on the principle that "the end justifies the means," the panel's chief ethicist quoted the man known as the father of situation ethics, Joseph Fletcher: "If the end doesn't justify the means, what does?"[6] He did not mention that Fletcher in turn claimed to be quoting Nikolai Lenin, who reportedly used it to justify the killing of countless men, women and children in the Russian revolution of 1917.[7] History has provided us with little reason to favor utilitarian thinking about human life—for even judged by its own terms, making moral judgments solely on the basis of consequences has so often had terrible consequences.

In modern discussions of human embryo research, it is often said that providing medical benefits and maintaining ethical norms against the misuse of research subjects are both important values to be "balanced" against each other—with some participants giving more weight to one, and some giving more weight to the other. However, this analysis of the issue is misleading.

The positive obligation to promote benefits for suffering patients, through medical research and other means, is important and generally valid.[8] However, it is a general norm that can be pursued in many different times and circumstances and in many ways, and it has no upper limit: that is, it will always be true during our earthly life that more could be done to promote this human good. The negative norm, that one should not harm or exploit human life in the service of such positive goals, is equally demanding, but it can only be pursued in one way: by refusing to violate the norm. These values are not in con-

---

[5]World Medical Association, Declaration of Geneva, reprinted in Stanley Reiser, Arthur Dyck and William Curran, eds., *Ethics in Medicine* (Cambridge: MIT Press, 1977), p. 37 (emphasis added). In the 1994 revision of the declaration, this phrase was amended to "human life from its beginning"; see <http://www.wma.net/e/policy/c8.htm>
[6]Ronald Green, speaking on April 11, 1994, at a meeting of the NIH Human Embryo Research Panel.
[7]Joseph Fletcher, *Situation Ethics: The New Morality* (Philadelphia: Westminster Press 1966), pp. 120-21.
[8]"The Church has a great esteem for scientific and technological research, since it 'is a significant expression of man's dominion over creation' (*Catechism of the Catholic Church*, n. 2293) and a service to truth, goodness and beauty." Pope John Paul II, "Address to the Jubilee of Scientists," May 25, 2000, par. 4.

flict, much less capable of being "balanced" against each other, because they are not commensurable. One cannot ethically kill one innocent human being on the grounds that this may produce results that could save the lives of several human beings. Rather, the negative norm sets a *lower* limit for ethically acceptable research: it requires us to pursue our positive goals in ways that will not violate the negative norm.[9]

When the NIH Human Embryo Research Panel proposed federal funding of human embryo research in 1994, it based its conclusions on exactly the opposite approach. It dissolved any possible tension between the negative norm against harming research subjects and the positive norm to advance medical progress, and it did so by subordinating the former entirely to the latter. Its ethical analysis cited an article by the panel's ethics co-chair, Professor Ronald Green of Dartmouth, in which he argues that there are no realities "out there" in human beings that require us to respect *anyone* as a person. It is the task of the educated and articulate members of society, he writes, to decide which qualities in others are morally relevant, based on their own enlightened self-interest. If we deny "personhood" or moral worth to too many people, we may risk denying it to ourselves or others we care about; if we bestow it on too many people, we may be depriving ourselves and our loved ones of the benefits of lethal human experimentation on those people.[10]

Professor Green called this deconstructionist approach to human dignity a "Copernican revolution" in medical ethics. It is exactly the opposite. Copernicus, a devout Catholic, no doubt felt he was striking a blow against human presumption by showing that we are not at the center of our physical universe. The panel's ethical revolution revived human presumption by denying any objective reality in human beings that could limit our own sovereign ability to choose to treat them as means to our ends. In this approach, if respecting a particular kind of human subject would prevent us from pursuing particularly promising research, that is a sufficient reason for refusing to respect that individual. This is to turn the Nuremberg Code upside down.

Researchers and those eager to be helpful to their enterprise are, and always have been, impatient with such intractable limits. That is one reason why society cannot allow the research community itself to be the sole arbiter of research ethics.

The risks of allowing the research community to set the policy agenda can be seen in several states where bills on stem cell research have been introduced

[9]See Pope John Paul II, *Veritatis Splendor* (The Splendor of Truth), 1993, par. 52, 67.
[10]Ronald Green, "Toward a Copernican Revolution in Our Thinking About Life's Beginning and Life's End," *Soundings* 66 (Summer 1983): 152-73, cited in National Institutes of Health, *Report of the Human Embryo Research Panel*, September 1994, p. 49 n. 13.

with the support of state biotechnology alliances. These bills are designed to authorize the use of embryonic, fetal or even (in some cases) adult stem cells derived from human cloning (somatic cell nuclear transfer, or SCNT). This extreme policy seems to envision the creation and "farming" of fetal and even newborn humans as sources of tissues and organs.[11]

Taking the bill proposed in Maryland (which was defeated in committee in the spring of 2003) as an example (H.B. 482, 2003 reg. sess.), two declarations in the bill's findings are especially noteworthy.

The first declaration is this: "The United States and the State of Maryland have historically fostered open scientific inquiry." The truth is that our federal and state governments have insisted that scientific inquiry not be pursued if it will mistreat human subjects. Granted that historically there have been lapses when the desire for medical progress was allowed to outweigh ethical concerns, these are generally recognized as the darkest pages of our nation's medical history. Maryland, in fact, has been in the forefront of states insisting on clear ethical and legal limits to medical research, and its courts have found that researchers can be sued for negligence when they give insufficient attention to the safety and well-being of children who are too young to consent to research. In *Grimes* v. *Kennedy Krieger Institute*, Maryland's highest court found that the Institutional Review Board at Johns Hopkins University had "abdicated" its responsibility to protect children from research risks, and had shown that it "was willing to aid researchers in getting around federal regulations designed to protect children used as subjects in nontherapeutic research."[12] Researchers at Johns Hopkins University nonetheless testified in support of the new cloning bill in 2003, citing the state of Maryland's support for open scientific inquiry.

The second and closely related declaration in the Maryland bill was that "public policy on stem cell research must *balance* ethical and medical considerations." This statement sounds moderate, until one realizes what a departure it is from Nuremberg's and Helsinki's insistence that the lure of medical progress must *never* outweigh ethics.

Researchers must be warned not to "balance" ethics and medicine, for that would mean one can pursue *even research that one knows is unethical*—if the potential medical benefit is great enough. The researchers who conducted the Tuskegee syphilis experiment on African-American men, those who deliberately infected retarded children with the hepatitis virus at the Willowbrook home, those who approved the Cold War radiation experiments on unsuspecting American civilians, those who allowed children to be exposed to lead poi-

---

[11]See Americans to Ban Cloning, "State Bills on Human Cloning," March 26, 2003 <http://www.cloninginformation.org/info/ABC-State-Laws.htm>.

[12]*Grimes* v. *Kennedy Krieger Institute*, 782 A.2d 807 (Md. 2001) at 813-14.

soning in the research condemned by the Maryland Court of Appeals—these researchers "balanced" ethics and progress, and progress won. We should not pursue such "balance," but instead should take to heart the warning expressed by a survivor of Dr. Josef Mengele's notorious "identical twin" experiments: "Human dignity and human life are more important than any advance in science or medicine."[13]

Respect for the Human Embryo as a Developing Human Life

To some the principle that the human embryo is among the human beings who deserve protection from research risks may not seem a consensus value. Yet four major advisory groups recommending federal policies on human embryo research over the past twenty-three years have agreed on this principle—or claimed to agree on it. For example, the Ethics Advisory Board to the Department of Health, Education and Welfare (EAB) concluded in 1979 that the early human embryo deserves "profound respect" as a form of developing human life (though not necessarily "the full legal and moral rights attributed to persons").[14] The NIH Human Embryo Research Panel agreed in 1994 that "the preimplantation human embryo warrants serious moral consideration as a developing form of human life."[15] In 1999 the National Bioethics Advisory Commission (NBAC) cited broad agreement in our society that "human embryos deserve respect as a form of human life."[16] And in 2002 a committee of the National Academy of Sciences acknowledged that "from fertilization" the embryo is "a developing human."[17]

None of these bodies could be described as having been appointed with any input from pro-life groups. The EAB was appointed under President Jimmy Carter, the NIH panel and the NBAC under President Bill Clinton, and the NAS panel, of course, by NAS's leadership. Moreover, all these bodies wanted to authorize at least some research involving destruction of human embryos; in the case of the NIH panel, it was publicly announced at the outset that approval of embryo research was its mandate and that anyone who objected to such research on moral grounds was ineligible to serve on it.[18] These

---

[13]Eva Mozes-Kor, quoted in A. Caplan, ed., *When Medicine Went Mad: Bioethics and the Holocaust* (Totowa, NJ: Humana Press 1992), p.7.
[14]Ethics Advisory Board to the Department of Health, Education and Welfare, "Report of the Ethics Advisory Board," *Federal Register* 44 (June 18, 1979): 35056.
[15]National Institutes of Health, *Report*, p. 2.
[16]National Bioethics Advisory Commission, *Ethical Issues in Human Stem Cell Research* (Rockville, Maryland: September 1999), 1:ii, cf. 1:2.
[17]National Academy of Sciences, *Scientific and Medical Aspects of Human Reproductive Cloning* (Washington D.C. : National Academies Press, 2002), p. E-5.
[18]Chairman Steven Muller, speaking on February 3, 1994, at a meeting of the NIH Human Embryo Research Panel.

bodies all nonetheless conceded that the subject of embryo research is a developing human life, because this fits best with the evidence.

The most recent embryological findings have strongly underscored the fact that from the very beginning the early embryo is a unified, sophisticated and organized living member of the human species, a human organism. According to an article in one of the world's most prestigious scientific publications, these new findings were scientific "heresy" only a few years ago. For example, human and other mammalian embryos were once thought to become organized and give their constituent cells definite fates only after implantation in the womb; now it is found that the embryo begins differentiation and develops a "top-bottom axis" guiding future development almost immediately after conception. The journal notes that from now on, "developmental biologists will no longer dismiss early mammalian embryos as featureless bundles of cells."[19]

While it makes no sense to say that any of us was once a body cell, or a sperm, or an egg, it makes all the sense in the world to say that each of us was once an embryo. For the embryo is the first stage of my life history, the beginning of my continuous development as a human organism. This claim makes the same kind of sense as the claim that I was once a newborn, although I do not have any recollection of cognitive or specifically human "experiences" during that stage of life.

This is distinct from the question of whether the embryo has the moral status of a person. However, one need not make claims about personhood to understand a moral obligation to respect and protect developing human life. Without making such claims, for example, federal regulations since 1975 have treated the human embryo in the womb (from the time of implantation onward) as a human subject to be protected from research risks. Moreover, by secular reasoning one can make a strong case in favor of treating every fellow member of the human species as a person. Indeed, any other standard—assigning personhood on the basis of appearance, cognitive ability and so on—will exclude many more people from personhood than just the embryo. This is readily apparent from the writings of ethicists who have started out to justify early abortion and have found themselves unable or unwilling to make an absolute or principled case against infanticide or euthanasia.

Christians are called to treat each and every living member of the human species, including the embryo, as a human person with fundamental rights, the first of which is the right to life. But even the less exalted claims made by

---

[19] H. Pearson, "Your Destiny, from Day One," *Nature* 418 (July 4, 2002): 14-15. For more on recent embryological data and their significance, see the appendix to the testimony of Richard M. Doerflinger on June 12, 2003, on behalf of the U.S. Conference of Catholic Bishops, before the President's Council on Bioethics <http://www.usccb.org/prolife/issues/bioethic/embryo/appendix61203.htm>.

these past advisory panels—"profound respect" and "serious moral consideration"—say a good deal about the ways the human embryo should *not* be treated. "Respect" is due to individuals who have inherent worth, who must be seen as ends in themselves and not merely as means. This should mean, at the very least, inviolability from direct lethal attack in the pursuit of benefits for others. (You may value the family pet, for example, but you *respect* your child, so you know which of the two must *never* be sacrificed for a dangerous nontherapeutic experiment.)

Tragically, some advisory panels that found the embryo worthy of "respect" then proceeded to set this finding aside when they made their policy recommendations. The NIH Human Embryo Research Panel, for example, favored a view that the embryo has chiefly "symbolic" value as a kind of harbinger of later human life—or that it has no inherent value at all, but can be assigned a status based on how beneficial it may be to destroy the embryo for research. In light of the fact that the panel approved a wide array of lethal experiments on human embryos—including some that required specially creating embryos solely to destroy them—even some panelists publicly observed that the panel had come to use the word *respect* merely as a "slogan" with no moral force.[20]

Five years later, NBAC tried to give more definition to what "respect" for the embryo might mean in the research context: "In our judgment, the derivation of stem cells from embryos remaining following infertility treatments is justifiable only if no less morally problematic alternatives are available for advancing the research."[21]

While this standard does not fully respect the embryo as a person with inviolable rights, it does create a presumption against research that requires killing the embryo: such research was to be a last resort, pursued only after it is found that research benefits cannot be pursued in any other way. However, the commission then evaded the implications of this standard by ignoring the emerging evidence about the promise of adult stem cells and other alternatives. To be sure, the commission did concede that its factual claim on this point would have to be reevaluated as scientific knowledge advanced.

As the NIH acknowledged in 2001, the burden of proof needed to justify human embryo research by NBAC's ethical standard has never been met. The NIH's review of stem cell research concluded that any therapies based on embryonic stem cells were "hypothetical and highly experimental," and that it could not be determined at that time whether these cells would have *any* ad-

---

[20]Dr. Bernard Lo, speaking on April 11, 1994, at a meeting of the NIH Human Embryo Research Panel.

[21]National Bioethics Advisory Commission, *Ethical Issues*, p. 53.

vantages over the less morally problematic alternatives.[22]

Since that time, in fact, scientific and practical barriers to the medical use of embryonic stem cells have loomed larger, while nonembryonic stem cells have moved quickly into promising clinical trials for a wide array of conditions. Yet many researchers have responded by simply abandoning the NBAC's approach of treating embryo research as a last resort. Instead, their claim is that research using both embryonic and nonembryonic stem cells should be fully funded now to determine which source is best for various functions.

This approach simply reduces "respect" for the embryo to nothing at all. For that is the approach one would take if there were no moral problem whatever, if the only factor determining our research priorities were relative efficiency at achieving certain goals. "Respect" must mean, at a minimum, that we are willing to give up some ease and efficiency in order to obey important moral norms instead of transgressing them.

Interestingly, the principle of respect for human life at the embryonic stage has fared better in the more representative branches of government, among policymakers who lack graduate degrees in ethics but have a keener sense of public moral sentiment. The NIH panel's recommendations were partly rejected by President Clinton (who refused to fund experiments requiring the creation of embryos for research purposes) and then completely rejected by Congress, which banned funding of any harmful experiments on preimplantation human embryos. In effect Congress decided to treat the embryo as a human subject, to be protected from research risks as fully as the unborn child in the womb has been since 1975. Congress's provision has been reenacted every year since 1996 through annual appropriations bills, with an amendment since 1998 to ensure that embryos produced by cloning are protected.[23]

Some states have gone further, prohibiting harmful experiments on human embryos outright regardless of the source of funding.[24] In one state, Louisiana, the embryo produced by IVF is protected as a juridical person—a standard that not only forbids harmful research, but also limits clinics' ability to perform any intervention unless it is designed to serve the embryo's opportunity for survival and live birth. The most recent state law on embryo research gen-

---

[22]National Institutes of Health, *Stem Cells: Scientific Progress and Future Research Directions* (Dept. of Health and Human Services, June 2001), p. 17; also see p. 63 (any possible advantages of embryonic cells remain to be determined) and p. 102 (not known whether these cells are better suited for gene therapy).

[23]For fiscal year 2004, this provision can be found as Sec. 510 of division E of the Consolidated Appropriations Act of 2004, Public Law 108-199.

[24]See USCCB Secretariat for Pro-Life Activities, "Current State Laws Against Human Embryo Research" <http://www.usccb.org/prolife/issues/bioethic/states701.htm >. See also US-CCB Secretariat for Pro-Life Activities, "Current State Laws on Human Cloning" <http://www.usccb.org/prolife/issues/bioethic/statelaw.htm>.

erally, enacted in South Dakota in 2000, also prohibits stem cell research using stem cells that one knows were obtained by destroying human embryos. Laws like those in Louisiana and South Dakota are the best current examples of how respect for the life of the human embryo should influence public policy on embryo research.

Is a policy of funding embryonic stem cell research consistent with the principle of respect for embryonic human life? When the NIH proposed such funding during the Clinton administration in 1999, it was argued that researchers would not be causing any net loss of life. The "spare" embryos from fertility clinics "would have been discarded anyway," so the policy would influence only how the embryo dies rather than whether it dies.[25] One is tempted to observe that this is true of any and all killing of mortal creatures. Such a justification could certainly have horrendous implications for lethal experimentation on terminally ill patients or death-row prisoners. In the realm of fetal research, federally funded researchers are barred by law from using the "will die soon anyway" defense to do harmful research on the unborn child intended for abortion (or the child dying outside the womb from an abortion).[26] In any case, the final NIH guidelines issued in 2001 were not restricted to embryos slated for discarding; they extended to any embryo deemed "in excess of clinical need," which only means that the parents do not need that embryo to reproduce at the present time.[27] Many of these embryos are kept in frozen storage and eventually transferred to a womb later (if they are not requisitioned for destructive research first). A recent study by the fertility industry concluded that fewer than 3 percent of the embryos now in frozen storage are available for research; the NIH guidelines would have encouraged researchers to press parents to choose this option more often.[28]

Still others have argued that by funding embryonic stem cell research, the government is not complicit in any destruction of embryos because the research only occurs after the embryos are destroyed. Yet Congress since 1996 has banned federal funding of any research "in which" embryos are harmed or destroyed, and it is difficult to see how embryo destruction is anything but an integral and essential first step in any embryonic stem cell research project. The Clinton administration's argument that such destruction and the use of the resulting cells were completely separate activities was criticized as hypo-

---

[25]See NBAC, *Ethical Issues*, p. 53.

[26]See 42 USC sec. 289g.

[27]National Institutes of Health, "National Institutes of Health Guidelines for Research Using Human Pluripotent Stem Cells," *Federal Register* 65 (August 25, 2000): 51980.

[28]D. Hoffman et al., "Cryopreserved Embryos in the United States and Their Availability for Research," in *Fertility and Sterility* 79 (May 2003): 1063-69.

critical and evasive even by supporters of federal funding.[29] Offering funds for research projects that rely on the destruction of embryos encourages such destruction to be done.

The policy articulated by President George W. Bush on August 9, 2001, is a more subtle and complex matter, but is not without difficulties of its own. The president's stated goal is to promote the possible benefits of embryonic stem cell research without encouraging future destruction of human embryos. Therefore, he said, federal funds would only support research using cell lines already created by destroying embryos in the past.

Yet the limited number of cell lines the Bush administration approved for federally funded research is meant to be adequate only for basic research, designed to determine the most promising avenues for further exploration. Some researchers have already complained that the currently eligible cell lines are of insufficient volume for treatments (on the assumption that treatments will ever emerge), have inadequate genetic diversity to treat most of the patients who may want cell implants, and might be inappropriate for human transplantation because they are grown in cultures of mouse feeder cells.[30] It is important to recognize that these researchers will ultimately want to develop thousands of cell lines with different genetic profiles, or to develop human cloning—to create and destroy embryos that are a genetic "match" to each individual patient. Limited research on existing cell lives may prepare the way for such broader agendas.

Recently a campaign was launched to reverse the current policy and authorize funding for research on new embryonic stem cell lines, cultured without the use of mouse feeder cells. Proponents have said that this expansion is necessary to take advantage of new advances in the use of embryonic stem cells. On closer examination, however, it turns out that the only advances cited are simply advances in growing the stem cells without mouse feeder cells.[31] No breakthroughs have occurred to indicate that embryonic stem cells are ready or almost ready for clinical use. Use of new cell lines from frozen embryos has not been shown to be necessary for current basic research; and such use would still be completely inadequate for any large-scale clinical research. This suggests that the proposed policy expansion is itself merely a transitional step to-

---

[29]Says ethicist Glenn McGee, who supports embryo research: "Pretending that the scientists who do stem cell research are in no way complicit in the destruction of embryos is just wrong, a smoke and mirrors game on the part of the NIH. It would be much better to take the issue on directly by making the argument that destroying embryos in this way is morally justified—is, in effect, a just sacrifice to make." Quoted in J. Spanogle, "Transforming Life," *The Baylor Line*, Winter 2000, p. 30.

[30]Editorial, "Downside of the Stem Cell Policy," *The New York Times*, August 31, 2001, p. A18.

[31]R. Weiss, "Stem Cell Strides Test Bush Policy," *The Washington Post*, April 22, 2003, p. A1.

ward mass-producing embryos (by cloning or other means) solely for harmful experimentation.[32] Oddly, the new cells proposed as a medium for growing embryonic stem cells are human bone marrow cells, which have themselves shown great clinical promise in both animal and human trials. Thus when the new mixture of adult and embryonic cells is transplanted into a patient, any clinical benefits may well arise from the adult cells—but would be attributed by embryo researchers to the embryonic stem cells, and used to justify funding even more embryo destruction. This campaign illustrates that to some proponents, preferentially advancing research that relies on the destruction of embryonic human life has become virtually an end in itself.

Ultimately the Bush administration's policy will lead to one of two outcomes. If new advances arise using existing embryonic stem cell lines (or from research in the private sector using new cell lines), political pressure for expanding the policy and involving the government in active and direct support for the destruction of developing human life will likely increase. If those advances do not come forward, or are rendered less relevant by more rapid advances using nonembryonic cells, interest in funding research on embryonic stem cell lines will likely fade, as occurred in the case of research using fetal tissue from abortions some years ago—but in the meantime scarce research funds will have been diverted to the most morally problematic and medically oversold avenues of investigation.

In vitro fertilization (IVF) itself has also come under closer scrutiny in recent years because it has produced so many "spare" embryos whose fate is now uncertain. More generally, IVF has given rise to a mentality in which human lives can be subjected to "quality control," selective discarding, intentional overproduction and "selective reduction" (abortion) when more embryos than expected begin to develop in the womb. In addition, evidence has accummulated to document an increased rate of serious birth defects among children conceived by IVF, especially among those conceived by particular

---

[32]By recent estimates, if all the human embryos in frozen storage up to the present time that are designated for research use were destroyed solely to obtain stem cells (deemed a "highly unlikely" scenario), this might produce a total of 275 cell lines. See Hoffman et al., "Cryopreserved Embryos," p. 1068. Clearly frustrated by most fertility patients' reluctance to donate their embryonic offspring for destructive research, the *New York Times* has proposed that these couples should be "pressed" to determine the fate of their frozen embryos "after a reasonable period." Editorial, "400,000 Embryos and Counting," *The New York Times*, May 15, 2003, p. A34. A more recent opinion piece in the *Times* cites two prominent researchers in support of the claim that merely determining the "best options for research" will require "perhaps 1,000" stem cell lines—about four times as many as could be obtained by destroying every available human embryo placed in frozen storage up to the present day nationwide. S. Hall, "Bush's Political Science," *The New York Times*, June 12, 2003, p. A33.

IVF procedures such as intracytoplasmic sperm injection (ICSI).[33] For all these reasons, efforts to promote the value of respect for human life in its earliest stages should include efforts to help move our society away from use of IVF as a reproductive procedure.

The Integrity of Marriage and Family

Protecting the integrity of the relationships that make up families—particularly relationships between husband and wife and between parents and children—is another value implicated in modern technologies affecting the beginning of human life. These relationships are essential to our full appreciation of our own humanity.

Besides affirming that children need "special safeguards and care, including appropriate legal protection, before as well as after birth,"[34] human rights declarations by the United Nations have recognized the family as "the natural and fundamental group unit of society" which is "entitled to protection by society and the State."[35] According to the U.S. Supreme Court, "the Constitution protects the sanctity of the family precisely because the institution of the family is deeply rooted in this Nation's history and tradition."[36]

That institution's integrity, hence its proper role in maintaining the order of society, can be eroded when relationships between husband and wife or between parent and child are blurred or redefined in some reproductive procedures. Without ignoring the needs of infertile couples, society must take care that procedures designed to help build families will not undermine the social and legal status of the family and treat children as mere instruments of others' wishes.

Of special concern are methods that introduce outside third parties into the marriage relationship for purposes of reproduction. It is now possible for a child to have as many as five parents: the "genetic" parents or sperm and egg donors, the gestational mother, and the couple that intends to raise the child. In such arrangements the child is denied his or her right to a unified family, and the moral and legal responsibilities traditionally seen as inherent in being a biological parent are diffused and rendered problematic. These practices have given rise to lawsuits in which several parents sue for custody of a child, or in

---

[33]See, e.g., B. Strömberg et al., "Neurological Sequelae in Children Born After In Vitro Fertilisation: A Population-Based Study," *Lancet* 359 (February 9, 2002): 461-65; M. Hansen et al., "The Risk of Major Birth Defects After Intracytoplasmic Sperm Injection and In Vitro Fertilization," in *The New England Journal of Medicine* 346 (March 7, 2002): 725-30; E. Maher et al., "Beckwith-Wiedemann Syndrome and Assisted Reproduction Technology (ART)," in *Journal of Medical Genetics* 40 (January 2003): 62-64.

[34]Preamble to the Declaration of the Rights of the Child (1959).

[35]Universal Declaration of Human Rights (1948), art. 16.

[36]*Moore v. City of East Cleveland*, 431 U.S. 494, 503 (1977) (plurality).

which no parent is willing to claim parental responsibility. Family relationships tend to be redefined in terms of commercial contract law, risking the reduction of human beings to the status of objects. Surrogate motherhood has rightly been criticized along these lines for its tendency to exploit the biological mother as a "surrogate uterus" and to reduce the child to a commodity for sale.

A more difficult but equally important question is whether even the "simple case" of in vitro fertilization, performed using sperm and egg from husband and wife, undermines values inherent in the institutions of marriage and family. Catholic moral teaching, as well as some other Christian accounts and some analyses not based on specifically religious principles, holds that it does.

In ordinary sexual procreation, a man and woman physically express their love for each other *and* are open to engendering a new person whom the two will love and care for together. This *openness* to new life sets the stage for parents' lifelong attitude toward their children. Their child's makeup will be a new and unpredictable combination of traits from both parents, for no one is involved in designing or forcing the production of a particular kind of child. In this way parents show respect for their children as free and equal members of the human family with their own open future—as persons over whom we adults have stewardship, not absolute dominion.

Some reproductive technologies assist this natural process, but some ignore or violate its central features. These technologies make children result from the meeting of sperm and egg in a Petri dish, rather than from their parents' union. They create opportunities for introducing third parties into the procreative act, and allow technicians to manipulate and control life at its beginning.

Human cloning is the final step down this path of depersonalized procreation. It involves no meeting of male and female at all; in fact, a child produced this way may have no "mother" or "father" in the ordinary sense, but only a template or model. Instead of revealing an openness to life, it involves domination over life, for a technician manufactures the new embryo in a laboratory and even controls his or her genetic makeup to be identical to that of someone else. This act has the nature of a manufacturing process, suited to a commodity rather than to a human being.

Nor is this only a Christian insight, for it is imbedded in our human nature. Says ethicist Leon Kass, now chairman of the President's Council on Bioethics: "Human cloning would . . . represent a giant step toward turning begetting into making, procreation into manufacture (literally, something "handmade"). . . . We here would be taking a major step into making man himself simply another one of the man-made things."[37]

When we manufacture offspring according to preset specifications, we are

---

[37]Leon Kass, "The Wisdom of Repugnance," *The New Republic*, June 2, 1997, p. 23.

violating a fundamental aspect of human procreation. We are treating our children as our "creatures." The other abuses of human cloning—the fixation on producing a child "just like me"; the willingness to subject cloned humans to high risks of death and disability; even scientists' willingness to clone embryos solely to exploit and destroy them—flow from this first fundamental error. Human cloning would create a human being who deserves to be treated as our equal, but it would do so in a way that undermines or fails to appreciate this equal dignity.

Though to a lesser extent, and despite any positive motives on the part of couples who resort to it, the procedure of IVF poses this same problem. By its nature, it fosters (at least among the scientists and technicians who actually perform it) an attitude toward children at their embryonic stage of development that invites further abuses, such as destructive experimentation and the creation of embryos for research. This has become increasingly apparent even to Christians who may not share the Catholic Church's view that IVF is inherently immoral. As a major Christian periodical has editorialized,

> We feel more concern than ever that IVF too often sets couples on a course of parenthood at all costs—not only financially, but also ethically and spiritually. Medical science has progressed to the point of offering us many ways to bring a child into the world, whether using our own bodies or those of complete strangers. But what threats might this Promethean offer pose to our very souls—or, just as important, to the bodies and souls created in vitro?[38]

Because of these moral concerns, government should not promote IVF through public funding but should discourage its use, instead promoting infertility treatments that do not pose such serious moral questions.

In 1979 when the Ethics Advisory Board (EAB) reported to the Secretary of Health, Education and Welfare on the advisability of funding in vitro fertilization projects involving humans, the board concluded that federal support for some projects along these lines would be "acceptable from an ethical standpoint." However, the board hastened to explain that this meant such support would be "ethically defensible but still legitimately controverted." The board declined to make any policy recommendation on whether such support should actually be given, citing "uncertain risks" to both mother and offspring, "the dangers of abuse" such as experimental manipulation of the embryo, and the fact that the procedure is "morally objectionable to many."[39] Since that time, no administration has funded human in vitro fertilization. None should consider doing so now.

---

[38]Editorial, "Souls on Ice," *Christianity Today,* June 2003, p. 28.
[39]See Ethics Advisory Board, "Report," pp. 35056-58.

Legal and Regulatory Goals

Christians concerned about the moral aspect of public policy seek to bring civil law into ever greater conformity with the moral law. Yet some practices that are immoral may not be appropriate subjects for legal prohibition, or it may not at times be possible to prohibit them without giving rise to greater harms. Practices that endanger the common good, including those that violate fundamental human rights such as the right to life, should be forbidden by law; but even this goal at times can be achieved only partially or by intermediate steps. This morally grounded realism is at least as old as Saint Augustine: "The law which is framed for the government of states, allows and leaves unpunished many things that are punished by Divine providence. Nor, if this law does not attempt to do everything, is this a reason why it should be blamed for what it does."[40]

Thus while one should never support legislation to promote or endorse unethical practices, one may support legislation to correct the most egregious wrongs when that is the most that can be achieved at a given time, as a step toward a legal system that is completely just.[41]

Even in a society that has come to accept IVF and other morally problematic practices regarding the beginning of life, then, there is much that the concerned Christian can and should do to reform the current situation or at least to prevent it from becoming worse. What follows is a partial list of suggestions.

Human cloning. State and federal bans on human cloning by the somatic cell nuclear transfer procedure, for any purpose, are urgently needed. Because it is expressly designed to create humans to preset specifications, as a means to duplicating certain traits deemed valuable, this technique is uniquely suited to treating new human lives as mere means rather than as ends in themselves. Its use invariably violates the dignity of human life—whether used for so-called reproductive purposes (where animal trials show a 90 to 99 percent death rate for cloned embryos) or for so-called therapeutic or research purposes (where death is to be deliberately inflicted 100 percent of the time).[42]

Human embryo research. Laws against destructive human embryo re-

---

[40]Augustine, *On Free Will* 1.5, cited approvingly in Thomas Aquinas, *Summa Theologiae* 1-2, 96.2 ad 3.

[41]"Though it is true that sometimes it is lawful to tolerate a lesser moral evil in order to avoid a greater evil or in order to promote a greater good, it is never lawful even for the gravest reasons to do evil that good may come of it (cf. Rom. 3:8)." Pope John Paul II, "Address," par. 90, quoting Pope Paul VI. On the issue of "imperfect" or incremental legislation, also see Pope John Paul II, *Evangelium Vitae* (The Gospel of Life), 1995, par. 73.

[42]For more on the pro-life case against human cloning, see "Cloning/Cloning Legislation," United States Conference of Catholic Bishops website <http://www.usccb.org/prolife/issues/bioethic/cloning/index.htm>.

search, like South Dakota's 2000 law, should be considered and enacted in other states. Consideration should be given to a federal law against creating human embryos for research purposes in general, a legislative goal now enjoying very broad support in Europe. However, such a law may not be effective unless it is combined with legal restraints on the overproduction of embryos for reproductive purposes (see my thoughts on regulating IVF below). Otherwise it may be virtually impossible to prevent fertility clinics from overproducing embryos precisely in order to have "spare" embryos available for research at the end of the process.

Patenting human beings. Despite a longstanding administrative policy at the U.S. Patent and Trademark Office that human organisms at any stage are not fit subjects for patenting, it was recently discovered that at least one patent has been granted on a cloning procedure that seems to allow patenting of the human embryos produced by it. It would be difficult to imagine a more egregious way of reducing fellow human beings to objects in which others can claim a proprietary interest. The cause of human dignity will be well served by a federal law forbidding the patenting of all human beings, including human embryos. A one-year ban on such patenting was approved by Congress in January 2004.[43]

Federal funding of embryo research. The annual appropriations rider forbidding federal funding of harmful experiments on human embryos should be maintained, and its policy permanently incorporated into federal regulations or statutes on research involving human subjects.

Federal funding of embryonic stem cell research. Efforts to expand the current policy, which allows the government to fund research on cells already obtained by destroying human embryos, should be strongly opposed. Continued diversion of scarce federal research funds toward embryonic stem cell research, at a time when the disease conditions for which it was hailed as a treatment (diabetes, Parkinson's disease, sickle cell anemia, immune deficiency, spinal cord injury, etc.) are being more rapidly and safely addressed by other means, now threatens to slow medical progress.

Federal funding of in vitro fertilization. The EAB's reasons for not recommending federal funding of IVF in 1979 remain valid and are better documented than ever. The federal government should not begin funding IVF, even on the grounds that this may allow an opportunity to regulate the IVF industry and prevent more egregious abuses. It is precisely the insistence by some that the government must fund this practice in order to regulate it that has produced an impasse regarding regulation of IVF for twenty-five years. It is the inherent nature of IVF that inevitably leads to abuses. In our society a decision to provide

---

[43]See sec. 634 of division B of the Consolidated Appropriations Act of 2004, Public Law 108-99.

federal funding is inevitably taken as a declaration that a given practice is ethically acceptable and should be promoted as a public benefit. IVF fails this test.

Regulating IVF. Public policy on IVF should help move our society away from this practice and toward responses to infertility that do not pose its many risks and moral problems. The strongest reason for legislating in this area is the protection of developing human life. Louisiana's law recognizing the laboratory-produced embryo as a person, for example, discourages harmful experimentation, overproduction of embryos, routine embryo freezing and other abuses; some European countries have enacted laws with similar goals. Yet the only current federal law in this country regulating IVF, a voluntary registry documenting "success" rates, has many deficiencies.[44] It rates success in terms of the percentage of ovarian stimulation procedures that end in live birth, rather than the percentage of embryos produced who survive to live birth—a standard that actually encourages the irresponsible use of fertility drugs to produce many eggs at once, and the transfer of multiple embryos to the womb at one time. And this law addresses neither the issue of whether less invasive or problematic fertility procedures have been fully considered before IVF is recommended nor the issue of the effects of superovulatory drugs on women's future health. Through careful amendment, this law could be reformed to help protect women and children endangered by the fertility industry.

Conclusion

The values and specific proposals outlined above could become a focus for agreement and cooperation among Christians and others concerned about technologies for manipulating human life at its beginning. These proposals should not be seen as arising from a negative assessment of medical research or technical progress in general. Rather, by rejecting research avenues that rely on the destruction and manipulation of developing human life, our society should be able to devote itself all the more enthusiastically to ethically responsible medical research and the dissemination of its benefits to all human beings, especially the poorest and most vulnerable.

The reality is that research avenues posing no moral problem are rapidly advancing to treat previously incurable diseases, offering us opportunities to work together on forms of medical progress that all can support and that all patients can benefit from with a clear conscience. In this area of policy there is no conflict between religion and science, or between ethics and medical progress. Rather, medical research can and should always be guided by fundamental ethical norms to benefit all members of the human family.

---

[44]See 42 USC secs. 253a-1 to 263a-7 (Fertility Clinic Success Rate and Certification Act of 1992).

APPENDIX

The Sanctity of Life in a Brave New World

A Manifesto on Biotechnology and Human Dignity

Our children are creations, not commodities.

PRESIDENT GEORGE W. BUSH

If any one age really attains, by eugenics and scientific education,
the power to make its descendents what it pleases,
all men who live after are "the patients of that power,"
slaves to the "dead hand of the great planners and conditioners."

C. S. LEWIS

1. The Issue

The debates over human cloning have focused our attention on the significance for the human race of what has been called "the biotech century." Biotechnology raises great hopes for technological progress; but it also raises profound moral questions, since it gives us new power over our own nature. It poses in the sharpest form the question, What does it mean to be human?

2. Biotechnology and Moral Questions

We are thankful for the hope that biotechnology offers of new treatments for some of the most dreaded diseases. But the same technology can be used for good or ill. Scientists are already working in many countries to clone human beings, either for embryo experiments or for live birth.

In December, 2002, the Raelians, a religious cult that believes the human race was cloned by space aliens, announced that a baby they called "Eve" was the first cloned human. But it is not just the fringe cults that are involved in cloning; that same month, Stanford University announced a project to clone human embryos for medical experimentation.

Before long, scientists will also be able to intervene in human nature by making inheritable genetic changes. Biotechnology companies are already staking claims to parts of the human body through patents on human genes, cells and other tissues for commercial purposes. Genetic information about individuals has already made possible advances in diagnosis and treatment of disease, but it may also make those with "weaker" genes subject to discrimination along eugenic lines.

3. The Uniqueness of Humanity and Its Dignity

These questions have led many to believe that in biotechnology we meet *the* moral challenge of the twenty-first century, for the uniqueness of human nature is at stake. We believe human dignity to be indivisible: the aged, the sick, the very young, those with genetic diseases—every human being is possessed of an equal dignity; any threat to the dignity of one is a threat to us all. This challenge is not simply for Christians. Jews, Muslims and members of other faiths have voiced the same concerns. So, too, have millions of people who intuitively understand that humans are distinct from all other species; at every stage of life and in every condition of dependency they are intrinsically valuable and deserving of full moral respect. To argue otherwise will lead to the ultimate tyranny in which someone determines who is deemed worthy of protection and who is not.

4. Why This Must Be Addressed

As C. S. Lewis warned in his remarkable essay "The Abolition of Man," the new capacities of biotechnology give us power over ourselves and our own nature. But such power will always tend to turn us into commodities that have been manufactured. As we develop powers to make inheritable genetic changes in human nature, we become controllers of every future generation.

It is therefore vital that we undertake a serious national conversation to ensure a thorough understanding of these questions and their answers so that our democratic institutions will be able to make prudent choices as public policy is shaped for the future.

5. What We Propose

We strongly favor work in biotechnology that will lead to cures for diseases and disabilities, and we are excited by the promise of stem cells from adult donors and other ethical avenues of research. We see that around the world other nations have begun to develop ethical standards within which biotech can flourish. We note that Germany, which because of its Nazi past has a unique sensitivity to unethical science and medicine, has enacted laws that prohibit all cloning and other unethical biotech options. We note that the one international bioethics treaty, the European Convention on Human Rights and Biomedicine, outlaws all inheritable genetic changes and has been amended to prohibit all cloning.

We therefore seek as an urgent first step a comprehensive ban on all human cloning and inheritable genetic modification. This is imperative to prevent the birth of a generation of malformed humans (animal cloning has led to grotesque failures) and the establishment of vast experimental embryo farms with millions of cloned humans.

We emphasize: All human cloning must be banned. There are those who argue that cloning can be sanctioned for medical experimentation, for so-called therapeutic purposes. No matter what promise this might hold—all of which we note is speculative—it is morally offensive since it involves creating, killing and harvesting one human being in the service of others. No civilized state should countenance such a practice. Moreover, if cloning for experiments is allowed, how could we insure that a cloned embryo would not be implanted in a womb? The Department of Justice has testified that such a law would be unenforceable.

We also seek legislation to prohibit discrimination based on genetic information, which is private to the individual.

We seek a wide-ranging review of patent law to protect human dignity from the commercial use of human genes, cells and other tissue. We believe that such public policy initiatives will help ensure the progress of ethical biotechnology while protecting the sanctity of human life.

We welcome all medical and scientific research that is firmly tethered to moral truth. History teaches that whenever the two have been separated, the consequence is disaster and great suffering for humanity.

SIGNATORIES AS OF FEBRUARY 5, 2003

Carl Anderson, Supreme Knight
Knights of Columbus

Gary L. Bauer, President
AmericanValues

Robert H. Bork, Senior Fellow
The American Enterprise Institute

Nigel M. de S. Cameron, Ph.D., Founding Editor
Ethics and Medicine; Dean, Wilberforce Forum; Director, Council for Biotechnology Policy

Dr. Ben Carson, Neurosurgeon
Johns Hopkins Hospital, Department of Neurosurgery

Charles W. Colson, Chairman
The Wilberforce Forum
Founder, Prison Fellowship Ministries

Paige Comstock Cunningham, J.D., Board Chair and Former President
Americans United for Life

Ken Connor, President
Family Research Council

Dr. James Dobson, Chairman
Focus on the Family

Dr. Maxie D. Dunnam, President
Asbury Theological Seminary

C. Christopher Hook, M.D.
Mayo Clinic

Deal W. Hudson, Editor and Publisher
Crisis Magazine

Dr. Henk Jochemsen, Director
Lindeboom Institute

Dr. D. James Kennedy, Senior Pastor
Coral Ridge Presbyterian Church

John F. Kilner, President
Center for Bioethics and Human Dignity

C. Everett Koop, M.D., Sc.D., Senior Scholar
C. Everett Koop Institute at Dartmouth

Bill Kristol, Chairman
Project for The New American Century; Editor, *The Weekly Standard*

Jennifer Lahl, Executive Director
The Center for Bioethics and Culture

Dr. C. Ben Mitchell, Professor of Bioethics and Contemporary Culture
Trinity International University

R. Albert Mohler Jr., President
The Southern Baptist Theological Seminary

Fr. Richard Neuhaus, President
Institute for Religion and Public Life

David Prentice, Ph.D. Professor of Life Sciences
Indiana State University

Sandy Rios, President
Concerned Women for America

Dr. William Saunders, Senior Fellow and Director
Center for Human Life and Bioethics, Family Research Council

Rev. Louis Sheldon, Chairman
Traditional Values Coalition

Joni Eareckson Tada, President
Joni and Friends

Paul Weyrich, Chairman and CEO
The Free Congress Foundation

Ravi Zacharias, President
Ravi Zacharias International Ministries

CONTRIBUTORS

Nathan A. Adams IV, J.D., Ph.D., serves as chief litigation counsel for the Christian Legal Society, where he focuses on religious liberty litigation. He was formerly an associate attorney with Rothgerber, Johnson & Lyons LLP, where he focused on complex litigation, including church-state matters.

Nigel M. de S. Cameron, president of the Institute on Biotechnology and the Human Future, and research professor of bioethics at Chicago-Kent College of Law, was formerly dean of Charles W. Colson's Wilberforce Forum and continues to direct its affiliated Council for Biotechnology Policy. Founding editor of *Ethics and Medicine*, he has written widely on bioethics and recently represented the United States at the United Nations discussion of a convention to ban human cloning.

Charles W. Colson, formerly special counsel to President Nixon, is founder and chairman of Prison Fellowship and the Wilberforce Forum, and chairs the Council for Biotechnology Policy. Colson's *BreakPoint* daily radio commentaries are heard by more than one million listeners.

Paige Comstock Cunningham, J.D., is former president of Americans United for Life, a public interest law firm that is also the nation's oldest national pro-life organization. She has been pre-law adviser at Wheaton College, in Wheaton, Illinois, and is also adjunct faulty at Trinity Law School in Santa Ana, California.

Richard Doerflinger, M.A., is associate director for policy development at the Secretariat for Pro-life Activities, National Conference of Catholic Bishops, and an adjunct fellow at the National Catholic Bioethics Center. He has testified many times before congressional committees and other bodies.

C. Christopher Hook, M.D., is a hematologist who is assistant professor of medicine at the Mayo Clinic in Rochester, Minnesota, and director of ethics education at Mayo Clinic Graduate School of Medicine. He has a special interest in the ethics of nanotechnology and cybernetics, and is also a member of the Secretary for Health and Human Services' advisory group on human genetics.

Henk Jochemsen, Ph.D., is director of the Lindeboom Institute for Medical Ethics, Ede,

The Netherlands, and holds the Lindeboom Chair for Medical Ethics at the Free University of Amsterdam. He is an associate editor for *Ethics and Medicine*.

C. Ben Mitchell, Ph.D., is associate professor of bioethics at Trinity Evangelical Divinity School, editor of *Ethics and Medicine,* and has long served the Ethics and Religious Liberty Commission of the Southern Baptist Convention in both staff and consulting roles. His doctoral work addressed the patenting of human life.

David A. Prentice, Ph.D., is professor of life sciences at Indiana State University and adjunct professor of medical and molecular genetics for Indiana University School of Medicine. He has played a prominent role in national debate about embryonic and adult stem cell research, and serves as science adviser to Senator Sam Brownback.

William L. Saunders, J.D., serves as the director and senior fellow for the Family Research Council's Center for Human Life and Bioethics. He is a member of the Ramsey Colloquium of the Institute on Religion and Public Life, and a board member of the Fellowship of Catholic Scholars. He has also been appointed to the U.S. delegation to the U.N. Special Session on Children.

Wesley J. Smith, J.D., is an attorney and author who has emerged as one of the most prolific writers on biopolicy issues. He is general counsel to the International Task Force on Euthanasia and Assisted Suicide, and a special consultant with Center for Bioethics and Culture.

David Stevens, M.D., serves as the executive director of the Christian Medical and Dental Associations. He is the author of *Jesus, M.D.* and has appeared on the *Today Show, NBC Nightly News,* BBC-World Television and National Public Radio, among other news programs. Dr. Stevens has also served as a health columnist and is the host of the CMDA Healthwise Public Service Announcements and the *Christian Doctor's Digest.* He has completed graduate work in bioethics.

Subject Index